Jesus in Asia

Jesus in Asia

R. S. Sugirtharajah

Harvard University Press

Cambridge, Massachusetts

London, England

2018

Library of Congress Cataloging-in-Publication Data

Names: Sugirtharajah, R. S. (Rasiah S.), author.

Title: Jesus in Asia / R. S. Sugirtharajah.

Description: Cambridge, Massachusetts : Harvard University Press, 2018. |

Includes bibliographical references and index.

Identifiers: LCCN 2017033253 | ISBN 9780674051133 (alk. paper)

Subjects: LCSH: Jesus Christ—Oriental interpretations. |

Jesus Christ—Hindu interpretations. | Jesus Christ—Humanity.

Classification: LCC BT304.94 .S84 2018 | DDC 232.095—dc23

LC record available at https://lccn.loc.gov/2017033253

CONTENTS

Jesus in Asia

INTRODUCTION

The Asian Search
for the Historical Jesus

Existing books on the historical Jesus fall into two categories. The first, made up of works written largely from a Western perspective and giving the impression that the search for the historical Jesus is a Western enterprise, effectively began with the publication of Albert Schweitzer's *The Quest of the Historical Jesus.* The second comprises histories written outside of Europe, especially in far-flung outposts like India, China, Korea, and Japan. These situationally based articulations were dismissed by Western scholars as culture-specific, gender and racially biased, and confessional and mission-oriented. Here I offer a different perspective that not only expands the one-sided picture of the Western search to include Asian re-imaginings of Jesus's life, but also situates the quest for the historical Jesus beyond the narrow confines of the Western world.

Few of the Asian thinkers studied here wrote a full-blown account of Jesus, nor were they seriously involved in a search marked by mainly historical questions. They did not approach the text with the heavy artillery of historical criticism, though some of them were familiar with it. Nor did they use the well-tested criteria that Western scholars routinely employ to assess the accuracy of the stories and sayings of Jesus, such as "multiple corroboration," "criterion of dissimilarity," "criterion of coherence," or "criterion of multiple attestation." Instead what they

1

often used was an unspoken criterion—"continental self-reference"—an intentional, deliberate, and dignified method of self-discovery and decolonization in the face of colonial degradation. Asia was their anchoring point for the correction or removal of the West's negative perception of indigenous culture. They unearthed and rediscovered Asia's spiritual treasures as an anti-colonial strategy, approving some for their own purposes and rejecting others. They reflectively used the continent's cultural resources, at times essentializing them as an instrument of mediation and thus declining to recognize the inferior role assigned to them by some missionaries and orientalists. Their articulations can be seen as a notable early attempt at "provincializing Europe" and a rejection of the notion that only the West can provide the pathways to understanding Jesus. These Asian thinkers demanded a different foundation for faith than history, logic, and neutrality.

Sadly, some of these thinkers have been forgotten, although they were influential in their time. While they showed familiarity with Western scholarship, wrote in English, and published with reputable publishers in colonial India and abroad, there were no attempts by the "historical Jesus" practitioners in the West to interact with them. The Asian voices under discussion here never made it into the Western discourse. Thakur Kahan Chandra Varma's book, for example, despite going through twelve editions, and Francis Kingsbury's Jesus books, which had two revisions and a completely rewritten Tamil version, were ignored by Western biblical commentators. Ponnambalam Ramanathan's commentaries attracted so much attention in America that he was hailed as the new Vivekananda, who had become famous after the 1893 Parliament of the World Religions in Chicago, but again, there was no response from the practitioners. It is likely that some of them, such as Ahn Byung Mu or Shūsaku Endō, might have figured in the globalization classes of U.S. seminaries. What is more disappointing is that even now these thinkers and their works are rarely discussed in Asian theological seminaries, nor do they feature in their syllabi. Even on the rare occasions when they and their work are considered, it is not in Christological classes but in Mission Studies, or the History of Religions. These thinkers were not part of the academy but effective public intellectuals who knew how to explain a complicated figure to their home audiences. They described their search for the historical Jesus in a language that made it easily readable and approachable for the indigenous Anglophone world. Yet in their attempts to articulate and textualize for both local and foreign audiences, regretfully they were not taken seriously by either constituency. My hope is that this volume will rectify this oversight, drawing the interest of the present generation of scholars and other readers, even though their questions and constructions may sound dated and stale. These marginalized biographies of Jesus need to be incorporated into mainstream history, in part to prove that they were not mere historical curiosities. These articulations establish that Jesus is not the private property of Western scholarship or the institutional churches. They represent a different approach to the Western iconic Jesus that is at times illuminating and imaginative, although also sometimes infuriating and insulting. In short, their representations of Jesus demonstrate that Asian Christological thinking has been engaged creatively both with its own past and with the intellectual and Christological thinking of the broader world.

This Volume and Its Chapters

Well before the modern Western search for the historical Jesus began in earnest, Asian thinkers were exploring and writing about the life of Jesus. These reconstructions happened in China in the seventh century, and ten centuries later in India, and were encouraged by the patronage and openness of the Chinese and Indian imperial courts in what were probably the last instances of the Christian church having state sponsorship in Asia. Chapter 1 recalls the endeavors of the Church of the East missionaries who first took the Gospel to China and their portrayal of Jesus on the Tang Chinese stele popularly known as the Nestorian Monument, as well as in the eight scrolls that later came to be known as the Jesus Sutras. Also in this chapter, I describe the experimentation of the Jesuits at the Mughal court, when Jerome Xavier produced a life of Jesus *Mir'āt al-quds* (Mirror of holiness) for the Mughal emperor Akbar. The chapter highlights the distinctive nature of their approaches. The Church of the East missionaries created a Buddha-type Jesus who drew from Confucian, Buddhist, Taoist, and Christian traditions and was a supremely wise teacher, whereas Xavier played it safe, devising a supernatural biblical figure with superficial indigenous characteristics

3

(Xavier's Jesus, for example, wears a turban—significant attire in the Mughal court). And while the Jesus Sutras seem to declare that the Gospel is exceptional in the sense that it shares all the virtues of Buddhism, Taoism, and Confucianism, Xavier's text claims that the Gospel is unique because Christianity is more true than the other religions. These texts make it clear that they are not overly burdened with the historical questions that preoccupied the later Western quest for the historical Jesus but focus more on imaginative narrative representation. Regrettably, both the Chinese and Portuguese portrayals remained remote and elitist, and it took another two centuries before Jesus became accessible to ordinary Asians.

The Taiping rebellion was one of the earliest religion-inspired revolts in Asia, and it shook China. This nineteenth-century Chinese rebellion has been studied from various perspectives but rarely for its idiosyncratic portrayals of Jesus. Chapter 2 focuses on Hong Xiuquan, the leader of this insurrection, and his distinctive view of Jesus. By sidestepping the traditional biblical identities conferred on Jesus, Hong came up with his own versions such as "Heavenly Elder brother," "God's first born," "heir apparent," and the "holy one," which make Jesus not God's equal but instead subordinate to God. We'll see that Hong's Jesus, too, was much more than these titles suggest. An amalgam of Christian, Confucian, and indigenous Chinese traditions, his Jesus, although reminiscent of the one in the canonical Gospels, is not the admirable innocent Jesus but a shadowy and a darker figure who slays demons, curses people, and orders the execution of those who fail to uphold right ideals and conduct. Hong grafted himself into the divine family, calling himself Jesus's younger brother, which proved irritating to the missionaries. His quirky construction of Jesus confirms that historical facts are not the sole guide to determining who this figure was.

The first modern biblical commentary in Asia was produced not by a Christian but by the Hindu Ponnambalam Ramanathan, an aristocratic and erudite Sri Lankan. Chapter 3 explores the Jesus embedded in his commentarial writings. Ramanathan made use of a dichotomous version of the world that espoused a spiritual India and materially decadent West, and portrayed Jesus as a good Hindu man, a charismatic guru, and a Judean Saiva jnani, who besides possessing knowledge of

God, had paranormal powers. More pertinently, he had the potential to bring out a person's awareness of the divine. Unlike the Indian reformers who fit Jesus in with the Sanskritic advaitic tradition, Ramanathan used Tamil Saivism to make his case. His is a Jesus who does not usher in the Davidic messianic kingdom, or offer political redemption. Ramanathan's Jesus is restrictive in that his message is not available universally but only to a select few who are spiritually ripe to receive such divine communication.

The Jesus Myth movement of the late eighteenth and early nineteenth centuries in the West had its ardent followers in Asia. Chapter 4 looks at the writings of Kahan Chandra Varma and Dhirendranath Chowdhuri, who made use of the Jesus deniers to create doubts about the historical Jesus and to further their anti-Christian agenda. Their contention is that the early Christians created Christ out of different mythologies available at the time. The Gospel Jesus was a personification of myths derived from various sources such as the Greco-Roman world and Eastern legends. Their thesis is that the historical Jesus did not exist but was created, not on the basis of historical memories or oral traditions stemming from historical events, but through a purely literary process. There is a reductive simplicity in their work and they flimsily reassemble the arguments of the Jesus Myth practitioners without injecting into the debate any ideas of their own. As we will see, they distort the cherished Christian image and come up with a wayward life of Jesus in order to spite Christians and missionaries.

An earlier attempt by an Asian writer to seek the historical Jesus in the style of the Western quest was made by Francis Kingsbury (C. T. Alahasundram). Chapter 5 takes a closer look at his Jesus books, which resemble the Western liberal portrayals of the life of Jesus. While Asian thinkers were looking for elements of Jesus's life, Kingsbury was already bold enough to produce a full-blown biography. Showing familiarity with the Western scholarship of the time, his Jesus's life ended with the Crucifixion, which horrified his fellow Jaffna Christians. Kingsbury's humanistic Jesus was no more than an inspired teacher and a guru, since he was convinced that Jesus's moral teachings had little to commend to a modern audience. This liberal Jesus treats both the poor and the rich as equal before God, and judges them by their attitude to wealth. Kingsbury's Jesus remains a detached and distant figure, and Kingsbury's English biographies of Jesus drearily repeat the Western debate. (His Tamil version was daring and theologically adventurous, however, in that he drew from the Saiva texts to weave his Jesus.)

There are plenty of examples of Hindus, Buddhists, and Confucians interacting with the story of Jesus's life, but hardly any Jains have taken up the challenge. Chapter 6 analyzes a rare intervention by a convert from Jainism, Manilal Parekh. On the surface, Parekh's massive book looks like a routine inventory of the Old Quest for the historical Jesus, but a closer investigation reveals some uncommon features. Unlike other Asian thinkers, Parekh was attracted by the immaculate purity of the personality of Jesus rather than by his moral teachings. Imagining himself to be a latter-day Paul for the new Indian republic, he constructs a Jesus who attained the highest spiritual goal—divine consciousness—and who inspired and awakened such high spiritual principles in others. What distinguishes Parekh from the others is his interpretation of the Cross as *swahimsa*—immolation of the soul for the sake of others. This adventurous streak is entirely missing from his later writings. His Christology was tainted by his advocacy of the caste structure and by his offering of an aloof Jesus at a time of nation building soon after Indian independence. His book was probably the last biography of Jesus in the "No Quest" (or no-biography) era before Ernst Käsemann embarked on the New Quest to find the historical Jesus.[1]

There were many Hindu thinkers who attempted to present Hinduism to the West. One of the prominent reformers among them was Sarvepalli Radhakrishnan, who almost single-handedly made Hinduism into an open, flowing system that would have made deconstructionists proud. Chapter 7 explores the Jesus embedded in his voluminous writings on the topic, created at the height of the No Quest phase of the Western search. His enterprise traverses colonial and postcolonial India. His writings, like many of those by his Hindu contemporaries, were a protest against the negative and menacing propaganda of the missionaries and orientalists that had so hurt Hindu sentiments. Radhakrishnan was relentless in challenging the Christian claim that the singular revelation of Jesus was universal. While writing with assured style and exhibiting remarkable scholarship, he projected a Jesus who basically embodied the spirit of the Vedanta, and drew nourishment from the spiritual ferment of the Eastern religions, thus almost making him a Mediterranean Vedantin.

One of the most vibrant religious explorations to emerge in Asia in the 1970s was the Korean minjung theology—a response to the country's dictatorship of the time and to urban unrest. Minjung theologians took it upon themselves to speak on behalf of the culturally exploited, politically victimized, and economically weak masses. Chapter 8 considers Ahn Byung Mu, a pioneer of the movement whose involvement resulted in his imprisonment and torture by security guards. He was probably the first serious biblical scholar in Asia. Ahn struggled to move beyond the mesmerizing control of his mentor, Bultmann, whose kerygmatic Christ he found irrelevant to his own situation, and valiantly attempted to reconfigure Jesus not as a single person but as a collective event in which he and the minjung are conjoined and entwined. The chapter draws attention to Ahn's fascination with Galilee even before the current interest began among biblical scholars. He fashions a Jesus as a noncosmopolitan Galilean villager who spoke the language of the minjung and understood their struggle. But although Ahn moved beyond the sterile conclusions of the Western search for Jesus to include elements of minjung theology, Ahn's Jesus still offers no more than old-fashioned pietistic platitudes and no serious political agenda.

One of the Asian novelists who persistently dealt with Christian themes in his writings was Shūsaku Endō. The last chapter investigates his *A Life of Jesus,* a deeply historical text that is on a par with the Western search for the historical Jesus, though it was entirely ignored by Western scholarship. Endō's search for the historical Jesus occurred halfway through his writing career, which enabled him to evaluate the representations of Jesus in his earlier novels against the historical figure, and to intensify and strengthen these representations in his later literary works. The Jesus that emerges is not the Jesus of apocalyptic urgency, but one alienated from the Jewish scriptures and the Jewish God of wrath and judgment. Endō's Jesus radiates tenderness and maternal love, resonating with the Japanese fondness for warm-hearted Buddhas and gods (though feminists may find such a motherly image patronizing). An interesting aspect of Endō's reconstruction of the life of Jesus is the role accorded to Judas, who becomes central to Jesus's mission. He is seen not as the betrayer but as double-crossed by the hierarchy. Other alternative readings by Endō challenge the stock exegetical conclusions as well. Endō's book coincided with the emergence of liberation theology, which projected a Jesus who sided with the poor. Endō's Jesus, too, opts for the poor, but in this case the poor are not the economically disadvantaged but those who suffer for their faith. Disappointingly, the only solace that Endō's Jesus offers them is simply to stand with them, reminding them of his own suffering.

These Asian-incarnated lives of Jesus, which emerged at a time that scholars call the no-biography phase, call into question the standard scholarly sequential arrangements. That the life of Jesus was being recast as well in England and America, as Daniel Pals has drawn attention to, casts further doubt on such claims.[2]

These articulations are remarkable examples of a successful migration of the quest for the historical Jesus beyond the West and its academic disciplines. They are notable in another respect, too. While the Western quest for the historical Jesus was largely a Protestant preoccupation, the Asian search included a diverse array of religious thinkers such as Hindus, Jains, Roman Catholics, and members of the Church of the East.

Coherences, Clichés

This book is not arranged in a strict sequence; readers can enter any chapter as they wish. There is, nevertheless, a coherence to the volume: binding the chapters together are their hermeneutical presuppositions, their excavations of Asian resources, and their keenness to redeem Jesus from Western strictures. What runs through them are the "interventionist possibilities" of postcolonial thinking, where knowledge generated by the colonizer meets up with a refusal of the colonized to accept the colonizers' view that the colonized are innately inferior to them.

An astute reader will notice a number of absences in the volume. One is Asian feminist voices. Unfortunately, the quest for the historical Jesus is and has been a white, male, middle-class enterprise, so it is not surprising that Asian feminists' contributions are scarce. If there are such articulations, I would be happy to include them in subsequent editions. Another absence is T. C. Chao's *The Life of Jesus* (1935). His search was undertaken at a time when China was torn apart by warlords and threatened by the Japanese presence; he found the moral vision in the kerygmatic Jesus to be a remedy for those troubled times. My attempts to obtain the English version of his book proved unsuccessful. The other omission is the visual representation of Jesus. Asian artists have worked out brilliant and often subversive portrayals of Jesus, but the exorbitant costs of reproducing these images and my incompetence in art criticism prevented me from including them. No volume could cover such a vast topic completely. What I have included are fascinating glimpses and compelling snapshots of Asia's search for the historical Jesus.

It is almost a cliché to write that descriptions of the lives of Jesus are constructed to meet the political and ideological demands of nations and tailored to meet contemporary concerns. There is truth in this, and this volume and other Western attempts at the search for the historical Jesus are a testimony to it. It is clear that the Western claim to so-called scholarly neutrality has been overstated and oversold. The German, British, and American quests were motivated by national aspirations, racism, exceptionalism, and colonial intentions. For this reason, the secondary literature on an Asian Jesus, which is extraordinarily extensive, is not the principal concern of the present work. A lengthy engagement with that secondary material would mean business as usual, that is, giving importance to the work of Eurocentric scholars and not paying attention to the writings of Asians.

A word about the sexist language, especially in the quotations, which readers may find offensive. I left these objectionable passages as they were in the original as a reminder that the authors were people of a certain age and generation who thought that they were speaking for the whole of humanity, thus collapsing all voices, including female, into a male one. Cleansing these offending passages would mean controlling the past—a favorite activity of dictators and nationalists.

I would like to take this opportunity to rectify a decidedly mistaken comment I made long ago. In an earlier volume I edited on Jesus, I made an injudiciously inflated claim that among the faith traditions other than Christianity and Judaism, the Hindus had worked out elaborate and varied images of Jesus that demonstrated their personal "admiration and affection for Jesus."[3] Now, looking back after more than two decades, such a claim looks exaggerated. Working on this volume has shown me that the attitude of Hindus toward Jesus instead moved from antagonism, to judicious censure, to modest approval and admiration.

As I finished this volume, a question came to mind: is it possible to write about a continent and its portrayals of Jesus without reducing its regional, religious, and cultural complexities into a single version of truth and reality? One response, which is resoundingly true of this volume, comes from the narrator of Madeleine Thien's *Do Not Say We Have Nothing,* about writing Chinese history: "No one person can tell a story this large."

Any quest for the historical Jesus that deviates from historical questions and is not driven by Enlightenment ideals such as skepticism, rational inquiry, and objectivity, tends to be dismissed as confessional or sentimental, or condescendingly described as an "unacademic intermezzo."[4] In other words, portrayals of Jesus in ethnic, gendered, or theological terms are treated as having less academic purchase and as being high in syrupy spiritual content. I hope the Asian thinkers discussed here have proved that this patronizing attitude was plainly wrong, and that their search and their renditions of Jesus were as vigorous, scholarly, and enriching—and no more vapid, sentimental, or enervating—than any other quest for the historical Jesus.

1

Jesus in the Sutras, Stele, and Suras

Producing narratives that describe the life of Jesus has been the preserve of and the foremost task of Western scholarship. Remarkably, however, the first modern depiction of Jesus's life was not written in the Christianized West, as is often presumed, nor was it composed in a European language nor even aimed at a Christian audience. It instead appeared in religiously plural India and was written for a Muslim emperor. Written in Persian, the language of the Mughal rulers of the time, this first portrayal of the life of Jesus, *Mir'āt al-quds* (Mirror of holiness), was prepared at the request of the emperor Akbar (1556–1605), a Muslim famous for his religious tolerance and inquiring mind. The person behind the production of this book was Jerome Xavier (1549–1617)—nephew of the renowned Francis Xavier (1506–1552)—who signed off with the explanation that the book had been compiled at the request of the emperor in "the seat of the Caliphate of Agra." Abdul-Sattar b. Qasim of Lahore acted as the translator. The famous Western biblical scholar Albert Schweitzer later referred to Xavier's book, though he himself did not have time for anything but an apocalyptic lead character in his monumental but overtly European-focused quest for the historical Jesus. Without access to the text, Schweitzer uncritically accepted the anti–Roman Catholic thinking of its Latin translator, dismissing the book as a "skilful falsification of the life of Jesus." Schweitzer had a Eurocentric motive. He wanted to credit Reimarus as the first to write the life of Jesus. As he put it, "There had been nothing to prepare the world for a work of such power as that of Reimarus."[1]

Xavier's unusual text owes its existence to two foreign invaders—the Portuguese, who occupied the state of Goa in 1510, and the Mughals, who hailed from a dynasty founded by Babur from Uzbekistan, who had seized North India sixteen years later. It was the emperor Akbar who consolidated the power of the Mughals in India.

Before we scrutinize the Mughal Jesus, we need to go back nearly ten centuries to look at even earlier and often patchy construals of Jesus in seventh-century China: a monument and manuscripts that are probably the first portrayals of the lives of Jesus outside the Jewish and Hellenistic environment. The monument, known as the Nestorian Monument, was erected in 781 somewhere between Chang'an and the nearby town of Zhouzhi, and rediscovered in 1625. The Chinese texts were largely the work of the missionaries of the Church of the East, disapprovingly called the Nestorians, who took the Christian faith to China in the seventh century and tried to relate Jesus to the Chinese context. The discovery of these Chinese materials has been well documented elsewhere.[2] Another series of eight texts, once known as the Dunhuang Manuscripts, has since been christened the Jesus Sutras. Four of these are early sutras written probably in the late 630s to 650s by Persian monks: the Sutra of the Teachings of the World-Honored One; the Sutra of Cause, Effect, and Salvation; the Sutra of Origins; and the Sutra of Jesus Christ. A further set of four are sometimes known as liturgical sutras, and were produced during the eighth century, probably by Jing Jing, a Chinese convert: these are Taking Refuge in the Trinity; Invocation of the Dharma Kings and Sacred Sutras, or Let Us Praise; the Sutra of Returning to Your Original Nature; and Christian Liturgy in Praise of the Three Sacred Powers, or The Supreme. These theological articulations were largely undertaken by Chinese Christians unsupervised by missionaries. Martin Palmer, who produced his own translation of these Sutras, is convinced of the late Sutras' Chinese provenance: "They are original Sutras composed in Chinese, by Chinese, for Chinese."[3] If Palmer's assertion is correct, then along with the invention of gunpowder and paper, credit for producing the first Christian theological writing in Asia should go to the Chinese. What is remarkable about this monument and the manuscripts is that they mix creatively the teachings of Jesus with Eastern religious thought. These Chinese materials do not present a fully extended biography of Jesus in the modern sense but instead provide glimpses and sketches related to his teachings and life.

Jerome Xavier's *Mir'āt al-quds,* dated Agra 1602, comes nearer to a modern life. The text remained inaccessible to the English-speaking world until recently, when Wheeler M. Thackston brought out an excellent translation and annotation.[4] The book is a mixture of texts drawing from the Gospels, noncanonical writings, Roman Catholic documents, and Xavier's own fanciful imagination. Although the book is about Jesus, it opens with the conventional Muslim prayers and salutations to the prophet Muhammed: "Praise be to God, Lord of the worlds and final reward of the pious, and prayers and salutation upon his apostle Muhammed and his family and companions and all." The volume has four chapters, each with implicit interpretative aims suggesting that Xavier was consciously trying to answer the doctrinal concerns of Muslims, especially those of Akbar, about Jesus. The first, "The Christ's Childhood," dwells much on Mary, perhaps in order to curry favor with Muslims, who hold her in high esteem. The second chapter, "His Miracles and Teaching," describes the impeccable life of Jesus, the miracles he performed, and the precepts he preached, the aim being to demonstrate that Jesus was faultless and more than superior to the Koran's view of him as a mere "word of God" or "spirit of God." The third chapter, "His Death and Suffering," provides gruesome details of Jesus's death in order to challenge the koranic notion that Jesus did not die, as illustrated in the following sura: "That they said (in boast), 'We killed Christ Jesus the son of Mary, the Messenger of Allah.' But they killed him not, nor crucified him, but so it was made to appear to them, and those who differ therein are full of doubts, with no (certain) knowledge, but only conjecture to follow, for of surety they killed him not" (Koran: Sura 4.157). The last part, "His Resurrection and Ascension," supplies countless examples of the appearances of the risen Jesus to various disciples to counter another Islamic misperception that Jesus will appear again only on Judgment Day. Xavier fills his text with Gospel narratives that are left out of the Koran—the Sermon on the Mount, the parables of Jesus, and the Passion pericopes. In keeping with the koranic claim that the Gospel revealed to Jesus by God was reportedly a single book, Xavier collapses all four Gospel narratives into a single, unified version.

These seventh- and seventeenth-century constructions of Jesus, both in China and India, would not have been possible without the patronage of the secular rulers of the time. Unlike Paul, the Church of the East missionaries and the Jesuits did not face inhospitable secular authorities or audiences. Both emperors, Taizong of China and Akbar of India, were open to foreign merchandise, diplomatic missions, and foreign ideas. Emperor Taizong (598–649) himself sent his minister to welcome Aluoben (Alopen) and the Church of the East missionaries. The emperor, who was supposed to have studied the scriptures, was apparently convinced of their "correctness and truth" and issued an edict allowing their propagation. This was promulgated in the twelfth Cheng-kuan year (August 15 to September 12, 638) and states: "The Way has no immutable name, the sages have no unchanging method. Teaching is founded to suit the land that all the living may be saved." The edict continues: the "teaching has been carefully examined; it is mysterious, wonderful, calm; it fixes the essentials of life and perfection; it is the salvation of living beings, it is the wealth of man." It then encourages its propagation: "It is right it should spread throughout the empire."[5] Further evidence of the royal patronage was the building of a monastery in the I-ning quarter, which had twenty-one regular monks.

Similarly, it was Akbar who took the initiative to invite the Jesuit missionaries to his court. Apparently he was attracted by the action of two Jesuit priests in Bengal: they had refused to administer absolution to some Christian merchants who had illegally avoided paying Mughal government taxes. Just as the Emperor Taizong sent his minister Duke Fang Hsüan-ling—one of the four greatest officials of the three-hundred-year Tang dynasty—Akbar dispatched his ambassador Abdulla to Goa.[6] In his *farman* (decree) to the fathers, Akbar had asked them to send two learned priests "who should bring with them the chief books of the Law and the Gospel," which he wished to "study, and learn from the Law and what is best and most perfect in it." The *farman* also assures the Jesuits that the priests will be "received most kindly and honourably" and once the emperor has learned about the new faith, they will be free to leave. The emperor promises them "honours and gifts," and concludes with these reassurances: "Therefore let them not have the slightest fear to come. I take them under my protection. Fare you well."[7]

The Jesus Sutras and the *Mirror of Holiness* had different hermeneutical purposes: one was designed simply to explicate the precepts of Jesus, whereas the other had a mixture of motives. Aluoben, the supposed writer of the Jesus Messiah Sutra, saw himself as a humble servant of God trying to clarify the precepts of the religion of Jesus: "The one who serves the heavenly Lord wrote this book in order to explain the doctrines."[8] Xavier, by contrast, had a combination of reasons for his creation, ranging from reaffirming Roman Catholic identity after the Reformation debacle in Europe, asserting the superiority of the message of Jesus, the eventual conversion of Emperor Akbar, and, implicitly, the promotion of himself as the successor of the original disciples.

In his preamble, Xavier makes clear his intentions—to bring out the "good qualities of Jesus," to recount "everything we have in our books on the sayings and actions of Christ," and to impress on Emperor Akbar "the stages of Jesus' heavenly teaching and the levels of his greatness" so that they might serve as a "guide for the souls of righteous." Along with these elevated ideals, Xavier had a specific motive: the conversion of Akbar. Unlike Aluoben and Jing Jing, who did not perceive their task as rescuing the Tang emperor from his religious deficiencies, Xavier took it upon himself to save Emperor Akbar. The Jesuits, who were recovering from the aftermath of the Reformation in Europe, had brought the Christian faith to the East as a way of recruiting more believers and to compensate for the loss of the Protestants. Xavier's life of Jesus was designed as an enticement to ease the way for Akbar's conversion. The emperor, a Muslim, was a seeker of truth and he favored conversation and the exchange of religious ideas. He had devoted himself to the evolution of a new religion, which he hoped would "prove to be a synthesis of all the warring creeds and capable of uniting the discordant elements of his vast empire in one harmonious whole."[9] The Jesuits misread his diverse religious interests as an openness to becoming a Christian, and believed that they could convert him. With the loss of the English king Henry VIII in the Reformation, Akbar's conversion would have been a compensatory royal prize.

In this mission to convert, Xavier affirmed his credentials in two ways. One was to establish his closeness to Jesus. By describing Jesus's physical attributes with phrases like a "man of tall stature," "his face is without flaw and adorned with a harmonious redness," "his beard is full," "his eyes are blue," "his hair is parted in the middle of his head"—all features not mentioned in the canonical Gospels—Xavier implied a level of intimacy with Jesus that placed him implicitly within the ranks of Christ's disciples. Xavier reinforced this idea by announcing himself as the chosen disciple for the task, that is, as one of the disciples whom Jesus was supposed to have sent to King Abgar of Edessa. The inclusion of the following words reinforce Xavier's claim: "When I will have gone into heaven, I will send one of my disciples to teach you the path of salvation and to heal you, in my name, of the illness you have."[10] It is this manufactured closeness to Jesus that makes Xavier bold enough to declare to Akbar in the preamble that "people may say that all books are balm for the soul" but the book he has produced is "above all others" and "will give peace to your majesty's heart, as Christ has said—'My word is the balm for the soul, and eternal life.'" Xavier utilized his imagined proximity to Jesus to show Akbar that embracing Christ was the way to salvation, "a balm for the soul and life eternal." Xavier even had the audacity to suggest that the emperor should read his text "repeatedly in imperial gatherings."[11] The Sutras, by contrast, make no mention of Jesus's outward appearance.

Chinese Christ, Mughal Messiah

Both the Jesus Sutras and the *Mirror of Holiness* record the birth of Jesus, a fairly well mythologized moment of his life, but there is a stark contrast in their reporting of the event. Both establish historical credence to the incident by providing dates. The tone of the Sutra of the Teachings of the World Honored One seems to dispel any skepticism about the event: "This physical manifestation took place 641 years ago and now everyone in the world believes" (7.34). It gives the place of birth as Jerusalem and even records the time of the birth as five o'clock. The *Mirror of Holiness* is more precise and traces the date from the earlier extraordinary events of the history of the Jewish people. In this way, it provides historical continuity and credibility, divine attestation, and the theological importance of the birth:

> Then, on the eve of Sunday in the year 5199 from the creation of the world, or 2,957 after Noah's flood, 2,015 years since the birth of Abraham, 1,510 years since Moses and the children of Israel emerged from Egypt, 1,032 years since the anointment of David and his obtaining the kingship of Israel, in the sixty-fifth week Daniel had prophesied, 752 years after the founding of Rome, in the year 42 of the reign of Caesar Augustus, when most of the world was at peace, at the point of midnight, when everything was extremely silent and the blessed Mary . . . cast her eyes to the ground and saw Jesus born before her, and she heard the first sound he made crying like other infants.[12]

Although not all the Gospels refer to the virginal conception of Jesus, both the Chinese and the Jesuit texts make mention of it. The Sutra of Jesus Christ narrates the Conception briefly. It records that a cool wind entered the body of Mary according to the command of the heavenly Lord and she immediately became pregnant without the agency of a male. This act is not seen as the fulfillment of Hebraic prophecy but more as dispelling the stigma attached to such a birth, and more importantly, as revealing God's power: "The whole world saw this, and understood what God had wrought."[13] In the Jesuit version, an elaborate scene is set in which Mary is portrayed as the chosen one to beget the Messiah. Her impeccable purity is emphatically stated. Xavier even gives the age when she became pregnant as thirteen. In his version, the angel Gabriel, along with other angels, announce the divine purpose of her pregnancy and tell her that the name of the child should be Immanuel.

The birth itself also is treated differently in the Sutras and in Xavier's text. The Monument Sutra provides only minimal information about the birth and is succinct in its approach. It simply states that the angels proclaimed the good tidings; a virgin brought forth a Holy One in Judea; and a bright constellation announced the event. The Sutra of Jesus Christ, too, records Jesus merely as a man appearing on earth, born of a virgin but in a birth that is not accompanied by any extravagant supernatural fanfare. The significance of the birth is confined to a bright star proclaiming the occasion: "The whole world saw a bright mystery in the heavens. Everybody saw from their homes a star as big as a wagon wheel."[14]

Xavier, by contrast, situates the birth of Jesus within Jewish prophetic expectations. He provides frequent biblical references to the Conception and to the actual birth as a way of validating his text's credibility and to impute supernatural authentication to these events. At the time of the birth, Xavier describes Mary's mood as contemplative and worshipful, and notes that as the birth occurred, an astonished joy came over her. Unlike Eve and other women, Mary did not feel any pain upon childbirth. Instead her womb remained undamaged and "without any opening being made." Jesus emerged as the "rays of the sun pass through the glass without tearing anything." When she heard the first cry, Mary threw herself on the ground and worshiped him. Xavier embellishes the event with strange happenings that are not found in the Gospels, such as the appearance of a fountain of oil in the city of Rome; the flowing of oil into the sea; a sibyl foretelling Caesar that a child would be born who would be greater than him; the collapsing of a temple known as the House of Eternal Peace that people believed would last forever or until a virgin gave birth; as well as the appearance of three brilliant suns and a colored cloud in the kingdom of Spain.

While both the Sutras and Xavier's version record the gifts brought to the newborn, in the Sutras, they were brought by Persians who remain unnamed, whereas Xavier calls them kings and provides their names as Melchior, Caspar, and Balthasar. These additional exaggerated supernatural events, and the visit of royalty to the holy family, may have been intended to contrast the birth of Jesus to the relatively mundane and ordinary birth of the prophet Muhammed and draw to the attention of the Mughal court to the amazing and spectacular arrival of Jesus on earth.

In the Chinese Sutras, the only mention of Jesus's early life relates to his speech. According to the Sutra of Jesus Christ, Jesus spoke his first words when he was five, but it does not reveal what those words were. It states simply that he "assumed the Holy Word, and began teaching" when he was twelve, and went on preaching until he was thirty-two. The Jesuit version provides more information. It mentions his circumcision on the eighth day; his escape to Egypt with his parents after being warned by the angel; his visit to the Temple when he was twelve and his temporary separation from his parents; and his theological discussions with the learned men of the Temple that revealed him to be a wonder-child, with an adult's understanding of matters of religion. In Xavier's retelling, when Jesus's worried parents are reunited with their twelve-year-old son at the Temple and tell him they had been searching for him, Jesus's answer was: "Why were you looking for me? Didn't you know that I had to be occupied with the things of my Father?"—an early indication that Jesus would be willing to sacrifice the happiness of his mother in order to seek the "pleasure of his Father." Xavier portrays the magical abilities of Jesus in his early years. Resonating with the Infancy Gospel of Thomas, where miracles are attributed to the child Jesus, Xavier records the diapers of Jesus as having magical powers. To restore the fertility of a balsam tree that had failed to bear fruit, it was sprinkled with the water in which the nappies of Jesus were washed.

In the Jesus Sutras, Jesus is described variously as the "King of Dharma," "Radiant Son," "Compassionate Joyous Lamb," and "The Great Teacher." The honorifics often used for Sakyamuni (a name for the Buddha that referred to his Shakya clan origins), "Honored by the Universe," "World Honored One," as well as, in a more direct and radical move, one of the Chinese names for Sakyamuni, *shi-zun,* are also employed for Jesus.[15] The *Mirror of Holiness,* however, sticks largely with the conventional biblical titles. Jesus is called "Jesus of Nazareth," "a prophet powerful in word and deed," "Nazarene," and "King of Kings." In the preamble, Jerome calls him the "Spirit of God," a koranic reference.

The Monument Inscription describes Jesus as one who "appeared upon earth as a man."[16] It is unequivocal about the humanity of Jesus: "Therefore, my Lord Ye Su ... hid his true power, [and he] became a human." Jesus is presented as a vehicle through whom God made the divine perceptible to humankind. This is made clear in the Sutra of the Teachings of the World Honored One: "The Messiah is not the Honored One. Instead, through his body he showed the people the Honored One" (4.12, 4.13). Anyone who claims divine status is spurned by the Sutras: "Anybody who says 'I am a God' should die."[17] Whereas in the Monument Sutras Jesus is described as the "Illustrious honoured one who hid his true majesty and came into the world of men," Xavier makes an extra effort to present him as a God or a Son of God. In Xavier's portrayal, we see a devout and confident defense of Catholic orthodoxy at work. In describing the birth of Christ, Xavier's text proclaims: "Although this son wanted to be like humans in everything and to suffer pains, in this instance he wanted to be born as a god." This is the Jesus who continually affirms his divine status and frequently claims "I and the Father are one." To those fellow Jews who accused him of calling himself a Son of God, Xavier's Jesus replies, "believe that my Father is in me and I am in the Father," and tells his disciples that in the Son of Man's glory, God also has been glorified. Jesus is commended as the one who continues the acts of the Father: "Until now my Father acts, and I act too." Jesus was killed, in Xavier's view, not because he violated the Sabbath Laws, but because he "called God his Father, and put himself on a level with Him." Xavier seems to have had a hermeneutical agenda: in making Jesus more than a human being and equal to God, he challenged the Muslim view of Jesus as a mere man.

In the Sutra of the Teaching of the Honored One, the word God is not used; instead the narrative refers to the "World Honored One," or "One Sacred Spirit." The Sutra's conception of God resonates with the Buddhist idea of the emptiness and the incomprehensible nature of God: "The holy One of great wisdom (is so invisible as to be) equal to Pure Emptiness itself."[18] In the end, God is beyond all human understanding: "God cannot be grasped" and the Sutra reiterates the invisibility of the divine: "Nobody has seen God. Nobody has ability to see God. Truly, God is like the wind. Who can see the wind?" The God of Jesus is "beyond knowing, beyond words" so that "no eye can see your form or your unclouded nature." This God is also resolute: "You are the truth, Steadfast for all time," and "among all Spirits you alone are un-changing." In addition, the God of the Sutras is one who dazzles: "You live perpetually in light. The Light which enters every sphere."[19] These sayings all have the essential characteristics of Eastern mysticism, which the *Mirror of Holiness* lamentably lacks.

The God whom Jesus proclaimed in the Sutras is not the historical, patriarchal, and personal God whom Jesus invokes in the Gospels. This God is not restricted to one region, or aligned to one group of people, but is "present everywhere all over the universe."[20] The Semitic God has been replaced with the Buddhas or the great invisible emptiness that manifests itself in the Word as Spirit or Wind. The name of the Buddha is called on frequently in the Sutras: "When people are afraid they call upon Buddha's name"; and it is in the "Buddha's nature to bestow grace, and with this grace comes also a deep, clear understanding that lifts us above folly."[21]

This is not the God of the Bible, who provides new moral precepts. The Jesus of the Sutras encourages his followers to discern God in-stead through observing nature:

> Consider the earth. It produces and nurtures a multitude of
> creatures, each receiving what it needs. Words cannot express
> the benefits the earth provides. Like the earth, you are at
> one with Peace and Joy when you practice the laws and save
> living creatures. But do it without acclaim. This is the law of
> no virtue.[22]

Like the Eastern sages, Jesus in the Sutras discovers moral knowledge through the created order rather than deriving it from the revelation of God acting through the great historical events of the Israelites.

Those raised on the notion of Jesus as the eschatological prophet who announced the imminent end of the world, to be replaced with the Kingdom of God, will be deeply disappointed. The Jesus of the Sutras does not offer any eschatological message. The Kingdom he envisages is not the future eschatological intervention that most Western bib-lical scholars uphold, but one that has to be found within oneself. The Sutras embody the Buddhist / Hindu idea of the Kingdom as an inward awareness, an inner spiritual faculty. The Kingdom is to be found here on earth: "Where is that world really to be found? It is to be found right here in the world."[23] Instead of offering a message with an eschatological dimension, the Sutras offer the Buddhist idea of mindfulness. Jesus's parable about a house built on sand, for instance, is turned into an example of mindfulness: "When we lack mindfulness, we are like someone who builds a house out of ignorance . . . The wind comes and blows it away."[24] The principal emphasis seems to be on the transformation of the self through conquering desire. Jesus is seen as stipulating eight virtuous measures that should purge away the dust of defilement. These eight moral measures, the scholar Saeki surmises, come from the Buddhist Garbha Sutrua [sic], which were available at that time in three different Chinese versions. Expressions like "He purged away the dust," Saeki believes, strengthen his argument. The phrase is borrowed from Buddhism. The dust here denotes "guna," which may well be translated as "sensation," "objects of sensation," or "organs of sensation"—namely, eyes, ears, tongue, body, and mind. What is implied in the expression is the purification of the sense organs.[25]

The Kingdom that Jesus proclaims in the Sutras is anti-imperial and anti-national: "Do not think that a tribe or nation or empire can become the kingdom, for the kingdom will grow when and where it wills." The Sutras depoliticize and personalize the distinctive announcement of Jesus. Once again, however, the *Mirror of Holiness* takes a different line, with Jesus advocating a Kingdom that is the manifestation of God's will, the space where God actively reigns, a realm where God exercises authority.

Jesus in the Sutras is a teacher of wisdom, concerned with a larger humanity, rather than one who confines himself to the limited interest of the Jewish people. The Buddhist framework in which he is depicted also softens this Jewish-centric view. Jesus is represented as a Christian bodhisattva, a compassionate sage filled with mercy who provides the raft for salvation. The salvation he offers is to restore human beings to their original nature, "pure and void of all selfishness, unstained and unostentatious, . . . with a mind free from inordinate lust and passion." Because of desire and selfishness, human beings have departed from these ideals. But the salvation offered by Jesus has "purged away the dust from human nature and perfected a true character" and has thus opened three constant gates—a Buddhist expression meaning gates of perception, eye, ear, and nose.[26] In Xavier's portrayal, Jesus is projected as both the prescriber and the personification of perfect righteousness. The attainment of it is summed up in the eight statements that begin with Beatitudes: "Blessed are they . . ." The reward is that they will be "the Sons of God" and "theirs is the Kingdom of heaven."

In the Sutras, Jesus emerges as the embodiment of a mixture of Buddhism, Taoism, and Confucianism. He preaches virtues that make an individual truly a good human being. He is the one who opens the door of virtues that are purity of body, speech, and thought. The Jesus Messiah Sutra claims that Jesus came to establish a "new teaching" of nonassertion, which has "the power to dissolve the dark realm and destroy evil forever." Jesus sounds like a Buddhist preacher who proclaims the message of self-control and detachment: "We are always seeking and acting, and because of this we create movement and desire which cause unhappiness and make it difficult to attain peace and joy. Therefore I say we should live without desire and action."[27] The teaching of Jesus is encapsulated in the third liturgical Sutra, where four essential principles—"no desire," "no piousness," "no doing," and "no truth"—all resonate with the "redeeming power or emptiness" explicated in Buddhism and Taoism. The "no desire" indicates how craving "creates a multitude of problems" and cuts one off from the root of peace and joy; "no action" denotes not performing in ways that are apart from one's normal being and not engaging in activities for the sake of progress and material gain, which can cause one to lose sight of the Way; "no virtue" inculcates the idea of not showing off one's spiritual piety and so not gaining fame through one's piousness; and "no truth" emphasizes not judging or insisting that one's truth is the truth. Just like the mirror that reflects all, "those who have awakened to the Way," have "attained the mind of peace and joy," and can "see all karmic conditions" and should reflect "everything as it is without judging."[28] These four principles are the most essentially Buddhist of all the teachings found in the Sutras. These virtues describe emptiness and attaining peace and joy through nondesire. The quest for purity is discouraged, in case it should promote self-consciousness. Jesus is projected as a person who disapproves of anyone seeking piety, and even merit: "We are always seeking and acting and because of this we create movement and desire which cause unhappiness and make it difficult to attain peace and joy. Therefore, I say we should live without desire and action."[29] In one sense, what the Sutras do is to reiterate non-Semitic Eastern values such as renunciation and detachment. Xavier's Jesus, the Jesus of the Gospel, is instead explicated through the inherited teachings, which begin with the Incarnation and end with the Atonement and Ascension.

In the Chinese texts, Jesus emerges as a contradictory figure, socially reactionary but ecclesiastically radical. He seems like a model Chinese patriarch reiterating the traditional Chinese values of obedience to God, emperor, and parents: "You should honor your parents just as you honor God and the Emperor." Jesus teaches how one should behave toward the family and before ruling authorities. This was clearly an attempt by the Church of the East missionaries to encourage Chinese Christians to integrate Confucian morals with Christian principles. The early Church of the East missionaries knew well the intricate link between the power of the word and the power of the authorities. The Monument Sutra explicates the strange bond between message and authority thus: "Dao / Logos without (the support of) the Emperor would not attain its full development, the Emperor without (pursuing) Dao / Logos would not become great. If Dao and the Emperors come together, then the world will be well managed."[30] This is the Jesus who encourages undivided loyalty to parents and total allegiance to the emperor. It is not the Jesus of the Gospel who showed disrespect to a ruler, calling Herod a fox, or the Jesus who redrew family ties by claiming "Who is my mother, and who are my brothers?"

Nevertheless, the same Sutras project a radical Jesus who challenges the conventional ecclesiastical hierarchy. He does not envisage an institutional community with a chain of command that puts a man at the top. When an annoyed Peter asks Jesus why he allowed women to follow him, Jesus accuses him of being "blind" and tells him that the "seeds of the kingdom are planted both in men and women, and that in the kingdom there is no difference between them." Unlike the canonical Gospel, Peter here is not the preferred one. The Sutras, resonating with the Gospel of Mary, accord that privilege to Mary: "When I appear in glory, Mary shall see me first. She is my beloved disciple."[31] Jesus seems to be a believer in equal rights, someone who discourages holding male or female slaves, and supports treating noble and ordinary people with equal respect.

Given these two approaches, it will come as no surprise that in the *Mirror of Holiness,* Jesus is drawn as the person who strengthens the institutionalized church. The Jesuit's version repeats the canonical gospel narratives and inducts Peter as the chosen leader who has the power of the keys—the power to bind and loosen, and to admit and exclude. To this already investured ecclesiastical authority, Xavier adds words that invest Peter with earthly powers that further reinforce his role: "The faith of Peter, who is the first vicegerent (*khalifah*), shall never be injured and his work will be to strengthen others." By identifying Peter as *khalifah,* Xavier knew exactly what he was telling Akbar. *Khalifah* is not only the civil and religious leader of a Muslim state, but also is considered a representative of Allah on earth. In other words, Akbar was indirectly told of the power and the role of the Pope, whom Xavier represents.

Xavier's Jesus appears to be an appeaser or compromiser. Sometimes he is portrayed as diluting those essential Roman Catholic doctrines that do not make any sense to Muslims. For instance, one of the cardinal Roman Catholic doctrines, transubstantiation—the belief that the bread and wine given at the Mass become the body and blood of Jesus Christ when they are sanctified—is glossed over in Xavier's retelling: "Know that my body will be taken for you, and my blood will be shed for pardoning you and many others." At times, Xavier edits out hardline Roman Catholic moral positions that might harm the advancement of the Christian faith. Divorce is a comparatively uncomplicated practice among Muslims. Not wanting to offend Akbar who had several wives, Xavier conveniently leaves out the rather strong words of Jesus about the annulment of marriage, found in Matthew 5.31–32 and 9.3–12. Xavier also would have been familiar with the traumatic divisions caused within the church by the divorce of King Henry VIII, an event that had occurred barely fifty years prior to the arrival of the Jesuits at the court of the Mughals.

By contrast, the aggressive mission command of Jesus that is found in the Gospel of Matthew is absent in the Sutra. The Sutra's report of it is very concise: "Go you unto the world and preach all things that I have taught you and declare the same." More pertinently, it leaves out baptism in the name of the Father, the Son, and the Holy Spirit. The commands to conquer, grow the numbers of followers, and expand the reach of institutional power that are very much encouraged by the Matthean verse are all missing in the Sutra texts. The nonaggressive, nonexpansionist attitude of the Sutra resonates with the Buddha's mission command in Mahavagga, where the emphasis is the enlightenment of souls rather than the enhancement of institutional power or recruitment of new adherents. In contrast to the less aggressively phrased missionary command in the Sutras, Xavier's sole aim is the conquest. Needless to say, he reproduces Matthew's missionary command, which encourages overpowering other religions and cultures and strengthening the institutional power of the church.

Unlike the Church of the East missionaries who were trying to envisage a Jesus who would meet Buddhist, Taoist, and Confucian expectations, Xavier was endeavoring to present a Jesus whose approach contrasted with that of the Prophet Muhammed. He accomplishes this in three ways. First, the Jesus who emerges is a person who lives frugally, seeks the company of unwanted people, teaches these people the mysteries of God's ways, and shoulders the fate of the poor and the persecuted. This is in contrast with the decadent moral standards of the Prophet Muhammed, who is supposed to have enriched himself with commercial deals and engaged in several wars to acquire honor and fortune. Second, Jesus is portrayed as a person who led a pure and chaste life, whereas the Prophet Muhammed had several wives and was alleged to have had sex with slaves. Third, the miracle-working ability of Jesus is emphasized. Xavier reiterates what is already recorded in the Koran and amply reported in the Gospels—the accounts of Jesus healing the sick, raising the dead, walking on water, multiplying loaves. The subtext would have been clear to the Mughal court audience. Jesus's miracles are attested to not only by his enemies but also by the Prophet Muhammed whom the Mughals venerate, whereas the miracles attributed to the Prophet Muhammed are denied by all. To Xavier, only the wonderful deeds of Jesus are worthy of being called miracles.

While the portrayal of Jesus in the Sutras is suffused with Eastern religious references, Xavier's Jesus exhibits all the marks of a remarkably confident biblical and Catholic orthodoxy. What Akbar offered was a pure Chalcedonian Christ. Jesus is a Nazarene and Son of God. He was a man from Nazareth who showed all human emotions but he is also the Son of God who knows what is awaiting him, and for whom every event of life has been confirmed by supernatural attestation and had analogical precedent in the life of the Jews.

A description of the final week in the life of Jesus is found in both the Chinese Sutras and Xavier's version, but one provides only the basic information supplied by the Gospels, whereas the other provides elaborate details. The Sutras are very frugal in documenting these events. They limit their portrayal to the plot against Jesus by the Jews, and to the Jews arguing their case in front of Pilate, the Roman prefect, who finds him innocent and washes his hands of the case. The narrative reaches its climax, recalling the Crucifixion, burial, and death in an unimpassioned way. The Jesuit version, however, records faithfully some of the memorable events surrounding the last days of Jesus's life, such as his triumphal entry into Jerusalem, the cleansing of the temple, and his meal with his disciples.

The atoning death of Jesus in the Sutras is described as a "sacrificing transformation," but its explication is entrenched very much in Buddhist terms. Jesus is portrayed as a "visitor" who offers his redemptory power as a means of breaking the cycle of cause and effect. He is the solution to the existential issues of rebirth and karma. The Messiah figure in the Sutras does not die specifically to forgive the sins of humanity but rather to release humanity from past karmic deeds and the cycle of rebirth.

Unlike the Christ of the Gospels who offers redemption from the worthlessness of unredeemed humanity, the Jesus of the Sutras, especially the Sutra of Cause, Effect, and Salvation, addresses the notion of the "karmic impact" of past actions: "All creatures should know that the karmic consequences of what is done in this life will shape the next life" (Second Sutra 4.22). Jesus is seen as offering a way out of the wheel of existence, the karmic cycle, for all the lives "affected by the karma of the past": "God suffered terrible woes so that all should be freed from karma, for nobody is beyond the reach of this Buddha principle" (2.26). As the Fourth Liturgical Sutra put it, Jesus is the "compassionate joyous lamb" who will "free us of the karma of our lives" and bring us "back to our original nature." A Jewish predicament is replaced with a Buddhist dilemma, and the Sutras come up with a Buddhist solution. The only way to unshackle oneself from the cycle of birth and rebirth is to break free from the law of karma, and the only way to achieve this is to become a Buddha or an "enlightened one." Biblical scholars who disregard as Eastern philosophical nonsense the idea that the consequences of past events affect the present should bear in mind that this Eastern notion of reward and punishment is not totally absent from Jesus's teaching: "Likewise, every good tree bears good fruit, but a bad tree bears bad fruit. A good tree cannot bear bad fruit, and a bad tree cannot bear good fruit" (Matthew 7.17–18). Biblical commentators tend to overlook the karmic implications of this verse and treat it as a way of distinguishing between good and bad prophets.

Although there are a few details in the Sutras of the historical Jesus, he is clearly not thought of as a figure who paid humanity's debt and saved them from their sins, thus bringing about forgiveness. Rather, he is perceived as someone who awakens the divine potentiality in human beings, leading humanity to the Way. The emancipation that Jesus dispensed is couched not in the image of a sacrificial lamb but in the Buddhist image of a raft on which one is ferried away from a turbulent life. Jesus is presented as the new raft that delivers people from ignorance and anxiety: to save mankind, he "took an oar in the vessel of mercy and ascended into the Palace of Light."[32] The idea of rescuing people resonates with the Buddhist Guanyin, a female bodhisattva, a savior of the people. She is often represented with a ship on her back as a testimony to her ability to save people from shipwreck. The prototype for the salvific work of Jesus is not male but female. In their compassionate effort, Jesus and Guanyin are engaged in a similar task. The liturgical Sutra continues with the raft image. The worshippers petition: "Send your raft of salvation. To save us from the burning streams!"[33] The reference to the burning stream could be Buddha's Fire Sermon, which addresses burning with desire.

Although Jesus was depicted as a bodhisattva who guides people to liberation and purges humanity from its pollution, the Chinese texts do not deviate from their doctrinal position, which caused a schism within the early church. In keeping with the belief of Nestorius, the founder of the Church of the East, the Sutras make it clear that only his human nature suffered, while his divine nature remained unscathed: "For instance, it seems to be plain, therefore, that, though the Messiah suffered death in his body of 'the five attributes,' his life did not end therewith."[34]

The *Mirror of Holiness* treads on the path of orthodoxy and describes the death of Jesus as the "best service ever rendered to God in this world, because he sacrificed to God the best thing he could and yielded himself voluntarily for the redemption and salvation of men." What is hinted at in the Gospels was enough to enable Xavier's fertile mind to indulge in his version of magical realism. Although the first three Gospels have only one sentence about the flogging of Jesus, and the fourth makes no mention of it, Xavier's narrative relentlessly focuses on the physical savagery that Jesus faced in his final hours. It depicts explicit details of violence meted out to Jesus that are not recorded in the canonical Gospels. Jesus seemed to have experienced every possible physical punishment: the modern torture of waterboarding must have been unknown to the Romans, otherwise Xavier would have included that too. In Xavier's version, Jesus was beaten mercilessly and six men were employed to carry out the thrashings. He was given 5,780 lashes with the result that "pieces of flesh were cut off and fell on the ground, so that the whole body became one wound."[35] Many more gory details are provided about when he was nailed on the cross. When the soldiers drove the nail into the right hand of Jesus, they found the other hand too short to reach the hole, "therefore they pulled it with all their strength, and made it reach the hole so that they could drive the spike through." While all this happened, Xavier records that Jesus did not say a word.

All these brutal acts are missing from the Sutras except that his agony lasted for five hours. The Sutra of Jesus Christ has a matter-of-fact tone about it: "They hung him high upon a wooden scaffold."

Xavier probably included these barbarous deeds to bring home to Akbar two important points. One was presumably to show that after such terrific beatings and gruesome nailing to the cross it would have been impossible for a man to survive, thus challenging the Muslim view that Jesus did not die. The other is to demonstrate the goodness and kindness of Jesus in spite of extreme agony and torment. To illustrate this, Xavier included an imaginary event—one unsupported by the Gospel—whereby the blood of Jesus heals the nearly blind soldier who had pierced Jesus with his spear.

In the *Mirror of Holiness,* Jesus plays the role already assigned to him in the Jewish salvation history. He provides resolution to a Jewish problem that has universal significance, redeeming humankind from its fallen state. In the Sutras, Jesus offers a Buddhist analysis and Buddhist solution to the human predicament. Humans have become corrupted by desire, and the cause of that desire is the false sense of self. The Sutras do not generally address the predictability of sin due to the transgression of humanity. Those readers raised on Paul, Augustine, Luther, and John Wesley regarding the inevitability of the sinfulness of humanity will find the Sutras uncomfortable. In the Sutras, Jesus still sacrifices his life and dies, but the object here is to teach the way rather than to absolve and forgive humanity for its sins.

The Sutras present a range of pictures of one of the main theological tenets of the Christian faith—the Resurrection of Jesus. The Monument Sutra makes the event less special than one would expect, and uses symbolic language to describe it: "The religion of light teachings are [*sic*] like the resplendent sun: they have the power to dissolve the dark realm and destroy evil forever" (2.22). The Resurrection is described as a light sent down to conquer death and wickedness. But in the Sutra of the Teachings of the World Honored One, there is an explicit reference to the event—"the Messiah had risen from the dead"—and a claim that it was attested to by a female disciple. The appearance of the risen Christ to a woman is seen as a reversal of the miseries brought about by the action of the first woman, Eve. The Sutra of the Teachings of the World-

Honored One puts it thus: "As the first woman caused the lies of humanity, so it was women who first told the truth about what had happened, to show all that the Messiah forgave women and wished them to be treated properly in the future" (5.32). Jesus here comes out as an advocate of women's emancipation. The gender equality that the Sutras seem to advocate is radical by the standards of the time, since the Chinese, like any other ancient culture, paid little attention to gender issues. According to the Sutras, the risen Messiah remained on earth for "fourteen days and one month," not forty days as recorded in the Gospels.

Xavier, in contrast, describes the Resurrection appearances in detail, and includes events not found in the Gospels; for example, Jesus appearing to Mary, his mother. The fact that he devotes the entire last section of his book to recording the various sightings of the risen Jesus accords with one explicitly clear motive. The Prophet Muhammed died and his body and his tomb were still in Medina, whereas Jesus died but was resurrected, an event seen by many.

In short, the Sutras effectively remove Jesus from his Jewish environment and the expectations of his people. They also effectively disconnect Jesus from the seminal moments of salvation history, such as the Fall, the covenant with the Jewish patriarchs, and the establishment of the dynasty of David. These were decisive events in Jewish history, pointing toward Christ's Crucifixion, Resurrection, and salvation. The Sutras include only an oblique reference to Jesus "fulfilling the old laws— by the twenty-four sages' writings." The sages mentioned here could be the Hebrew prophets.[36] Jesus is also isolated from the rest of the New Testament. Paul is completely absent from the Sutras, which distance themselves as well from what Paul dared to proclaim: "For sin shall not have dominion over you" (Romans 6.14). Paul, as a European hero, is yet to be discovered. The Church of the East missionaries realized from the beginning that the Semitic view of God and Jewish religious concepts tinged with Hellenistic ideas needed to be carefully reformulated.

Imperfectly and haltingly, these Sutras try to project an understanding of Jesus that sets the tone for detaching Jesus from his environment and articulating him in a wider multi-religious context, an

31

approach that was later vigorously pursued and practiced by Ponnambalam Ramanathan and Sarvepalli Radhakrishnan, whom we will meet later in this volume. Xavier, in contrast, situates Jesus in a salvation history that has no relevance to India, which has its own multiple salvation histories. Xavier treats the life and work of Jesus—his birth, the place of his birth, his miracles, and his death—as part of the salvation history of the Jews predicated by influential prophetical figures such as Isaiah in order to interpret the events related to Jesus, even though there is no evidence that these great prophetical sayings were related to Jesus. This elaborate historical and cultural documentation from Jewish history and heritage was used perhaps as a way of contrasting with the life, birth, and work of the prophet Muhammad, who had no such prophetic attestation. The Islamic messenger came into the world like any other ordinary human being with no such anticipations of his coming, whereas Jesus becomes the object and fulfilment of divine foretelling.

When Asia Ruled the World

Both texts—the Jesus Sutras and the *Mirror of Holiness*—had a hostile reception in the West. John Foster dismissed the Chinese reworkings as "hopeless syncretism."[37] Samuel Hugh Moffett found some of the Sutras "closer to syncretism."[38] Another criticism often leveled against the Church of the East missionaries was that they had compromised the Gospel and neutered the power of the Christian message. James Legge blamed the Monument Inscription for being "too passionless altogether for mission," and accused the missionaries of the Church of the East of not being able to challenge "the emperors and men in power, and placing their reliance so much on them."[39]

Likewise, Xavier's text was criticized for not being faithful to the Gospels. Louis de Dieu, a Dutch Protestant who translated the work into Latin with the sole purpose of discrediting Roman Catholicism, accused Xavier of omitting incidents in Jesus's life and incorporating elements from noncanonical sources—facts that Xavier himself acknowledges in his preamble.

For these critics, the missionaries of the Church of the East had compromised too easily. Ramsay MacMullen, in his study of the growth of Christianity in the West, has demonstrated how the Christian message was significantly "paganized" when it was introduced into Europe. But critics' generosity regarding cultural concessions made by the Western churches in this European scenario was hardly extended to the Church of the East. These critics also failed to see that the Church of the East missionaries did not have any theological precedents to go by but valiantly wrestled through issues that were bewilderingly new to them.[40]

In fact, the type of Christianization that happened in the West could not be replicated in the East. First, Chinese and Indian cultures at that time were too powerful to be simply dislodged. The Christian missionaries in Asia had to face a totally different kind of religious landscape to that encountered by their counterparts in the West. They experienced in China and India a formidable array of written sacred texts that their colleagues in the West rarely encountered. They had to confront a culture that, as Legge put it, possessed a literature "venerable for its antiquity, subtlety, variety." In addition, these missionaries had to face awesome Confucian, Taoist, and Buddhist thinkers who had received much higher intellectual training than those who had come to teach them. These thinkers' intellectual reasoning, Legge reckoned, was too "strong" for the newly arrived Persian missionaries.[41] Unlike the missions to the West, which faced less sophisticated Germanic tribes, and the Anglo-Saxons in England, the Church of the East was dealing with ancient, highly literate, civilized cultures and peoples.

The story was similar in India. The stock European assumption that the Portuguese had found an inferior primitive people was far from true. The Indians, according to John M. Hobson, were "more advanced than their European discoverers." Indeed, Vasco da Gama would not have reached India without "superior Asian nautical technologies and scientific ideas."[42] The Indian rulers treated the Portuguese not as a superior power but as pirates. Far from being "overawed" by their arrival, the Indian rulers were "completely underwhelmed."[43]

By the time the Portuguese landed in India, K. N. Chaudhuri reckons that Indian civilization had "already scored a series of triumphant near 'firsts' in human discoveries of the mind: scientific theories of linguistics, grammar, the mathematical concept of empty set, zero, and negative numbers." These "dazzling intellectual achievements" were further heightened by India's progress in technology, economics, and the arts, which were there for the "whole world to see."[44] The Jesuits faced an extremely erudite and enlightened Mughal court.

The second reason that the success of the early church in the West could not be repeated in Asia was that the Gospel did not come with political power. Unlike the later missionary propagation, which came with the might of modern European colonialism, this earlier Christian activity occurred in the seventh and seventeenth centuries without the support of a powerful and prestigious Christian ruling elite or secular authorities. In fact, as a Christian community, the Church of the East was often persecuted by the Persian rulers of the Sassanian dynasty such as Shapur II (309–379) and Bahram V (421–438). Although the Jesuits came with the Portuguese invaders, Portuguese dominance was confined to coastal areas of India. Their influence was highly restricted, and after the Reformation it became further constrained as the Jesuits became less energized.

Third, the Persian missionaries and the Jesuits in India found that the Chinese and Indians were less rigid than Europeans about adhering to one religion. In China, people were attached to three systems—Confucianism, Taoism, and Buddhism—without erecting any boundaries. In India, the Emperor Akbar built a House of Worship, Ibādat Khāna, that was open to different religions. The supreme example of Akbar's liberality was his promotion of a universal religion known as Suhl-i-kul. In this atmosphere of relaxed, untroubled eclecticism, and loose organizational structures prone to absorbing elements from outside, those promoting an inflexible Christianity would have found it difficult to have any influence, let alone to replace indigenous religious beliefs.

Reflections, Observations, Comments

Even a cursory glance at the Jesus Sutras and the *Mirror of Holiness* shows that they are as different as Chinese dim sum and an Indian vegetarian thali meal. The Jesus Sutras reflect the importance of the "luminous religion," as the Chinese called it—an intricate, sensitive faith that is supple enough to incorporate Taoism, Buddhism, and Confucian thinking and yet retain its religious identity and distinctiveness. Xavier's version makes biblical religion seem overpowering and leaves no room for compromise. In contrast to the terse, spiritual, complex, theologically adventurous, and profound Jesus Sutras, the *Mirror of Holiness* is verbose, theologically staid, sensationalist, and often deviates from the received text.

These Tang dynasty Christian documents are as significant as the Dead Sea scrolls and the Nag Hammadi library. The Dead Sea scrolls, a corpus of writing dating from the late Second Temple period, a time when Jesus of Nazareth lived, help in examining Judaism, and the Nag Hammadi library assists in our understanding of the canonical Gospels and Gnosticism. The Jesus Sutras and *Mirror of Holiness* should be seen as apocryphal writings that continue the practice of the early Christians in creating gospels to meet new, and, in their case, non-Semitic, complex situations and demands. In keeping with the apocryphal style of writing, Xavier provides additional materials that are not found in the canonical Gospels. Besides naming the Magi, and spicing up the Crucifixion, Xavier declares that the day Mary was born is a holiday; recounts a story about a cow that Joseph and Mary owned that carried their belongings but had to be sold to meet their travel expenses; and includes the well-known Catholic story about a woman called Veronica, who, seeing the agony of Jesus, wiped his face with her apron and when opening it later, found in "each of the folds his very image." These embellishments are meant to help the *Mirror of Holiness* appeal to the Mughal court.

Although scholars have tended to reject these texts, especially the Jesus Sutras, as full of dubious interjections and extrapolations, as dissentient and theologically spurious, and as insignificant outliers in the development of the church's theology, they are in fact indispensable guides to post-canonical Christianity. They challenge the church's traditional notion that theology reflects only biblical revelations. Instead, they offer creative speculations on the church's received understanding of Jesus.

The Chinese and Xavierian texts emerged before the current search for the historical Jesus began in the West. As their depictions of Jesus show, the authors were not restricted by the same questions of historicity that characterized the modern quest. Their representations of Jesus were at times speculative and spectacular, and at times clerical and eccentric, because they were not intended for a Christian audience: instead they were written to instruct and win the confidence of their patrons, a Chinese emperor and a Mughal ruler who welcomed them warmly to their imperial courts.

Both the Chinese and the Jesuit texts emerged within the religiously pluralistic worlds of China and India. The Sutras are ambivalent about religious pluralism, both affirming and negating pluralistic thinking. On the one hand, they announce that there is not just one path to truth: "There is no single name for the way, Sages do not come in a single form."[45] This resonates with the Bhagavad Gita's notion of many ways to truth. In addition, the Sutras do not have any qualms about assigning the term Buddha to the God of the Bible, and the Law of the Buddha is employed to convey God's law.[46] The Sutras also point out the possibility of God's presence everywhere. Faced with the existence of numerous religions, worship of many gods, and a variety of philosophical schools, the authors of the Sutras did not overtly press the case for a Christian God. Instead they drew attention to the one true God: "All things manifest only one-God. All things are things made by the One-God . . . There is only one—God"—a God that provides "for all beings" and "cannot be grasped." Or, in the words of the Fourth Liturgical Sutra: "All great teachers such as the Buddhas are moved by this Wind and there is nowhere in the world where this Wind does not reach and move." The Sutra *Secret Sayings of Ye Su* goes still further. When James asks Jesus about other preachers who offer wisdom, Jesus answers: "The seeds of the kingdom are everywhere. Do not think of the kingdom as your personal possession . . . Where there is light, rejoice in it."

On the other hand, there are instances where these Chinese documents reveal an exclusivism: "But, the rest of the people of (Persia) all worship the Lord of the Universe and are united in declaring that I-shu (i.e. Jesus) is the Messiah."[47] The Sutra of the Teaching of the World-

Honored One states: "Pay no attention to outsiders but worship the One sacred spirit. The One will become visible to you, and then you should worship only the One."[48] A clear and strong Christian exclusivism is found in the Discourse on the Almsgiving: "Only by the succour of the Holy Mystery through the Messiah can people be saved."[49] There is also an acknowledgment of the superiority of the Christian God, at least in the liturgical Sutra Taking Refuge in the Trinity: "Your virtues are greater than those of all the Holy Ones and Dharma Lords." Such exclusive sentiments are reminiscent of the uncompromising attitude of the Jesus of John's Gospel: "I am the way, the truth and the life."

Xavier produced his text as if other religions did not exist or matter. He was trying to present the open-minded emperor with a glorious but dominant Jesus whose aim seemed to be to conquer individual souls, replace existing religions (in this case Islam), and eventually conquer the entire nation.

The Jesus Sutras and Xavier's biography of Jesus contain some delicious indigenous images. Jesus not only dispenses Buddhist precepts, but also appears in *jiasha*, a gown worn by Buddhist monks, and wears a turban in keeping with the Mughal habit: when Peter entered the tomb, he sees "the linen and the turban that had been on his head lying aside folded." Instead of literal translations, too, the Chinese and the Jesuits' texts offer homegrown equivalents. In the Sutras, angels and archangels and hosts of heaven are replaced with Buddhas, kinaras, and superintending devas. Satan is renamed Yama, the archetypical demon god of Eastern religions. Xavier, too, substitutes some difficult-to-comprehend biblical terms with Islamic ones. The Roman tax collector becomes "usurer" and the biblical heathen become "idolaters," both terms that would have been familiar to a Muslim reader. When listing the witnesses to the first Pentecost, Xavier names the nationalities that are most likely to be recognized by the Mughal court: Iraqis, Shrivanis (modern Azerbaijan), Turanians, inhabitants of Diyarbekir, Egyptians, Africans, and Arabs who take of the place of Parthians, Medes, and Cappadocians. Xavier's Jesus is attributed with the Muslim practice of saying "peace be upon him," a phrase often said after the name of prophet Muhammed. Similarly, after Mary's name, "May God be content with her" is added, which is a phrase often used for Ai'sha, the wife of the prophet. These Islamic salutations, along with the other indigenous details used in Xavier's retelling of Jesus's life story, seem designed to please and impress the audience at the Mughal court rather than to convey any biblical truth. Knowing very well that Friday is a hallowed day for Muslims, Xavier claims, without any historical evidence, that several biblical events happen on a Friday, including Mary's birth, her presentation in the temple, and John's birth. Whereas the King James Version describes the room where the Last Supper took place as "a large upper room furnished," Xavier makes it more elegant by replacing the room with a pavilion—a building style that Akbar would have been familiar with: in 1556, at the age of twelve, he had been crowned at a pavilion in Kalanaur, Punjab, India. In his reimagining, Xavier also furnishes the room with carpets, an item produced in Mughal India.

Sometimes Xavier's cultural references are rather flat-footed. Vineyards in the parables of Jesus are replaced with "gardens," which the Mughals were fond of, but the Mughal emperors were not averse to wine; indeed, there is evidence that they imported Shiraz and maintained vineyards in the Deccan.[50] And Malchus, the high priest's servant whose ear Peter cut off, is given a Muslim name—Malik.

Although *Mirror of Holiness* originated in the subcontinent, there are only a couple of references that are Indian. When the parable in Matthew refers to a thousand talents, Xavier converts it into Indian currency—"several lakhs of rupees"—and in another story he uses the Hindi word *opchi* for an armed soldier. Xavier is unsure how to contextualize the biblical truths for an audience that is totally unfamiliar with Semitic idioms and concepts. His attempts at Indianization are superficial and limited to a few external objects, rather than a radical incorporation of essential Indian philosophical ideas. This was in contrast to the Sutras, which creatively wove Buddhist, Taoist, and Confucian ideas into the text.

On a surface level, it appears that the Sutras tend to offer the standard Christian story. The basic components of the biblical story are all there. The Sutras contain the Virgin Birth, the teachings of Jesus especially on obeying the governing authority and respecting parents, a condensed version of the Sermon on the Mount, the record of Jesus's miracles, his command over nature, his denunciation of idols, his substitutionary atonement, and his Crucifixion and Resurrection. Where these Sutras differ is the way they tell the Christian story by mixing it with Buddhist, Taoist, and Confucian images, a practice that Moffet found "troubling."[51] The text is littered with expressions like "eight cardinal virtues," "He took the ore of the vessel of mercy" (a Buddhist concept), "the new teaching of non-assertion" (Taoist), "how to rule both families and kingdoms" (Confucian) and the "two principles of nature"—a reference to the Chinese philosophical idea of yin and yang. The image of Jesus that emerges in the Sutras is that of an Eastern sage who dispenses wisdom and embodies compassion rather than the conventional biblical image of a preacher who is preoccupied with sin, sacrifice, and redemption. This is a Jesus who attempts to answer Chinese questions rather than Judeo-Christian ones. Thus he is presented as addressing the issues of karma and rebirth rather than sin and salvation. Jesus is seen as the person who frees people from their past karmic deeds and restores them to their original nature.

While Chinese writings were adventurous and willing to take risks, and incorporated Eastern thought in order to present the Gospel and Jesus to people who found these Christian ideas utterly new and alien, Xavier's version was cautious, confrontational, conciliatory, and ambassadorial, and at times very robust in driving home the Christian message. There is no interaction with indigenous Hindu notions, or even Buddhist ideas or concepts. In the Mughal court, Persian culture and Islamic thinking were so potent that the Hindu aspects of Indian society were marginalized. Hinduism was regarded as a "kind of eastern paganism, a country religion of the villagers."[52] Europeans had yet to discover the intricacies of Indian philosophy and the treasures of Sanskrit and Tamil literature. It was only a century later that orientalists like William Jones would make them aware of the riches of Indian literature and philosophy. But even if these Indian writings had been available, Xavier would not have dared to incorporate them. He was too much of a propagandist. On reading Xavier's text, one notices that it lacks the theological range for a multi-faith context, and is unsure as to how to go against the grain of the traditional narrative. Like the master in the Parable of the Banquet, Xavier has a definitive weakness for "compelling them to come in"—in his case, into the Christian fold.

Reading Xavier's version now, it sounds rigid and simplistic, with dubious stereotypes and a fondness for narrative embellishments. The openness on the part of the Sutras and the rigid, narrow, and cramped style of the Jesuit version can be attributed to the geopolitics of their different times. Just three years before Christianity reached China, Muslim armies defeated the Persian Empire and brought Assyria, Mesopotamia (modern Iraq), and southeast Anatolia under Arab control. The Sassanian Empire came to an end with the defeat of Yazdgerd III in 651, while his son Peroz II escaped, ending up in Tang China. Under these circumstances, the Church of the East missionaries were insulated from the mother church and thus had no institutional pressures from home. They were able to intermingle indigenous thought patterns with biblical texts. By contrast, the Jesuits after the Reformation were spurred on by the idea that what was lost in Europe could be won in India and China. Jerome Xavier, the grand-nephew of Francis, exemplified this zeal and his text reflects this uncompromising mood.

Sadly, the Jesus Sutras and the *Mirror of Holiness* both remained outside the reach of ordinary people. The Chinese documents were often obscure in their "expression and allusions" and the chosen literary form was not "very appealing to a larger audience."[53] This may have been due to the poor scholarship of the Church of the East missionaries. The Nestorian Monument, which was supposed to have been written by Jing Jing, is seen as a "mockery of his ignorance." The Buddhist records of the time show that he neither knew Sanskrit nor understood Buddhism.[54] Christianity, too, was seen primarily as the faith of the foreign communities, merchants, soldiers, or missionaries, and it remained dependent on foreign leadership and the support of those who had power at court, including some of the Persian missionaries who became high court officials. The Church of the East in China not only became closer to political power, but also gave the impression of being ostentatious. A sign of this flamboyance was "using pearls as the door-curtain."[55] Most of all, the Christian faith in China at that time could not shake off its foreign connections. Aluoben was known as the "Persian Monk," and the worship places of the Church of the East were called "Persian Temples."

Likewise, because the story of Jesus was told in Persian by Xavier for the Mughal court, Jesus remained a distant and unapproachable figure for the inhabitants of North India, who had to wait another two hundred years to read about his life and work in their own languages. Only upper-class Hindus and Muslims knew the Persian language and were familiar with Persian literature.[56] It wasn't until 1805 that the first Urdu version of the four Gospels was translated by the learned natives of the College of Fort William; a year later, Henry Thomas Colebrook, the president at the bench of Calcutta, brought out a Hindi version.[57] The whole earlier Xavierian enterprise was geared toward the conversion of the emperor; ordinary people were a "matter of somewhat secondary importance."[58]

The Jesus Sutras and the *Mirror of Holiness* represent two models for presenting Jesus to an Asian audience. The Sutras' approach was to reconfigure Christian teachings in the light of local theological limitations and requirements. Instead of translating the conventional theological agenda of sin, death, and redemption for an audience unfamiliar with these categories, this approach took seriously the indigenous Chinese concerns regarding ignorance and anxiety and redevised and reshaped the story of Jesus's life and mission to address them. The Sutras thus engage not with Semitic concepts of sin and human depravity, which were completely alien to the surrounding culture, but with vernacular Buddhist, Taoist, and Confucian categories that were recognizable to their audience.

The other approach, which Xavier took in his *Mirror of Holiness,* was the straightforward transference of the Semitic message without consideration of the receiving population's culture and context. Biblical insights imbued with European values were transmitted without paying any attention to indigenous needs and nuances. The underlying subtext: the Christian message is universal and therefore applicable to all people.

These construals of Jesus's life were probably the last attempts at Christology that had the support of royal patronage in Asia. Aluoben and Jerome Xavier belonged to an age in which the church benefited from the support of the rulers of the country. An earlier example is that of Augustine and his forty monks. When he reached Britain in 597, although it was a Roman province, he sought royal approval and support from King Aethelbert. Much like Xavier's approach, the strategy here was to first convert those in authority, in the hope that doing so would facilitate the monks' work in persuading the populace. The court support for the missionaries of the Church of the East and the Jesuits was brief and never replicated. Asia never had a Hindu Constantine or a Christian Asoka. This was also probably the last time that Christianity and Eastern religions met as equals. The subsequent theological articulations that developed in Asia emerged as minority exercises, without state patronage and often as a counternarrative to the state, and indeed were frequently pitted against the Christian missionaries' own colonial impositions and hegemonic attitudes. The rest of this book is a witness to those sometimes valiant, at times vainglorious, and often aggressive endeavors by Asian thinkers.

2

The Heavenly Elder Brother

Ever since the Gospels reported that Jesus came preaching the Kingdom of God, the desire to establish that Kingdom on earth has been the chief desire of Christians. One man who was able to achieve this elusive goal, though controversially and for only a brief period, was Hong Xiuquan (1814–1864), the Hakka-born leader of the Taiping rebellion. He founded his contentious Taiping Heavenly Kingdom in Nanjing, the rebel capital located in the southern part of China, where he reigned for nearly thirteen years, from August 1851 to May 1864. The Taiping rebellion had an impact on sixteen of China's eighteen provinces. The kingdom he set up was not the spiritual, intangible Kingdom that the missionaries had been preaching about and aspiring to, but a real physical, territorial, political kingdom on earth, with its own set of moral rules, standards for military discipline, and canonical literature that posed a threat both to Chinese rulers and foreign invaders. It is reported that his soldiers "advanced everywhere, the sword in one hand and the Old and New Testaments, in Chinese translations, in the other."[1] Hong's "Ode on the Sword" reinforces this popular (mis)perception: "Holding the three-foot sword in hand, I consolidate the mountains and rivers. I capture all the demons and return them to the web of earth . . . Collecting the remaining evil ones, I drop them into the net of heaven."[2] The establishment of the kingdom, at least for some missionary enthusiasts, made it seem as though the prophecy of Isaiah had been realized: "Behold, these shall come from far: and, lo, these from the north and from the west; and these from the land of Sinim."[3]

Hong started his Taiping movement in Guangxi province in 1846. A highly emotional individual, he had the energy of an insurgent, as well as an infectious religious zeal. The reasons behind the insurrection need not detain us here; they have been covered expertly elsewhere.[4] It is sufficient to note that the following factors played a considerable part: Chinese anger at the misgovernance and racial policies of the foreign Manchu rulers; overpopulation and a lack of adequate lands for farming; resolute attempts by Western nations to obtain favorable trade and diplomatic concessions, and to enact humiliating international treaties such as the Treaty of Nanjing (1842); poverty caused by annexation of lands; and a famine so severe that starving people had to fight for the food waste meant for the pigs. When the rebellion began, the protesters were known as the Bai Shang-ti Hui (Society of God Worshippers). The Taiping rebellion, in Thomas Reilly's view, was the "first movement to advocate not just the removal of the then-ruling emperor or the end of one particular dynasty but, along with this, the abolition of the entire imperial system and the institution of a whole new religious and political order."[5]

Once the Taipings took over, they transformed everything from the dress code and hairstyles to the conventional spelling system. They ordained that the Taipings should let their hair grow instead of shaving, which had been a mark of subjugation to the Manchus. They even proclaimed a new Heavenly Calendar that did away with the old system of dating from the reign of a new emperor, and removed all the lucky and unlucky days in the old calendar.[6] What Sir Walter Scott said of the French Revolution could be equally applicable to the Taipings—they "changed everything from the rites of religion to the fashion of a shoe buckle."[7]

Hong was born into a peasant family, but because he had an extraordinary capacity to study, he was sent to school when he was seven. Within a short period, he had mastered and memorized the Four Books, Five Classics, and the Book of Filial Piety.[8] His ambition was to be part of the Chinese establishment. After becoming a village schoolteacher, he immersed himself in Confucian scholarship for the civil service exam, but he kept failing, and after his third failure experienced a nervous breakdown. In his delirious state, Hong began to have strange visions that made a deep impression on him and set him on his mission. In these visions, he was taken up into heaven and saw a "venerable man, with a golden beard, and dressed in a black robe" sitting on a high place. Tearful and angry, the man told Hong: "All human beings in the whole world are produced and sustained by me; they eat my food and wear my clothing, but not a single one among them has a heart to remember and venerate me; what is however still worse than that, they . . . worship demons; they purposely rebel against me, and arouse my anger. Do not imitate them."[9] Hong was given a sword and sent as "the true ordained Son of Heaven to exterminate the depraved and preserve the upright."[10]

Hong was not attracted to the Christian faith through traditional evangelical preaching or the educational efforts of the missionaries. His contact with missionaries was minimal, and by all accounts, his initial dealing with the American missionary Issachar J. Roberts did not go well: Hong failed to win his confidence. Theodore Hamberg, the Swedish missionary who produced one of the earliest accounts of the Taipings, reports that Roberts did not have any confidence in Hong's visions and preaching, and, more crucially, he failed to understand Hong's character and motives. Even so, after the capture of Nanking, Hong wanted Roberts to assist him:

> I have written to you several times, but have yet received no answer to my letters . . . I have promulgated the Ten Commandments to the army and the rest of the population, and have taught them all to pray morning and evening. Still those who understand the Gospel are not many. Therefore, I . . . request you, my elder brother, to [come and] bring with you many brethren to help to propagate the Gospel and administer the ordinance of baptism.[11]

Hong's conversion to Christianity was remarkable in that his exposure to the foreign faith was limited apparently to a single set of texts written not by a foreign missionary but by a Chinese convert, Liang Fa, a colporteur who produced nine slim volumes called, collectively, *Good Words to Admonish the Age.* Liang's tracts were Hong's "only doctrinal source for Christianity."[12] He revered these tracts so much that he warned anyone wanting to read them that they should not mark or alter them because what was "written therein (Ps. 33.4), Jehovah's word, is correct."[13] He may have obtained a Bible (Robert Morrison's Chinese version) when he was briefly instructed by Roberts. Liang's volumes, however, were presented to him when he attended the examination in Canton. He did not pay much attention to them at the time. They were simply lying among his books, six years after his visions, when Hong read them again at the instigation of his cousin Li. It was then that he realized how they provided a key to the strange events in his visions. As he recalled later: "These books [were] certainly sent purposely by heaven to me, to confirm the truth of my former experiences; if I had received the books without having gone through the sickness, I should not have dared to believe in them ... If I had merely been sick but not also received the books, I should have had no further evidence as to the truth of my visions, which might also have been considered as mere productions of a diseased imagination."[14] Now he understood that the old man was none other than God the Heavenly Father; the middle-aged man who had instructed him and assisted him in exterminating the demons was Jesus, the Savior of the World; and the demons were the idols. In these visions, he also saw himself as Jesus Christ's "Divine Younger Brother," with the Heavenly Father's mandate to govern China, and that he was charged with a Jesus-like mission to "rescue mankind."[15]

Under this new conviction, Hong began to preach his newly found doctrine, and used both Liang Fa's volumes and his own visions to authenticate the truth of the other. He created a community that attracted initially two thousand believers and began to proclaim the new message, going along with his cousins Hong Renan and Feng Yunshan on a campaign to destroy idols—that is, tablets of Confucius—from classrooms. Initially, the state authorities treated Hong and his group of believers as religious extremists and did not pay much attention to them, but their fierce iconoclastic activities, and Hong's opposition to the corrupt and declining foreign dynasty, eventually incensed the rulers and led to conflict with the Manchu imperialist forces. In January 1851, after the first major victory against the government troops, Hong proclaimed the advent of the Heavenly Kingdom of Great Peace, himself as the Heavenly or Peaceful King, and Nanking as the heavenly capital. The result was the creation of a complicated theocracy led by divine guidance, a complex bureaucracy, an elaborate system of graded positions and ranks, an economic program that abolished private ownership of wealth and land, and an inflexible and rigorous form of Christian faith complete with its own canonical literature. This new and toxic amalgam of ideology and organization attracted anyone to Nanking who had religious, economic, or religious grievances against the ruling Manchus. It also proved attractive to foreign powers.

But Hong's kingdom did not last long. As with all revolutionaries, the Taipings had their weaknesses: unrealistic ambitions, internal dissensions, suspicions of outsiders, and a disregard for law and property all skewed their understanding of Christianity and led to their downfall. Hong's version of Christianity, according to Teng, "alienated the Confucian scholar-official class."[16] External and foreign pressures also played a considerable role in undermining the Taipings, as well as another crucial element: Hong and the Taipings gradually lost their anti-imperial, anti-feudal revolutionary spirit and resorted to embracing the "Chinese traditions of provincialism."[17] This was a major deviation from their original rebel spirit. They were defeated in 1864 by a combination of a disgruntled indigenous elite and foreign forces.

The role of the foreign powers in the fall of Hong's kingdom was critical. Mao Zedong, true to form, blamed the foreign imperialists when commenting on the rebellion: "Earlier Revolutions failed in China because imperialism strangled them."[18] The British imperial forces, which had been used to put down upstart Hindu and Muslim rulers in their far-flung colonies, this time helped to bring down a mass movement of converted Christians—the very conversion they tacitly supported. Charles George Gordon, a pious Christian whose reading was "confined almost entirely to the Bible," had delusions of being the chosen instrument of God, appointed to put down a rebellion that was based largely on the very Bible he adored.[19] His Chinese adventures earned him the name "Chinese Gordon." Ironically, in 1885 in Khartoum, he was to die at the hands of an equally enthusiastic religious charismatic, Mahadi, a Muslim messiah.

Hong's Uterine Elder Brother

Hong's construction of Jesus is both interesting, and, at times, irreverent in the sense that he himself sought to identify with God's family. Hong called himself Jesus's "uterine brother" and "Elder Brother"—imaginings that went well beyond the missionary presentation of Jesus at the time.

Hong's writings are copious, and for our purpose the important ones are "The Taiping Heavenly Chronicle," "Ode on the Hundred Correct Things," "Ode on the Origin of Virtue and the Saving of the World," "An Exhortation on the Origin of Virtue for the Awakening of the Age," and "The Trimetric Classic." Also important, of course, are his biblical annotations, which are called the "Taiping Bible."[20]

Hong provides only minimal information about Jesus, and the few events he does refer to were chosen to reinforce his ideological and theological views. Hong gives the birthplace of Jesus as Judea, and mentions the supernatural events associated with him—the virginal Conception, the voice at his baptism, and the Transfiguration—in order prove his pet guiding idea that Jesus was the son of God, heir apparent, and not God himself. There is no mention of Jesus's Galilean life apart from his flight as an infant to Egypt, his Temptation, his healings, and the nature miracles that he performed. Two parables are mentioned in passing without any details: the Wheat and the Tares, and the Mustard Seed. The Wheat and the Tares is used to support the idea that Jesus came to the world to destroy the heterodox and preserve the orthodox. The Mustard Seed is employed to demonstrate the growth of Hong's own kingdom from tiny beginnings to a large-scale organization. Unlike Xavier's elaborate details of Jesus's agonizing death, Hong restricts the account to a minimum. The manner of Jesus's killing is described as "nailed on a cross," and he is noted to have "bled and suffered" without referring to his trial. Then, after his death, Hong reports that Jesus "came to life again in three days" and after that, ascended into heaven. The crucial event in Jesus's life, the Resurrection—which Christians

48

view as a decisive happening that rejuvenated and radicalized the disciples and the early church—is interpreted instead as an event that enabled Jesus to return to earth. Hong is fairly certain about the reason for the appearance of Jesus on earth: to save humanity and, more pressingly, to help Hong "sweep away and exterminate the devilish spirits"—the Manchus and the devils. In this task of annihilating the demons, Jesus is depicted as "holding the golden seal" whose shining made these evil spirits run away. Hong's frugal use of historical detail stands in contrast to the other Taiping document, "The Imperially Composed Thousand Word Edict," which was meant to be used as a primer, and whose purpose is the same as that of the "Trimetric Classic," which follows faithfully the Gospel accounts and blames the Jerusalem authorities for Jesus's death.[21]

Hong is very clear about his idea of Jesus. In his view, Jesus was the first son of God, not to be equated with God and not God. Nowhere in the Taiping documents are the coexistence or coeternity of the Father and the Son declared or mentioned. The birth of Jesus was looked upon as a "marvellous event" but not as the incarnation of one who existed eternally.[22] As Thomas Meadows put it in his extensive account of the Taipings, as far as Hong was concerned, Jesus the Son was a "created or produced Being."[23] In Hong's own words, the "Elder Brother is the First Son of God." He was "inferior to the Father but superior to angels."[24] While Hong did not hesitate to accord divine status to the Holy Spirit, the most he concedes to Jesus is holiness: "The Heavenly Father and Heavenly Elder Brother alone are holy."[25] Jesus is evidently not God, "yet he is to be revered as God," or, on another occasion, "Christ ought to be honoured as God."[26] Hong was also clear that sonship was not limited to Jesus only, and that there could be other potential sons as well. In his communication with Roberts, his one-time tutor, Hong deleted the word '"only" where Jesus is spoken of as the "only begotten Son of God."[27] In addition, Hong told Roberts, "You also are a son of God," which may well have startled the American, who had been raised as an evangelical.[28]

Hong emphasized very clearly that Jesus should not be equated with the Father, but in one of his exchanges with Joseph Edkins of the London Missionary Society, who almost became the spokesperson for the Taipings, Hong informed him with conviction: "God has no form; Christ is his form."[29] This sort of contrived position occurs a good deal in his annotations on various New Testament passages. In his comments on Mark 12.29, Hong rebuked those who had unwittingly blended the identities of the Father and the Son: "The Great Brother stated quite clearly that there was only one Great Lord. Why did the disciples later suppose that Christ was God?" The separate existence of the Father and the Son comes out very distinctly in Hong's comments on Stephen's witness before his martyrdom: "Stephen clearly proved that Christ stood on the right side of God. Thus God is the Divine Father and Christ is the Divine Son, one passing into two."[30] Similarly, Hong quashes any misunderstanding that could be found in the late, marginal passage in 1 John 5.7–8, which seemed to coalesce the Father, the Son, and the Holy Ghost into one. In an assured manner he writes: "The one and only true God says: 'Beside myself, thou shalt have no other Gods.'"

To reinforce his idea of Jesus being subordinate to God, Hong brings in two biblical witnesses: Jesus himself, and Paul. Commenting on the two great commandments (Mark 12), Hong makes it clear that the Elder Brother proclaimed only "one Supreme Lord" and castigated the disciples for supposing that Jesus was God: "if he was, there would be two Gods." On another occasion, Hong commented that the Elder Brother should not be tempted because he himself was not God. Hong brought in Paul to support his nondivine status of Jesus. His annotation on the first chapter of Romans reads: "Paul also proved that Christ is the Son of God, not God."[31] Again in Romans 9.5 he sees the same point: "There is only one God, and Christ is the Son of God, and not God."[32] His comments on Romans 9.5–8 further emphasize the idea of a single God: "God alone is the Supreme One. Christ is God's heir apparent and is not God. Respect this."[33] To Jesus and Paul, one could add Arius, the North African theologian who, like Hong, held a view that emphasized the Father's divinity over the Son. Apparently Hong held him in high regard. In his communication with Roberts, he said the council that had condemned Arius was wrong; Arius was in the right.[34]

The subordinate status of Jesus is further established in two other ways: by denying his agency, and by divesting him of his powers. In Hong's retelling, Jesus's words and actions were not presented as innate abilities but attributed to God: "A word from the Great Elder Brother was indeed a word from God."[35] All of Jesus's healing miracles, too, were divine actions simply carried out through Jesus. When the man with the palsy was healed, Hong pointed out that "at that time they glorified God and did not glorify the Elder Brother as God."[36] He claimed that "the deeds of the Great Elder Brother were those of God."[37]

Hong is very sparing in using traditional Christological titles for Jesus. He employs two titles, "Son of God" and, on one occasion, "the prophet." To Hong, "Son of God" meant simply that Jesus was intimate with God, and, more importantly, below the level of God. This did not prevent Hong from identifying divine attributes in Jesus, but he could not accord him the title of God. Hong comes up with three titles—all were his own creation and had no Semitic equivalent—the "Elder Brother," the "Crown Prince," and the "Elder Prince." All these titles were designed to pave the way for proclaiming Hong as the second son, next in line to take over from Jesus. Just as Jesus reigned and was killed, now it was Hong's turn to take up the cudgels on behalf of God.

The work of Jesus that Hong envisaged is found in "The Trimetric Classic," which echoes the famous passage from John 3.16:

> But the great God out of pity to mankind, Sent his first-born son
> To come down into the world. His Name is Jesus, The Lord and
> Saviour of Men, who redeems them from sin by the endurance of
> extreme misery. Those who believe will be saved and ascend up
> to heaven; but those who do not believe will be the first to be
> condemned.[38]

On the face of it, this passage does not say anything about the atoning nature of Jesus's death. Hong does not see Jesus's sacrifice in the orthodox Christian way—as an atonement for the sins of humanity—but as the filial duty of a Chinese son, an obligation that others are also encouraged to fulfill: "The Great Elder Brother does not forbid people to make offerings as the duty of sons should be to feel gratitude and make offerings to the Divine Father."[39]

Jesus's redeeming activity includes not only saving the world but also slaying the "devilish demons": "When the impish fiend did strange things in injuring the children of men, (God) repeatedly sent his own son down into the world. (Then) he swept away the impish fiend and the world was at peace." Jesus is often described as descending into to the earth to "slay the vicious and save the righteous, to gather the wheat and burn the tares." More pointedly, this is a Jesus who accepts some and condemns others.

Whereas the New Testament writers were expecting the second coming of Jesus, in Hong's scheme of things, God and Jesus had already returned to earth to establish the Kingdom in Nanjing and fulfill their mission to help out Hong. Hong's comments on the Book of Revelation make it clear that, as far as he was concerned, the end time had arrived: "Now God the Heavenly Father and Christ the Great Elder Brother descend upon earth to guide myself and the Junior Lords as the Lords."[40] He claimed that the present capital was "the New Jerusalem" where "God and Christ descended upon earth to guide" him to establish the heavenly dynasty. The paradise of God was "now among the people."[41] He went on to ask, "now God and Christ have come; why are the saints not overjoyed? . . . how can you not believe?" He reminded the Taipings that these claims were in accordance with the Gospel and were exactly what the Elder Brother had prophesied: "I should come like a thief, when no one knows. It is fulfilled. Respect this."[42]

In Hong's vision, Jesus is portrayed as part of a divine family rather than as the wandering solitary figure depicted in the Gospels. Hong's concept of God as having human characteristics and an entire family places him beyond the biblical record. The Heavenly Father had a wife referred to as the Heavenly Mother, who is portrayed as "kind, and exceedingly gracious, beautiful and noble in the extreme, far beyond all compare."[43] Jesus's family status is clarified by making him the elder son with a wife whom Hong identified as his own heavenly sister-in-law. She is described as "virtuous and very considerate" and consistently urges the Elder Brother to "do things deliberately."[44] The passage in the Book of Revelation—"for the marriage of the Lamb is come, and his wife hath made herself ready" (19.7)—appears to have led Hong to believe that Jesus had a wife. Hong's comments on the Lamb's bride substantiates this: "The wife of the Divine Lamb is the Heavenly Sister-in-Law, whom I saw several times in Heaven. The Heavenly Sister-in-Law also descends on earth, and calls me Younger Brother."[45] In contrast to the Gospel records, where Jesus almost disowned his family and they in turn viewed him with suspicion, in Hong's portrayal, Jesus is preoccupied with family relationships. Jesus is imagined as a family man married with five children: three boys aged eighteen, fifteen, and thirteen, and two girls, one sixteen and the other born since Hong was last in heaven. In addition to his own children, and in keeping with the Chinese idea of adopting the first born of the younger brother, Jesus has an adopted son, Tiangui, who was Hong's elder son. Hong insinuates himself into the divine family by having his elder son live with Jesus's mother, and by having his wife, First Chief Moon, live with Jesus and his wife.

Hong, in one of his poems, describes his Elder Brother, Christ, as one whose "grace and compassion are broad and profound."[46] But in Hong's other writings we find an angry Jesus, frequently enraged at Hong's slowness in reading and reciting Psalms, and then restrained by his mother: "Whenever the Heavenly Elder Brother, Christ, was too harsh with and treated him sternly, His Heavenly Mother would persuade the Heavenly Elder Brother to desist." Jesus was also portrayed as angrily scolding people for "being selfish and for not being public-minded and [having] loyal hearts." One of the rare instances where a Gospel-attributed saying of Jesus appears almost exactly in Hong's work is the extreme injunction: "If your right eye deceives you, pluck out your right eye. If your left eye deceives you pluck out your left eye. Rather should you ascend to heaven with one eye, for it is ten million times better than falling into hell with two eyes." This Jesus, too, has a strong streak of patriarchy in him, warning Hong's wives: "if you show the slightest aversion or negligence of my younger brother, the sword shall fly." An example of the intolerance of this Jesus is that he often thunders at Confucius: "You created books of this kind to teach the people, so that even my own blood brother, in reading your works, was harmed by them."[47]

Hong's Jesus shows no compassion. When Confucius kneels before him and begs for mercy when getting lashed, Jesus—who in Matthew 18.21–22 preached that one should forgive "No, not seven times, but *seventy times seven!*"—remains unmoved. It is the Father of Jesus who intervenes and pardons Confucius because of his earlier meritorious work. Even this pardoning comes with a condition, that Confucius should not return to earth. Jesus hates Confucius so much that he burns his books. Another example of Jesus's intolerance is his treatment of the Buddhist Goddess of Mercy, Guanyin, whom he calls "sister." He keeps her as a hostage in heaven and will not permit her to come down to earth because he fears that people might get wrong ideas from her teaching. Clearly, Hong's Jesus is not the gentle, kind person in whom generations of Sunday School students were taught to believe. Jesus instead comes across as a strict disciplinarian who is not afraid to punish and even execute those who violate the Heavenly Command. Jesus tells the assembled troops:

> If, after having been instructed, there are any of you who still violate the Heavenly Commandments, still disobey orders, still wilfully disobey and answer their superiors, and still, when advancing into battle, flee from the field, you should not blame me, the Heavenly Elder Brother, if I give orders to execute you.[48]

In Hong's portrayal, Jesus does not come across as a dispenser of moral precepts but simply as an issuer of edicts or proclamations. These are often in the form of enigmatic parables. In one of these edicts, Jesus orders the Taipings to be "pure." The Sermon on the Mount is reduced to the announcement of the arrival of the Kingdom, except for a passing reference to "Blessed are those with pure hearts."[49] Such sterling qualities as meekness and detachment, which enable one to inherit God's kingdom, are omitted. The Golden Rule—"Whatever you wish that others would do to you, do also to them, for this is the Law and the Prophets"—is another notable oversight. Apart from a few allusions to not tempting God, and a reference to the forgiveness of sin, the major sayings of Jesus are left out. Instead of the great commission to the disciples, Jesus gives a series of instructions to the multitude composed of Hong's followers. These include obeying the commandments; being in harmony with others; shouldering responsibility mutually among the weak and the strong; showing no hatred toward enemies; not plundering other people's goods; not being infatuated with money; and not fleeing from the battlefield. Unlike the Sermon on the Mount where the weak and the poor are blessed, in these instructions the weak and cowards are the object of his ire and severely punished. Hong's Jesus even warns him to stay out of sight when demons are killing each other.

In Hong's rendering, Jesus comes across as a rhetorical leader rather than as a moral teacher. During one of his earthly visits, Jesus says: "To become a real human being one must not be at ease, he that is at ease cannot become a real human being. The more you endure sufferings, the greater will be your dignity."[50] Rather than engaging in moral discussions, Hong converses about military matters with Jesus. When asked who should be Taipings' commanding generals, Jesus issues a list of names. He further informs Hong that one of his commanding generals will be a foreigner. When asked whether that leader was already in China, Jesus told him not yet, but named him as Cai. When Hong had a dream in which he was attacked by demons with guns and was rescued by angels and heavenly generals, he asked Jesus whether this dream was authentic. He was assured by Jesus that it was indeed true and that a general had been sent from heaven. Based on the type of destruction carried out by a general against the Qing, Jonathan Spence, in his history of the Taipings, surmises that the foreign general could have been Lord Elgin, whose cultural vandalism destroyed so much of China's finest architecture and treasures.[51] His destruction of the Summer Place was akin to the smashing of statues and shrines by the Islamic State in the Iraqi city of Mosul, the demolition of the ancient Assyrian city of Nimrud, and the blowing up of Palmyra's Temple of Bel in Syria.

Unlike Jesus in the Gospels, Hong's Jesus bestows his blessings not on little children but on the Taiping leaders, especially on nearly twenty-three staff officers, all of whom were taken to heaven and instructed by Jesus. Instead of being accompanied by disciples like Peter and John, Hong's Jesus is flanked by an army general. Hong's Jesus instills in these army personnel a sense of loyalty and obedience, and warns them that their refusal to comply with military regulations is as grave as disobeying the Word of God, of Jesus, and of Hong himself. In Hong's representation, Jesus does not tolerate any dissension, in contrast to the lenient historical Jesus who had among his ranks Judas, a dissenter, and disciples vying for privilege and position. He confers authority on commanders to "kill any such rebels before reporting them to higher authorities, since killing these rebels won't lessen the strength of our armies, whereas having rebels in our army ranks harms the entire kingdom."[52] This belligerent Jesus is unlike the historical Jesus who urged his disciples to turn the other cheek, though he resembles the one who is supposed to have said "sell your cloak and buy a sword."

Hong's Jesus preaches not the biblical idea of justice, mercy and redemption, but the Confucian values of respect, uprightness, goodness, truthfulness, and righteousness—which are attained not through repentance but through purification and obeying the edicts. The overturning of people's wicked ways listed by Hong, such as licentiousness, gambling, unfilial behavior, and homicide, are all common objectives of Confucian moral teaching. As Philip Kuhn observes in his critique of the Taiping rebellion, it is hard for Hong to "shake off either his literary heritage or his self-image as a transmitter of orthodox culture."[53] It was clear that Hong envisaged his task as bringing the Christian revelation to the people in a way that reconciled that revelation with Chinese Confucian values.

If the Hindu concept of *avatara* enabled Hindu thinkers to fit Jesus into their framework, it was the Chinese concept of *xiafan,* "descending to the earth," that helped Hong explain the manifestation of God, the appearances of Jesus, and the divine commissioning of Hong himself. Archie Lee notes that the use of the term *xiafan* shows the impact of the traditional Chinese notion of "descending to the profane," where "divine beings come down to earth to perform saving deeds when there is social disorder or injustice. The Taipings surely reappropriated the concept for the numerous ascents and descents of Hong and God in both directions."[54] Hong's annotation of Matthew 10.32–33, with its comment that the Father and the Elder Brother "descend upon earth to exterminate the vicious and save the righteous," resonates with Krishna's words to Arjuna: "for the protection of the good, and destruction of evil doers, for the sake of establishing righteousness, I am born in every age" (Bhagavad Gita 4.8).[55] In Hong's reckoning, the incarnation of Jesus was not a once and for all event, as Christian theologians claimed, but an ongoing process. Jesus comes back to earth several times and brings wide-ranging messages to Hong. Like the Hindu *avataras,*

Hong's God and Jesus visit the earth a number of times, displaying "innumerable powers and innumerable proofs."[56]

The single God that Hong proclaimed was not the tribal God of an exclusive group but the "Father" of all. Hong's idea of the total oneness of God helped to democratize God. It challenged the traditional monarch's association with the divine and heaven, and the claim that only emperors could worship God. At a time when the Chinese "mind had been deluded" by the idea that only the monarch could "worship the Great God," Hong boldly claimed that the "Great God is the universal Father of all in the mortal world." To reinforce this point, Hong tapped into the Chinese idea of filial piety: "If you say that monarchs alone can worship the Great God, we beg to ask you, . . . is it only the eldest son who can be filial and obedient to his parents?" The idea of one God was Hong's way of helping his people return to what he believed was the proper manner in which they had worshipped God from the very beginning, because for the past two thousand years they had been "erroneously follow[ing] the devil's path."[57]

The God of Jesus, Hong proclaimed, was not the biblical God but the Chinese God, Shang ti ("Supreme Deity" or "Highest Deity"). In the "Trimetric Classic," he tries to reclaim not the God of the biblical patriarchs but this Chinese God of Shang ti, and to place the dealings of Shang ti in a universal context. Although this God resembles the biblical God in creating heaven and earth in six days, this God is basically from the Chinese classical past, and Jesus is seen as the incarnation of this Chinese God rather than begotten of Yahweh. Informing his followers that "Throughout the whole world, there is only one God," Hong explains that out of all the earth's people, Shang ti chose the Chinese for special treatment: "The Chinese in early ages were looked after by God; together with foreign states, they walked in one way."[58] Hong believed that in ancient times, before Taoists, Buddhists, Barbarians, and the devil himself had perverted their minds, the Chinese had known how to worship the One True God, Shang ti. Hong reminded his fellow Taipings that the deviation began in the time of Cheng of Chen, who was "infatuated with the genii and all were deluded by the devil, those two thousand years," and the Ming of the Han, who was "foolish, and welcomed the institutions of Buddha; He set up temples and monasteries, to the great injury of the country."[59] Examples of this deviation included sacrificing to the "Empress Earth," honoring shamans, searching for Buddha's bones, seeking for the Jasper cock and golden horse, and sending people to India to get Buddhist books. His message to his people was that while "various barbarian countries of the West have walked continuously in the great way," the Chinese have "erroneously followed the devil's path." His plea was that the time had come to restore the true God, the all-wise creator and sovereign sustainer of the universe.

In the face of widespread idolatrous worship and the polytheism prevalent in China at that time, Hong wanted to establish that there was only one God. For him, "the Heavenly Father, God is the only true deity, the only holy deity." As God said, "aside from me you cannot have other deities, other gods." His point was that "if we mistakenly explain that Christ is God that is to have another God; what peace of mind could this bring to the Elder Brother?" One of the instructions that Jesus gives to Hong further strengthens the notion that there is only one God: "Hsiu -ch'uan, my own brother, later on you must not proclaim yourself *Ti* (God or emperor). Our father is *Ti*."[60]

Hong's Jesus is not the Jesus of the Gospels. He is more akin to the Jesus of the Gnostic Gospels. The tantrum Jesus throws resonates with the Infancy Gospel of Thomas where he curses the son of Annas for disturbing the water Jesus had collected, and similarly curses a child who accidently bumps against his shoulder. The married Jesus, too, had already been featured in the Gospel according to Philip. There is no evidence, however, that Hong read these extra-canonical Gospels. Hong's Jesus sings songs composed by the Heavenly Father, and teaches them to the congregations. He talks to Hong about events in Heaven since he left eleven years previously.

Although Hong's Christian admirers would have liked to believe that Hong's inspiration and vision were based on biblical values, Hong's ideas were an amalgam of Christian, Confucian, Buddhist, and popular resistance literatures and beliefs. His promotion of the worship of a single God was patterned on the Jewish-Christian monotheistic ideal, but his abhorrence of idols, and his ordinances on moral behavior, were influenced by traditional Chinese wisdom and thought. The Jesus he conceived resembles a Chinese son who fulfils his filial duty rather than a descendent of the Davidic dynasty. Jesus assumes "responsibility and heavy burdens" on behalf of the Father.[61] The voice in which Jesus speaks is the voice of Confucius. The spiritual virtues that Jesus upholds—humility, charity, purity of heart, forgiveness—have all been turned into a Confucian explanation of right conduct. What Hong advocates is the moral principle of correctness. In his rendering, Jesus demands that all sovereigns, ministers, husbands, wives, fathers, and sons act correctly. As his "Ode on the Hundred Correct Things" makes clear, correctness and incorrectness lay at the root of not only personal good fortune and calamities, but also the rise and fall of empires: "The truly correct make the people peaceful and the country stable."[62] Needless to say, this Jesus is never proclaimed as a kind of Messiah in keeping with Semitic expectations. The Christianity that the missionaries introduced was instead used by Hong as a mold into which he forged an amalgam of Confucian, Taoist, and Buddhist elements into a potent weapon to resist both foreign invaders—the Manchus and the British. Buddhist ideas such as the thirty-three heavens and eighteen hells, future life and the infinite transmigration of souls, are sprinkled throughout the writings of the Taipings.[63]

Hong's borrowing was not limited to the classical tradition; instead he seems to have been influenced as well by popular Chinese resistance novels. Much of the symbolism found in Hong's writings, such as the magic sword, magic mirror, esoteric books, the heavenly net, and the earthly trap, come from these popular novels.[64]

Like the Koran and the Book of Mormon, Hong's Taiping Bible contained material with new divine disclosures beyond those seen in the already available Old and New Testaments.[65] He firmly believed that he had the divine authority to improve, add, and correct these ancient revelations. To those missionaries who doubted his divine mandate, he would shoot back: "Why do you feel uncertain of the fact of divine communications to me?"[66] Hong's heavenly revelations are his own fabrications. Some of the sayings purported to have been uttered by Jesus are not found in the Gospels but were instead made up by Hong. To cite a few examples: "Those who seek to climb high fall into the depths," and "There is no secret that does not expose itself." Hong and the Taipings accorded more authority to direct revelation from God than to the written word that had come to them via the West.

The Missionaries and the Hakka Warrior

The missionaries had a mixed response to Hong's version of Christianity.[67] On the one hand, there was secret admiration for an indigene doing their work for them. Missionaries approved of Hong's fierce stance against idolatry, his desire to serve the one living God, and his promotion of a belief in future life, high moral codes, the Bible as the standard of teaching, and the saving content of Christian prayers and hymns. Even Roberts, who disapproved of the Taipings, admitted: "The bright side consists chiefly in negatives, such as no idolatry, no prostitution, no gambling, nor any kind of pubic immorality, allowed in the city. This might be well esteemed one grand step towards religious improvement."[68]

Ironically, some of the missionaries even defended the Taipings' unconventional theology. Thomas Meadows of the China Inland Mission wondered whether Hong's humanistic and household aspects of the Godhead were his way of counterbalancing the understandings of God prevalent at that time. His anthropomorphic treatment of God could be attributed to his "reaction [against] . . . pantheism"; his "unity of one *Shang te*" could be seen as opposed to the multiplicity of idol worship prevalent during the period; and the "distinct human-like personality" of God that he described stood in opposition to belief in a "non-personal ultimate principle" propagated by the educated classes.[69] W. A. P. Martin, an American Presbyterian missionary, taunted his fellow European doubters: "When has Christianity in its incipient stages not presented the appearance of being spurious? . . . was not the religion of the Middle Ages exceedingly crude and imperfect? And yet light was made to shine out of darkness." His plea was that this "false religion" would still be "a more fruitful soil in which to plant the true seed than that afforded by Taoism and Confucianism."[70] The validation of the missionaries came with a strongly patronizing tone. The general regret was that these Taipings were not "rightly directed."[71] It was thought that the rebellion was "the fruit of an unguided Confucian mind" and would have greatly benefited from the teachings of intelligent missionaries like themselves.[72]

But not all missionaries were so enthusiastic about Hong's theological articulations and political activities. In fact, some found them troublesome and disturbing. Hong's disregard for the verbal inspiration, his tampering with the texts, his devaluing of the Trinity, and his indifference to the vicarious suffering of Jesus—a staple tenet of evangelical Christianity—infuriated some of the missionaries. Hong's claim to be the brother of Christ was a plain blasphemy to them. His excessive representation of God in human form, his claiming of supernatural characteristics to himself, and his assertions of visions and hallucinations did not endear him to them. Yet while the missionaries viewed these mystical experiences negatively, the Chinese people were attracted to them. Indeed the "ecstatic dimension" of Taiping Christianity came from the remote mountain areas where trances and spirit possessions were already features of the Hakka community.[73] The missionaries, in criticizing Hong, overlooked two factors—that the Gospels themselves record numerous incidents of visions and of people being controlled by spirits, and that Christianity includes a tradition of mystics expressing their religious encounters in similar supernatural ways.

Some missionaries detested Hong's political involvements, dismissing his posture as the "error of the half-enlightened mind," and wished that the Taipings would embrace Jesus's announcement of the reign of God as a "spiritual kingdom, and not in the spirit of Fifth Monarchy men."[74] The most vehement denunciation came from Issachar Roberts, with whom Hong had an uneasy relationship, and who wrote after his visit to Hong's Heavenly Kingdom in Nanking that Hong was a *crazy man*, entirely unfit to rule." Roberts was equally annoyed at Hong's anti-trade stance, which thwarted Western commercial interests: "He is opposed to commerce . . . and has promptly expelled every foreign effort to establish lawful commerce." Martin, however, who defended Hong's theology, saw his politics as no different from those of Cromwell and his "abstemious, devout and image-breaking fighters."[75]

A Self-Proclaimed Divinity Makes His Mark

Hong's construction of Jesus, like the Chinese Sutras and the Jesuits' portrayal of Jesus for the Mughal emperor, was undertaken before the modern quest for knowing and recounting the life of Jesus began, and Hong was not unduly concerned about the historical veracity of the events surrounding Jesus. He instead used his imagination to forge a Jesus who helped to inspire what was probably the first Christian-based revolt in Asia. Hong's Jesus became the savior of China's subalterns before the marginalized enlisted Jesus's story for their own colonial and postcolonial resistance.

Like all reformers, for Hong the future depended on systematic raiding of the past, and recovery of the much-loved and imagined glorious Shang ti. In this quest, Hong was quite certain of his divinely ordained role. God, though angry, out of compassion had chosen Hong to deliver the Chinese from "the devil's grasp, and lead them about to walk again in the original great Way."[76] Like all dogmatists, he does not hesitate to restrict other people's choices and bring them to his way of thinking. Hong does not shy away from prescribing the newly recuperated Chinese God for all humankind. Shang ti became not only Taiping's God but the God of all people, including the barbarian nations. In other words, the resister himself had colonizing tendencies.

Hong's borrowing of Gospel details of Jesus is very minimal. His appropriation of salvation history is largely traditional and there is nothing revolutionary about it. He writes about how the first ancestors were tempted by the serpent, disobeyed God's commandments, departed from their true nature, and turned to idolatry, and of God's sending his beloved son to rescue humanity. Where he differed was in tailoring biblical concepts to suit his theology. There was no doubt in Hong's mind that Jesus "descended to take away sins."[77] The sin from which Jesus redeems humanity, however, was not seen as the transgression of heavenly commands but as incorrect behavior. As Hong put it, "correctness distinguishes men from brutes; . . . Correctness is mankind's original nature."[78] Similarly, the atoning death of Jesus was not regarded as reparation for the wickedness of humanity, but as Jesus's filial duty toward his Father.

Hong's self-deification as the second son of God, calling himself the savior and the true sovereign, had a great deal to do with the prevailing political and personal threats at that time. Such postures were a ploy to marshal the people against the oppressive Manchus rather than an attempt to meet the theological expectations of the missionaries. Hong had to face other contenders such as Yang Xiuqing and Xiao Chaoqui, who claimed to speak in the name of God and Jesus. His declaration of himself as the second son, his personal visits to heaven, his place in the divine plan, and his commission to bring the knowledge of God were tactics to appeal to the local Chinese populace. The sole purpose of his bombastic grandstanding and pompous claims to be the Son of God was not to affirm a natural identity with God, but to preserve the solemnity of his status before his followers and rivals. His declarations of divinity were aimed at the indigenous audience, and were not made for the benefit of the missionaries.

Hong was an unusual colonial convert. At the same time that he and Roberts were having their theological disputes, another colonizer-colonized dialogue was going on in South Africa. John Colenso, an Anglican missionary in Natal, was being questioned by his translator, William Ngidi, about the historical veracity and questionable morality of the Bible. Colenso's Zulu pupil was seen as the ideal native, a fitting monument to missionary work. Ngidi, who was "simple minded" and had "the docility of a child," was willing to learn from an erudite missionary about the literal truth and moral content of the Bible narratives, whereas Hong was declared to be a "crazy man" who, far from being compliant and willing to learn from the missionaries, had taken upon himself the task of tutoring them. While Colenso admired Ngidi's modernistic dilemma with the biblical narrative, Hong was postmodern and was prone to visions and hallucinations. Ngidi asked questions but remained silent. Hong, by contrast, often talked back to the missionaries, clarifying their questions and often correcting them. While Ngidi remained under the tutorial management of a colonial instructor, Hong went "beyond the control of any human advisor."[79] While doubting the historicity and the morality of the Bible, Colenso and Ngidi still believed that the Bible contained the true "Word of God," the "things necessary for salvation" and "profitable for doctrine, reproof, correction, instruction in righteousness."[80] Hong, however, found the Bible inaccurate and claimed that he had been commanded by God to correct whatever faults he discovered in it. He confidently informed the missionaries that he had corrected the books they had brought with them, at the behest of the Father, and they would be "published to the world in their amended form."[81] Colenso and Ngidi were dealing with the old revealed Word, whereas Hong claimed that the earlier disclosure was an "erroneous record" and that he had a "new revelation."[82] This conviction impelled him to add his own personal revelation to the biblical accounts.

The Christian gospel that Hong advocated was different from that of the sixth-century Church of the East Christians whom we encountered in Chapter 1. Their aim had been to influence the elite Chinese literati, and to find favor with the emperor. Hong's desire was instead to bring the gospel to ordinary people and challenge the autocracy of the Manchu, the feudal tendencies of the mandarins, and the foreign imperialists. As we saw, this alienation of the elite in a sense caused the failure of the rebellion. Aluoben and his missionaries had come with the Eastern canon, the *Peshitta*—twenty-two books of the New Testament—whereas the Taiping had the Western canon in the form of Morrison's Chinese version of the King James Version. Both deviated from the accepted words of the Bible they had received. Both diluted the Christological references to Jesus. Their method, too, was similar. Both Aluoben and the Church of the East Christians, as well as Hong and the Taipings, were attempting to situate themselves in Chinese culture and make sense of Semitic thinking in that context. Both were accused of syncretism—a prime sin at that time. In the postcolonial context, these cultural contacts would be treated in a more affirmative manner. Their attempt to relate the Gospel can be seen as syncretism from below—how the powerless shape the gospel and gain identity and power. In a culture that was strongly weighted against the colonized, the fusion of different systems of belief was a small but significant piece of weaponry in their hands.

Hong's interpretation of Christianity was often disapprovingly dismissed as "foreign righteousness." His reply:

Some also say erroneously that to worship the Great God is to imitate foreigners; not remembering that China has its histories, which are open to investigation . . . the important duty of worshipping the Great God, in the early ages of the world, . . . was alike practised both by Chinese and foreigners. But the various nations in the West have practiced this duty up to the present time, while the Chinese practised it only up to the Tsin and Han dynasties, since which they have erroneously followed the devil's ways.[83]

It is tempting to compare the Taipings with the basic ecclesial communities of Latin America.[84] These grassroots-level Christian communities came into existence in the 1980s, inspired by Latin American liberation theologies. The centrality of the Bible, the expounding of biblical passages, sermons critiquing idolatry and the ruling classes (in the case of Latin American communities, railing against the ruling military juntas and American interventionism), and weekly worship services all resonate with the basic ecclesial communities. But where Taiping Christianity differed from the Latin American version was in the way it was structurally organized. The Latin American basic ecclesial communities emerged voluntarily as an alternative to the institutionalized churches that had lost their pastoral energy. They hardly had any political ambitions of taking over or running the country. The Taipings, by contrast, were the singular achievement of one man, Hong, who ran the community like a strict army-style regime where the sergeants taught the Bible and expounded his writings and proclamations. Hong's "kingdom" was a puritanical one that prohibited smoking and drinking. There was gender discrimination where men and women sat separately at assemblies. Extreme punishments were meted out to those who neglected their duties. Perhaps Hong's Heavenly Kingdom was the first and last example and experiment of a Christian caliphate. Martin, who offered them support, lamented that "an opportunity was lost such as does not occur once in a thousand years."[85]

Karl Marx, watching the events from far-off London, called the Taiping rebellion a "formidable revolution." Surprisingly, though, in his filing of the event, he failed to mention the peasants or the Hakkas, the migrant minority of Chinese society who were responsible for it.[86]

Hong showed that peasant rebellion could work in the modern age. His spiritual message had a political dimension—a vision of equality and shared land ownership, with nothing for private use and everything to be held in common. Hong declared, "When all the people in the empire will not take anything as their own but submit all things to the Supreme Lord, then the Lord will make use of them, and in the universal family of the empire, every place will be equal and every individual well fed and clothed."[87] The idea was that there should be sharing and no one should go hungry, naked, or empty. The provisions from the public granaries were thus made available for the sustenance of the widowers, widows, orphans, the childless, the disabled, and the sick. The mutual sharing was not based purely on the primitive communism practiced by the early Christians, but was fused with Chinese one-world philosophy, which considers the empire as one large family. Teng explains the one-world family thus: "In this world-family, in which God was the Heavenly father, and men and women were brothers and sisters, and every one had an equal right to take what he needed, and to contribute what he could, no selfishness or private ownership is permitted."[88]

Chinese academics, Christians commentators, and Chinese politicians including Mao Zedong have an uneasy and complex relationship with Hong and his legacy. Was he an illustrious revolutionary, or a self-seeking racketeer? A restorer of ancient belief, or a nostalgic who wanted to return to an unadulterated earlier time? Was he a religious tyrant who introduced rigid moral codes, or was he patently crazy? Truthfully, he was all of these things. To allay the negative allegations, Hong could have summoned the words of Columbus, who himself was involved in a similar divinely sanctioned mission and came under suspicion and ridicule: "God made me the messenger of the new heaven and the new earth of which he spoke in the Apocalypse of St. John after having spoken of it through the mouth of Isaiah; and he showed me the spot where to find it."[89] Hong would certainly be disappointed if the latter-day theologians and historians were to dispute his accomplishments, but to this day, China and the Western watchers can't make up their minds about him.

3

A Judean Jnana Guru

In 1881, Swami Vivekananda (1863–1902), who came into prominence at the Chicago Parliament of the World's Religions, gave a series of stirring speeches in various South Asian cities, including Colombo, Sri Lanka. In these addresses, he depicted a materialistically degenerate West and urged Indians to conquer it with Indian spirituality. He was looking for "heroic souls" who would go and convert Westerners. Ponnambalam Ramanathan, the chief focus of this chapter, was one of those heroic souls who was destined to heed Vivekananda's call. Like the Indian delegates at the 1893 Chicago Parliament of the World's Religions twelve years later, Ramanathan was able to mesmerize America with his message of the greatness of Indian spirituality. He played a critical part in the cultural rejuvenation that accompanied the nationalism sweeping across South Asia.

Ramanathan (1851–1930) came from a very illustrious family in Sri Lanka, which distinguished itself in the island's public and political life. Several of the family, including Ramanathan, had knighthoods from the British government. Ramanathan himself became the solicitor general and entered the Legislative Council at a young age, as a member representing both Tamil and Sinhalese communities.

For our purpose, what is crucial is Ramanathan's meeting with a spiritual guru called Arul Parananda Swamigal of Tanjore in South

India. This was a major turning point in Ramanathan's life. M. Vythil-ingam, who wrote a largely reverential biography of Ramanathan, de-picted this meeting in quasi-religious terms, that is, as a predestined event where the Swamigal was sent to wean Ramanathan from "sen-suous materialism" and to "set him firmly into a path of piety and spiritual endeavour."[1] It was under the direction of the Swamigal that Ramanathan undertook the study of Saiva Siddhanta and the practice of yogic meditation. He often publicly acknowledged his indebtedness to the Swamigal. That Ramanathan published his commentaries under the name of Sri Parananda is itself a sure sign of his gratitude to the South Indian saint.

Ramanathan's sudden spiritual transformation did not lead him to withdraw from active worldly life. Unlike other enlightened Hindu sages, he did not escape to a detached life but continued to participate actively in politics. Even before Gandhi, Ramanathan introduced reli-gion and ethics into the mundane world of politics.

Ramanathan produced two biblical commentaries: *The Gospel of Jesus According to St. Matthew* (1898) and *An Eastern Exposition of the Gospel of Jesus according to St. John* (1902). These were probably the first modern biblical commentaries in Asia. If this is the case, ironically, the milestone was reached not by a Christian but by a Hindu. His other books include two lectures delivered in the United States: *The Spirit of the East Contrasted with the Spirit of the West* (1905) and *The Culture of the Soul among Western Nations* (1906). Both contain a fair amount of biblical exposition that extends and explicitly articulates what he had already stated in the commentaries. According to information given in one of his volumes, Ramanathan wrote three more books on biblical exposition: *The Exposition of the Psalms of David (I–XXX) According to Jnana Yoga; Lectures on the Sermon on the Mount;* and *Lectures on the Doctrine of the Resurrection of the Dead, Being a Commentary on the XVth Chapter of the First Epistle of Paul to the Corinthians.* These were listed as under preparation, and my attempts to obtain copies of them proved unsuccessful. I am not sure whether they were ever published.

Carnal Jesus, Sanctified Teacher

Ramanathan's Jesus appears on the scene preaching three simple messages, which at face value were recognizably common and predictable:
God's reign is here, now; a childlike nature is a prerequisite for entering
the Kingdom of Heaven; and Jesus is the revealer of the Father. But the
Jesus configured by Ramanathan was not as straightforward and conventional as these messages suggest. What differentiates Ramanathan's
reconstruction from other Indian portrayals of Jesus was his appropriation of the man from Galilee into the perspective of Tamil Saiva Siddhanta at a time when subcontinental depictions were full of Sanskritic
images.

Ramanathan, like most Hindu reformers and the liberal theologians
of the time, did not invest too much in the personality of the historical
Jesus, nor did he spend his energies in unearthing his original teachings uncontaminated by later accretions and doctrinal interpretations.
He was simply not interested in the flesh-and-blood historical Jesus, nor
was he interested in searching for the human Jesus hidden behind the
Gospel narratives and the teachings of the church. What intrigued him
was Christ the Sanctified, the Spirit hidden in the human body. To Ramanathan, what was attractive was "the Spirit named Christ who is
within the fleshy Jesus."[2] In keeping with Saiva Siddhanta thinking, Ramanathan believed that the fleshy, mortal, human body was "no better
than a carcass."[3] It did not have any value except "as a hut for the spirit."[4]
For Ramanathan, Jesus was the supreme example of a body that had
emerged as pure from the impure. What is found in Jesus is the subtle
body (*sukshma sarira*), which consists of "invisible instruments of
knowledge and action."[5] Ramanathan told his American listeners that
"Jesus found Christ within himself, and through the Christ within, he
attained God."[6] God speaks not through the fleshly body in which the
Son is encased, but through this sanctified body. Ramanathan's Jesus
boldly asserts:

> I, Jesus, may be the carpenter's son; but I, Christ, am a Son of
> God. When the Spirit within the flesh was healed of its worldli-
> ness or sanctified, it became godly and qualified to teach. I am a

true teacher, entitled by virtue of my spiritual experience to
teach. But as I have been born among you, I know you will not
honour me as a spiritual guide, but I shall be honoured
elsewhere.[7]

It was Jesus's spiritual experience that had made him a Christ. But this
spiritual experience was not unique to Jesus; instead other historical figures have had similar experiences and so have attained a hallowed
status.

Jesus was a redeemed soul who had discarded his fleshy body and
now enjoyed the bliss of fellowship with God. Ramanathan's Jesus
announced:

I speak of the spirit within the body. No man or woman begat
the spirit, and I say that, whoever may be the father or mother of
my body, the spirit within it has been sanctified by God and
ordered to teach the truths of the Spiritual Kingdom."[8]

No one knows where the Christ came from. In Ramanathan's view—

what was sanctified by the Lord was *not* his fleshly body but the
spirit within the body; that upon the Sanctification of the Spirit
or attainment of Christhood, he (i.e. the Spirit) knew the Lord
and was directed by the Lord to go forth and teach.[9]

With such an understanding, Jesus is basically disconnected from
his Jewish roots and divested of his Jewish heritage. Ramanathan describes Jesus variously as a "voice from the East" and the "great Eastern
Master," thus situating him within a larger oriental location than his
specific Galilean milieu.[10] He does not always provide geographical
markers but often simply calls the native land of Jesus the "land of his
ill-treatment."[11] He deemed the importance of Jesus's birth mother,
Mary, his birthplace of Nazareth, and his occupation as a carpenter's
son superfluous to the task that Jesus had been called to perform, although these maternal, environmental, and occupational descriptors
were "not inconsistent with the doctrine relating to the coming of

Christ."[12] The reference to Nazareth as his birthplace and Mary as his mother are associated with the human Jesus and his earthly, tangible body (*sthula sarira*). Ramanathan is of the view that only those "who gloried in nationality and other forms of fancied greatness" relied largely "on the supposition that the body is everything." Ramanathan declares any physical relationship Jesus had with his mother and the disciples an "unnecessary intrusion" once Jesus had attained Christhood. At this point Mary, too, becomes redundant: "When the Man-Jesus became the Christ-Jesus, through the Holy Spirit, *his* mother was the Holy Spirit not Mary."[13] That is why Jesus addresses Mary as woman, not as mother. The Christ-Jesus does not attach any importance to relationships based on the body.

Likewise, Ramanathan effectively removes from Jesus his Jewish genealogy, especially his descendancy from David. To Ramanathan, the idea that Jesus came from the stock of David was a "popular, but erroneous, belief among the Jews." The Christ as the son of David is a "violent mis-reading" of the Hebrew Scriptures, and the sporadic statements about Jesus's Davidic lineage found in the New Testament "cannot be supported; nor, even if supported, would such a conclusion be in the least consistent with godly experience."[14] His contention is that a pure spirit like Jesus does not require an ancestry going back to David to bolster his sanctified state. Ramanathan draws attention to the Gospel accounts where Jesus took "great pains to expose the popular fallacy that Christ was the son of David."[15] This effectively neutered the conventional idea of Messianism based on the royal and political ideology of Davidic kingship. As Jesus said, Christ came before Abraham and "Christ is the Soul that has been freed from its bondage to worldliness, and blessed with the knowledge of God."[16]

Jesus is not only cut off from his Jewish ancestry in Ramanathan's rendering, but also virtually displaced from Jewish prophetic expectation. Ramanathan remarks: "But in these days of deep research and enlightened criticism, the authority of Jesus as teacher cannot well rest on prophecy."[17] The Gospel writers might have used the prophecies to "validate his divinity" but what counts is his spiritual experience, which *"proved to be in conformity with* the spiritual experience of others who, like him, have attained God."[18]

71

In Ramanathan's portrayals of Jesus, the two cardinal events in Jesus's life—the Crucifixion and the Resurrection—have been drained of their traditional theological intensity. When Jesus yielded up his spirit, Ramanathan interprets this as *"seemed to die."*[19] What happened on the cross was that Jesus engaged in yoga—a spiritual communion where speech and breath are suspended—but such a loss of animation is not a sign of death nor a permanent state of unconsciousness, for after a time one resumes life and reenters everyday activities. Ramanathan's Jesus is not the Christ who dies on the cross to save the world. He is also not the crucified guru as in Thomas Thangaraj's condescending misapplication of the Christian concept to the Saiva gurus.[20]

Ramanathan treats the Resurrection as a "vulgar doctrine."[21] For him, the Resurrection has nothing to do with the carnal, fleshly body, which is useless for all things related to the kingdom of God. He does not interpret the Resurrection as a physical event. When the dead or the asleep are said to be aroused or awakened, it is not their flesh that is aroused or awakened, but their soul or spirit. As Ramanathan's Jesus explains, "resurrection referred to *an awakening to God*, a coming to *know God.*"[22] What it actually means is the regeneration of the spirit. It is the spirit that passes from "ignorance of God to knowledge of God."[23] When Paul claimed that he was "an apostle raised from the dead," he knew that he had risen from "darkness, ignorance or non-knowledge of the Spirit, and passed into Light or Knowledge of the Spirit."[24] Ramanathan did not rule out the likelihood of the physical rising of Jesus from the tomb, which was not at all an "impossibility." Some masters like the *siddhis* in India (more on them later), after being "entombed," have emerged and moved about. Jesus had such powers to overcome "physical obstacles of a certain kind."[25] Ramanathan also dismissed the general Resurrection, citing Jesus as one who distanced himself from such a notion. He assumes that the Jews mistakenly borrowed this idea when they were captives in Babylon and erroneously believed in "the *Individual* Re-birth or resurrection of every spirit, each in its own time or order," an idea reiterated later by Saint Paul when he wrote about a *"General* Resurrection of *Bodies* all in one day."[26] The general Resurrection was first thought of by Ezekiel in order to raise the spirits of the Israelites for the "purpose of raising the national faith from the slough of corruption and despondency into which it had fallen."[27] Resurrection basically meant being reborn or risen from within.

The work of God is not effected through events like the cross or Resurrection but through mundane activities like teaching, writes Ramanathan:

> The Gospel of God means the teachings of God, delivered
> through the Sanctified in Spirit (like Jesus and other masters),
> as to the way in which God carries on his work of illumination
> and emancipation, right in the midst of worldly life, unseen and
> unthanked by most men, through agencies of different sorts.[28]

The people were attracted to Jesus not because of his self-sacrifice, which led to his efficacious death. Instead "the wonderful acts he performed in the name of God—his overflowing love and pure disinterestedness, his unblemished life and utter contempt for things worldly, were the grounds upon which thousands and thousands were led to accept him as a true teacher, and to take on trust what he taught regarding God."[29]

In Ramanathan's reconception, Jesus comes across as a world-renouncer and one who lives frugally. This renunciation of the world includes both a subjective overcoming of attachments and desires, and an objective existence in which he came to have no dwelling-place of his own and abandoned all family ties. Ramanathan argues that in his early life Jesus went in search of a Master. After being duly instructed, Jesus reached godliness and became a Master himself by completely overcoming worldly attachments through undergoing intense yogic practices. After attaining sanctification, Jesus did not go back to his family, but went about his business without any care for home, clothes, or food. It is not clear where Jesus learned the mystical knowledge of inner renewal. Ramanathan refers to a teacher who taught Jesus the "art of arts," who came in the name of God, but does not reveal who this teacher was nor the name. He merely states that "Jesus was sanctified and sent into Judaea."[30]

Ramanathan's Jesus does not offer any social message, for social action is far more effective if people are first perfected inwardly: "This is the old Hindu doctrine, and it has been brought to you by your own religious teacher Jesus Christ."[31] While the missionaries at that time were presenting Jesus as meeting the physical needs of the people, Ramanathan was portraying Jesus not as a person who satisfies the bodily needs of people by offering food, clothing, or, as he put it, "corporeal necessities," but as someone who provides spiritual sustenance. He writes:

> To sympathise with others, to help them with words of comfort and advice, to teach them the way of righteousness, to establish them in God—these acts, relating to the *spiritual* necessities of man are the highest forms of charity or love."[32]

Caring for the physical needs of people, in Ramanathan's reckoning, was an inferior form of compassionate act: "It was of course competent to his disciples to give away the offerings, which had been made to them by devotees, to others in need of corporeal help. Such acts are lower forms of charity."[33] Jesus's task was instead to show the folly of worldliness.[34] The comfort that Ramanathan's Jesus offered was a manifestation of the divinity within oneself, which should enable one to bear thirst and hunger, cold and heat. Jesus gives an appearance of being unworldly and uninterested in the basic necessities of human life.

For Ramanathan, Jesus was essentially a "Sanctified Teacher" sent forth by God to bring salvation to humankind by changing natural human beings into spiritual ones. His task was to convince the doubters and deniers to abandon their worldly ways and find the new love of God. For generations, the priests among the Jews had persecuted the prophets and the apostles, and had lost the keys of knowledge, and now Jesus was in possession of that knowledge. Each person has a soul or the temple of God in his or her body, through which they must enter by their own efforts in order to be in God's presence. Ramanathan posed the question: "How is this temple in which God is enthroned to be discovered, and, when discovered, how is it to be entered?" His answer was that we should follow the example of one who had already entered, found God, and had the desire to pass that knowledge to others. Jesus was such a person. God does not teach directly but "through the Sanctified Spirits called Christs."[35]

Jesus, for Ramanathan, was "above all things a teacher" and was "eminently great at teaching." But the teachings he imparted were not really new; they had already been revealed by the sages of India, and were merely being echoed by Judean prophets and lawgivers. These principles of truth were made known to the people of Western Asia by Jesus. This is the Jesus who openly claimed that he did not come to oppose the teachings of ancient lawgivers such as Moses and the Prophets, but came "only to *develop* and carry to its due fulfilment the object aimed at by law-givers and teachers, namely, the *ripening* of Love in man's heart."[36] What Jesus preached—the mysteries of the kingdom—existed before Jesus was born, and what he announced was not his own. What he did was to proclaim what "he had heard in the ear and realized in actual experience."[37] What Jesus had was the authenticity of one who had personal knowledge of what he said; he was not like the scribes who simply followed the letter of the law. Similarly, the contrast that Jesus made between earthly and heavenly things in his meeting with Nicodemus was already known to the sages of India as spiritual experiences "*deha mukti* (state of freedom while in the body) and *videha mukti* (state of freedom while without the body)."[38] Ramanathan is also quick to point out that Jesus is not the only one set apart or selected for this task. When a sanctified teacher is removed or disappears from the earth, God will send someone else to learn until Christhood is achieved.

Jesus, in Ramanathan's view, was not "an idle dreamer nor a vain theorizer, but a man of the deepest spiritual experience, a true teacher of the kingdom of God, a veritable light unto the world, whose doctrine *must* be recognised by all other men of spiritual experience as leading to the sanctification or healing of the spirit, and thus to the attainment of God."[39] This is the Jesus who opposed ceremonies and rituals. Ramanathan observes: "Passover was utilised by Jesus to illustrate the truths that Christ and God should be worshipped, not by the formality of a sacrifice but, subjectively, within us, as a personal experience."[40]

Like the Eastern gurus, Jesus wanted his disciples to seek their own inner meaning rather than to slavishly follow him. Jesus did not bother to explain how this should be achieved even to his disciples, but left them to work it out for themselves, saying, "He that is able to receive it, let him receive it."[41] No good can come by simply following the master. The task of the master is to tell his disciples about "the purging process," then it is up to them to work at it.

Earthly Jesus, Oriental Christhood

Ramanathan carefully distinguished between the Jesus of the flesh and the spiritually sanctified Christ. He points out that Jesus himself took pains to explain to Philip, the night before the Crucifixion, that to know Jesus was very different from knowing Christ, and that only the knowledge of Christ could lead to knowledge of God. When he distinguished between the physical Jesus of history and the Christ of Christian faith, this distinction was not based on the familiar Enlightenment quandary over the authentic historical Jesus and the dogmatic Christ. Ramanathan's differentiation instead resonates with the Saiva Siddhanta's understanding of the body as worthless and the soul as eternal. In his physical form, Jesus is seen as born of the womb of Mary and given the name Jesus, but he was not Christ until his corrupted worldliness had been healed by the invisible spirit, called *pneuma* in Greek, *ánma* in Tamil, or *átma* in Sanskrit. For Ramanathan, "in the body of *every* man is an invisible spirit which, being tainted with worldliness, thinks and acts in a worldly way. But by suitable training it is possible to purge it of all worldliness, when it will stand forth as Christ and function in a godly way."[42] It was the historical person Jesus who became Christ. As Ramanathan puts it, "Christ is the Soul that has been freed from its bondage to worldliness, and blessed with the knowledge of God."[43] Christ thus existed before the carnal form of Abraham came into existence. Ramanathan interprets "seed" in "Christ cometh of the seed of David" as a Word of God. It meant that "Christ is born of the Word of God or Holy Spirit, of whom David sang or taught."[44]

Just as he does with the physical Jesus, Ramanathan strips his Christ of any Jewish connotations, and describes Christhood in vague terms such as "Godliness," "perfection," "fullness," "maturity," "Peace," and "infinite love." Sometimes Christhood is described in terms of an ideal sonship, or "the Spirit re-risen in Godliness *without the limitations of flesh*."[45] Christhood is essentially a state of inward illumination in which the divine wisdom has become the inheritance of the soul. The Messiah or Christ is not a person made of flesh and blood, "but a soul sanctified by apt methods." Ramanathan recalls the words of Isaiah, who explicitly states that Christ is without form or proportion and yet is "transcendingly beautiful."[46] The Christ that Ramanathan envisaged was not the Christ who summons "dispersed tribes," or sits in judgment over the house of Israel, intent on conquering all their "enemies" and establishing a "universal empire," the center of which is to be "Zion, the holy city." Ramanathan advises that these Messianic expectations should not be understood "literally."[47] The Christ is essentially the one who appears within a human person as "love and light."[48] This Christ is not the Christ who enters Jerusalem triumphantly in full view of the people announcing his Messiahship, or overturns the tables of the merchants in front of the crowd, or talks about truth to Pilate in the Roman council. He is not the Christ who needs a fleshy father ancestor like David, nor does he spring from the "seed" of David, nor does he appear publicly in the "Temple" or on "Mount Moriah." This Christ is the one known only to those who have been" blessed with the fundamental experiences" and he manifests himself to those who worship him "spiritually in truth and spirit."[49]

Ramanathan is relentless in his belief that there is no need to look for a historical Christ. The coming of Christ is not an event that takes place out there in history, "but is an experience within you, so that if any man says 'Lo, here is Christ,' or 'there is Christ,' believe it not. He is to be found neither in the desert nor in mountain caves."[50] Ramanathan consistently tells his followers: "You are the Temple of God, you, the Spirit, which is within the body. The signs occur in the spiritual temple. Therefore you have not to look for them outside of you."[51] Nor is the Christ event associated with external signs and wonders. A Christ with miraculous powers might look marvelous to worldly eyes, but these powers are vain and unprofitable and of no importance to saints. Christhood and miracle-working are two different things and "they have no necessary connection with each other."[52] Ramanathan dismisses biblical predictions of the coming of the end, such as earthquakes, wars, famines, and plagues, as having nothing to do with the coming of Christ. Instead, he asserts, these calamities are caused by natural developments over the course of everyday life. The true disasters, Ramanathan urges, occur within a human being. It is carnality that holds the spirit captive. The destruction of the carnal elements within oneself is "the end of the world."[53] In Ramanathan's reckoning, the two most amazing wonders granted to people by God are finding God within oneself and attaining sanctification.

The sanctified Christ envisaged by Ramanathan is not restricted to Jesus alone. John and Paul had attained Christhood themselves by going through the stage of being disciples and attaining this spiritual promotion, not through the "lips of man," but, on the contrary, by having their souls follow the holy spirit inward until the "last atom of the darkness falls off."[54] It is then that the mystery of conversion takes place: a human being is turned into Christ. In biblical terms, the old Adam is transformed into the new Adam. In India, this spiritual experience is known as Atma Darsana, or the appearance of the Atma. In the New Testament, it is referred to as the "'coming' of Christ (Matthew 24.3, 27)."[55] In all this, God functions as a gracious teacher. This experience is not for all people and all times, but is reserved for those who are poor in spirit. Two such people are John and Paul.

John saw God as light within himself, and when he spiritually discerned the "great spiritual experience of Holy Spirit within him as Light," he progressed "from manhood to Christhood." Paul, too, confessed: "I certify you, brethren . . . that the Gospel which is preached by me is not after man, for neither did I receive it from man nor was I taught it, but it came to me through the uncovering of Saviour Christ . . . When it pleased God . . . to uncover the Son within me." Paul's emphatic declaration is a sign of this newly found divine experience: "Know ye not that ye are the Temple of God; and that the *Spirit of God* dwelleth within you."[56] Biblical figures like John and Paul come to know the mysteries of the Kingdom upon the "uncovering of Christ" in themselves.[57] These are the saints who provide Western nations with the "key of knowledge" and "interpret truly the teachings of Jesus, and the earlier

Sages of Judaea!" These are the sanctified souls who have "attained Christhood, [and] can properly teach and guide the world."[58] There are many such Christs to be found in India. Whereas Western nations knew of only one Christ, India had all along known "scores in each generation, busy saving seekers from the perils of atheism and materialism, and leading them to God."[59]

Ramanathan blames a wrong translation of "the only begotten son" for the Christian church's belief in a single Christ. He found fault with the translation of *monogenenes huios* as "only begotten Son," which in his view made Christendom think that there could be "only one Christ in the universe, though Jesus, Paul, and other Apostles spoke often of the possibility of other persons also attaining the state of Christhood, called also Sonship of God, Perfection, Peace, or Rest."[60] Jesus himself taught that others could be as perfect as God in love (Matthew 5.48) and as exceptional as himself if they had faith. Ramanathan invokes the words of Jesus to challenge those who said that it was not possible for human beings to achieve Christhood. He provides a series of biblical texts that "have proved a stumbling block to those who are wedded to the belief there is only one Christ for all time in the Universe, and that that Christ is Jesus."[61] For Ramanathan the correct rendition of *monogenenes huios* should be "alone-become" and not "only begotten." He explains that the "alone-becoming" of the soul is known in India as Kaivalya, a state of loneliness in which the "soul knows itself and God who is in it."[62] "Alone-becoming" is a great spiritual experience "known only to those have succeeded in Jnana Yoga," namely the ones who have been emancipated from desires and selfishness and are now in constant fellowship with God.[63]

Although Ramanathan claims that everyone could attain Christhood in due course, such a realization is restricted to a few. The egregious example of one who did not attain such status was John the Baptist. Not all the disciples reached the hallowed position of Peter, who was on "the way to blissfulness."[64] Such higher spiritual status is possible only to a few individuals who have a "certain ripeness of soul," as indicated by a renunciation of the world and a generous interest in the welfare of others.[65] While the standard readings of Jesus forbidding his disciples to go to the Gentiles or the Samaritans were seen as a streak of xenophobia in Jesus, Ramanathan interpreted these injunctions as Jesus recognizing that some were "not ripe enough to receive the gospel."[66] When Jesus upbraided the cities of Chorazin and Bethsaida, and Tyre and Sidon, and thanked God for hiding the mysteries of the Kingdom from the wise and the prudent, Ramanathan saw a tinge of irony in Jesus's words because, for such people, understanding the ways of God was beyond their reach and, far worse, they would use it for their sensual purposes. Such mysteries, as he put it, are revealed to "those only who are like babes, pure in heart."[67] Ramanathan identified eight classes of people who were qualified to hear the final truth. They are the people who are listed in the Sermon on the Mount: the "poor in spirit," "they that mourn," "the meek," "they who hunger and thirst after righteousness," "the merciful," "the pure in heart," "the peacemakers," and "they who are persecuted for righteousness sake." These are exclusive groups of people who "are fit to *understand* them [i.e., the mysteries of Christhood] without difficulty, enter diligently upon the practice of them, and attain the blessedness."[68] Even for people who are qualified to receive the truth, Ramanathan cautions that it had to be imparted prudently, depending on one's intellectual and spiritual condition. Or, in Ramanathan's rephrasing of the biblical verse: "Many are called (drawn to the Sanctified Teacher), but few are chosen" (i.e., for the attainment of Christhood).[69] The way to attain Christhood is to love one another, and to conquer selfish desires and worldly attachments. Loving one another involves blessing the enemies who curse you, doing good to those who hate you, and praying for those who despise and persecute you. It may even mean laying down one's life.

Ramanathan differentiates between Christ and logos. For him these are not the same. The Word, for Ramanathan, is "the Bodiless and Still Voice of God that speaks in, or directs, the spirits of men and indeed of all flesh."[70] He makes it clear that when John spoke of the logos, he was not referring to Christ: "John did *not* mean Christ. If Logos is *like* Christ, Logos cannot be Christ."[71] The logos is greater than Christ. For Ramanathan, the logos is like the Indian notion of *vak*, the most spiritual and inaudible voice that arises in God as an "over spreading power." The word is an activity of God that is beyond the prowess of Christ and parallels some of the work of the Lord Siva—creation, maintenance, destruction, instructions, rewards, and punishments. Such conduct and actions are beyond Christ. For Ramanathan, the Word is universal and has been present from the dawn of history, whereas Christhood occurs only intermittently in history.

Ramanathan conflates the Son of Man and Son of God into one. For him, the Son of Man is an "elliptic for son embodied in human flesh" and is not to be distinguished from "Son of God," for it is the Son of God who in the flesh is called Son of Man. The Son of God is the spirit in humans who have been cured of carnality. Jesus has used both expressions to denote Christ.[72] Ramanathan solemnly declares that "when Christ within you is known, he will lead you unto God."[73] In his view, spiritual experience has proven that it is possible for human beings to attain the status of the Son of God, that is, to attain "Godliness" or Christhood. Ramanathan persistently urges his admirers to find Christ within themselves: "Uncover the Christ that is within you . . . and then, and then only, will you find that you are one with the Lord, and the mysteries of the Kingdom of Heaven will be laid bare to you."[74]

Semitic Siddha, Galilean Guru

In Ramanathan's construal of Jesus, two Tamil images emerge: that of a siddha, and that of a Saiva guru.[75] In Tamil, a siddha, according to T. N. Ganapathy, who studied the phenomenon, is a person who has "realized the ultimate" in knowledge, achieving a "state of spiritual enlightenment and / or mystical self realization," and so has become a god in "flesh and blood," that is, one who has achieved a "state of spiritual enlightenment and or mystical self realization."[76] A siddha is one who transforms the body into a different kind of body and treats it "as the best medium of realizing the truth."[77] Ramanathan sees Jesus as an exceptional example of this type. In addition to investing Jesus with the knowledge of God and the state of being most useful to the world, Ramanathan gave him spiritual powers of a "very high order," similar to one who possessed siddhis (spiritual powers).[78] Jesus, like an Indian siddha, suspends his mind and breath and returns to face life after being awakened from *samadhi,* the yogic sleep. The withdrawal of Jesus to

Capernaum after his temptation by Satan, his sleeping at the back of the boat when there was a great storm, and his withdrawal to pray alone, are looked upon as godly sleep or *Jnana sushupti,* in which the soul retreats from the "world of senses and thought; exists in a condensed form, in a state of *involution.*"[79]

Just as a siddha who has realized the nonduality of *jiva* (the state of being alive) and Siva, Jesus is seen as the one who has realized God or Christ consciousness. It is not a state of oneness with God but rather "the same in being as God."[80] Ganapathy's description of a siddha as a "God-realized being alive in the world for the sake of the mankind and all living beings" fits with his image of Jesus.[81] Other characteristics of siddhas—that they have "no sacred city, no monastic organization, no religious instruments"; their "indifference to formal religion"; and their insistence on enlightenment as distinct from belief in doctrine— resonate with Ramanathan's Jesus, who has no permanent abode, is critical of institutional religion, and emphasizes awakening souls rather than producing neat dogmas.[82] Jesus was wary of doctrines, apathetic toward rituals, and indifferent to legalistic piety. Another trait of a siddha that Ramanathan's Jesus exhibits is involvement with society. He does not withdraw himself from the world, but, like the siddha, labors for the well-being of the people out of a sense of deep compassion. As a fulfilled and accomplished being, he serves as a guide for others to live better lives.

Jesus, too, performs paranormal acts similar to those carried out by the siddhas, who have attained special psychic and supernatural powers. Among his powers, Jesus can expand infinitely, float through the air, reach everywhere, overcome obstacles, control natural phenomena, and dominate all of creation.[83] For instance, the risen Jesus entering the room even when the door was shut was like a siddha possessing supernatural powers. To those who questioned the correctness of the wording regarding Jesus riding on two animals—an ass and a colt—Ramanathan recalled that, just as Jesus controlled devils and walked on water, as a siddha he had the power to control animals as well. Ramanathan wrote: "Natural obstructions were of no consequence to him. This is a well-known *siddhi* or spiritual power possessed by many saintly men."[84] But for Ramanathan, these superhuman acts were not enough. Saints feeding the people, walking on water, or stepping on burning embers do not indicate "sanctification of spirit or attainment of peace."[85] For Ramanathan, the most strange and splendid experience of all was finding Christ in oneself and attaining Godhead.

There is also an allusion to the Saiva concept of *eluntharuli*—spirit rising or "gracious rising"—an act of Siva who rises from within to bring emancipation. The following from Ramanathan alludes to such a notion: "Just as the soul enshrined in the body 'rises' from the body, God enshrined in the Soul 'rises' from the Soul and manifests himself to the Soul."[86] The description of the coming of Christ as an event that happens not in the outer world but occurs as "an experience within" the body is only another indication of eluntharuli.[87] His writings are strewn with words such as "rising anew (*anastasis*) of souls," "re-risen spirit," "rising," and "coming," which refer to the Saiva notion of gracious rising. This totally contradicts the concept of avatara, where God comes from above to redeem the world. "Though when the subjective world ends, Christ will certainly rise in glory from amidst the melting rudiments of the flesh, no man, not even Christ himself, knows the time of rising, for it is only God who knows it, as the author of salvation."[88]

Beside the many prototypes of Indian *jnanis*, Ramanathan identifies Jesus as a guru. He might not have used the Saiva word guru explicitly for Jesus, but he refers to him as a "spiritual teacher," "spiritual guide and teacher," "a true Teacher from God," "a true teacher of the kingdom of God," and "this great teacher" with all the characteristics of a Saiva guru. His preferred term was *jnani*. Jesus as a jnani had the vision of the soul, *átma-darśana*, which is equivalent to Saivites having *Śiva-darśana*: "This is called by the Agamic jnanis *átma-darśana*, or knowledge of the soul, corresponding to the 'manifestation' or 'appearance' of Christ within man. Then is realised *Śiva-darśana*, or knowledge of God, who manifests himself only within the Spirit though He pervades all the Universe. This is 'His way,' His usual method, of manifesting Himself to those men who worship Him spiritually, 'in truth and in spirit,' as Jesus said."[89]

Much like Siva, who comes in the form of a guru to help the soul to get rid of its bondage and suffering, initiates the soul into finding its authentic identity, and brings together the soul and Siva not into a state

83

of oneness, but sameness, Ramanathan's Christ helps the soul to resist attachment and makes it possible for the soul to unite with Christ: in the words of Ramanathan, he heals the "souls of their worldliness, and so make them Godly."[90] In Saiva Siddhanta, liberation is a gift from God and it is the result of Siva's direct intervention; so too is the salvation offered by Jesus. Just as Lord Siva bequeaths his grace to devotees and comes to them in the form of a personal guru and leads them to overcome their illusion and realize their Siva consciousness, Ramanathan's Christ performs a similar function. When one loses interest in the pleasures of the world, "a man sanctified in spirit—a Christ in man—will appear and teach him how to discern the True from the False."[91]

In Saiva Siddhanta, the guru is said to be the very God who appears out of the fullness of his grace to help human beings in their struggle against carnality to realize their inner divine potential. He is a religious master who has the authority and the ability to impart and initiate such knowledge because he himself has personally experienced it. In Ramanathan's view, Jesus was such a person who, having known God himself, was able to direct "suitable pupils" to "the way to know God."[92] Only a rabbi who has attained Christhood can properly teach and guide the world. He comes in the form of a guru when a disciple is ready. The person must first become a "*mumukshu*, or seeker of Freedom" in whom the hunger for liberation from the material world has been awakened.[93] This portrayal of Jesus resonates with the Saiva Siddhanta idea of a guru. Siva appears as a guru only to those who are ready to receive the message "as the sun opens only those lotuses that are ready to bloom."[94] His task is not simply to pass on the knowledge but also to enable the individual to experience the divine. This is achieved not through moral statements but through sensible moral acts. In Ramanathan's configuration, Jesus emerges as such a mystic guru who has come to instruct those who are "fit for the manifestation."[95] For Ramanathan, Jesus, like the Saiva guru, is the supreme example of a person who believed and realized his inner light and who grew into a divine status, embracing a divine destiny.

Ramanathan's dismissal of the genealogy of Jesus, or his placement within a great Israelite institution, is in line with the Saiva guru tradition, which pays little attention to succession. His disregard for any filial affection resonates with the saying of Tirumular, one of the Saiva mystics, that one should not boast by saying "My father, my mother."[96] Such an indifference to historical lineage is an indication of the flexible, unrestricted, and evolving character and purpose of the guru. Similarly, Ramanathan's idea of Christ resembles that of Siva taking human form to display his saving qualities. Tirumular, in his *Tirumandhiram*, a Tamil poetic work, calls the body the abode of God and the best medium to realize the truth. Jesus is seen as a liberated soul who used his body as a vehicle for the manifestation of the divine. Unlike in the Vedic tradition, where the guru is seen as God, in the Siddhantic tradition God is revealed in the form of the guru. Jesus is such a guru.

Discovering the Jerusalem Within:
Saivising a Semitic Savior

It is clear that Ramanathan did not set out to write a full biography of Jesus. His writings are full of references to Jesus, and the Jesus that comes through is a devotional type whose sole interest is to awaken the latent divinity in humans. Ramanathan shows only a partial interest in the past life of Jesus; his focus instead is largely on the spiritual benefits that Jesus can bring in the present. It is tempting to place Ramanathan's work among the devotional biographies that were popular before the modern quest, but such a placement would be unfair to Ramanathan. His works show his astute use of the newly emerging tools of modern criticism, which he utilized to promote his interpretative agenda. At a time when Gospel harmonies were popular, Ramanathan applied the historical method to scrutinize the Jesus tradition for dissonances that could open the way for his alternate perspective. His work, unlike the German endeavor, was an early example of communicating the fruits of biblical scholarship to the general public.

The reception of Ramanathan's work varied. While in the West his commentaries, especially his exposition of Saint John's Gospel, were hailed in *Open Court* as "fertile and suggestive," in India they mustered only limited sympathy. A. J. Appasamy, who himself worked extensively on the Gospel of John, found that Ramanathan's attempt to make Jesus follow the doctrines of Saiva Siddhanta went against "fundamental laws of historical criticism." Robin Boyd, too, who did much to identify and classify Indian Christian thinkers, castigated him for manipulating the text to conform to Advaita Hinduism, and dismissed his commentaries as too remote from Christian tradition.

The Jesus who emerges in the writings of Ramanathan is not the figure who is recognizable from the pages of the Gospels, is at home within the dogmas of churches, or who is invoked in popular religious practices. An elusive, esoteric character known only to a few, Jesus in this manifestation is not a generally accessible Christ figure but a "special and private one," recognized only by those who are spiritually ripe enough to receive his message.[97] Jesus is seen not as announcing the message from the God of the Israelites, but as propagating Saiva philosophical, mystical, and ascetic tenets, with a particular emphasis on self-realization and finding God within oneself. What we have is a non-eschatological figure, an iterant Eastern mystic who embodied God and acted as God's *asariri vak,* or "bodiless voice."[98] A messianic figure who comes to rescue God's people at the end of time from whatever they need to be rescued is accorded a negligible role in Ramanathan's configuration of Jesus.

Those raised on the tradition of a Davidic king challenging the Roman power and restoring the political independence of Israel would certainly be disappointed with Ramanathan's Jesus. They would also miss the total absence of the promise-fulfillment motif, which was constructed by Christian apologists who exploited the Gospel genealogies to cast Jesus as the anticipated Messiah. Ramanathan's Jesus did not fulfill the Jewish national hope nor was he part of a renewal movement that envisaged the restructuring of Israel. For him, the expressions Kingdom of God and Kingdom of Heaven used by Jesus denote not political kingdom or kingly rule but "the *reign* of Godliness in the mind" or "the reign of Peace in our hearts."[99] This reign is established within oneself as a spiritual heaven, and cannot be inherited: it is a state of "perfect bliss" and "unspeakable calm" that, in Saint Paul's veiled language, is the "third heaven" (2 Corinthians 12.2).[100] Unlike in the traditional picture, Ramanathan's Jesus is not sent to the least and the lost, but to inculcate Godliness in those who, to use his favorite phrase, are ripe enough to receive it. It is clear that Ramanathan's Jesus is not at the vanguard of political liberation but has to do with spiritual renewal. Jesus is an individualist with no social or communal message, no interest in politics or national regeneration. Instead he directed his good news to individuals.

Ramanathan does not invest Jesus with any originality. Jesus is depicted as contributing nothing to Jewish life, religion, and culture; he simply echoes what the sages of India and Judea uttered before him. Ramanathan tells his American followers that the message Jesus brought—the Kingdom is within you, convert self-love into neighborly love, and neighborly love into perfect love—is the "old Hindu doctrine, and it has been brought to you by your own religious teacher, Jesus Christ."[101] Even the revelation that Jesus received is not exceptional to him. Paul had a similar divine disclosure, which put the master and the disciple at the same level: "The foundation which was revealed to Paul was identical with the foundation which was revealed to Jesus."[102] Christ's originality is further diminished when he is cast as someone who has no power of his own but relies on God for whatever power is given to him. Jesus himself has no doctrines of his own: "My doctrine is not mine, but His that sent me."[103] Jesus, like any other spiritual master, acts merely as an instrument of God's will. Ramanathan even divests the Hebrew sages of their inventiveness. He claims that, if their words are suitably interpreted, their conclusions "stand corroborated by the teachings of other Eastern masters."[104]

Ramanathan is a spiritual elitist and believes that the Messiah and his message are meant for an exclusive few: "Esoteric truths cannot be imparted to all alike in the same way, but only in ways suitable to each person, for fear that the information conveyed may take the person further away from the goal than he is already."[105] This Christ is not easily visible: "In everyman there is the spiritual substance called Christ which is invisible to carnal eye but visible only to those who have been healed or sanctified of all worldly pleasures." In Ramanathan's view, only people of culture may become as perfect as God. Paul, too, taught that culture was necessary "till we *all* come unto (that is, grow to be) a perfect man, unto the stature of the fullness of Christ."[106] Like the Saiva guru, Jesus influences, and dispenses salvation to, only those individuals who have "ripeness of the soul," which can be seen by their rejection of worldly pleasures and generous interest toward others, a status dictated not by law but by love. What we have is a Jesus who offers counter-elitism rather than anti-elitism.

Ramanathan is liable to be accused of anti-Semitic tendencies in his writings. His removal of Jesus from his environment and from prophetic expectations, and his denial of Jesus's ethnic extraction, could be used as prime evidence to indict him. But the reduced Judaistic role accorded to Jesus by Ramanathan is different from the discriminatory anti-Jewish thinking found in the West. Ramanathan never referred to Israel as rejected by God, nor entertained supersessionist ideas. For that matter, he certainly did not advocate Saiva texts replacing the Torah. His sole concern was to show that the Judean jnanis corroborated what the Indian sages had dispensed long ago. True to his character, and living up to his hermeneutical principle of finding God within oneself, he told the Boston Zionist Association that they should find Jerusalem within themselves. Attaining Jerusalem within one's soul is better than longing for the physical, geographical Jerusalem.

Ramanathan shared a number of characteristics with the Hindu reformers of the time. Like them, he was ready to provide an analysis of what was wrong with the West, and was only too willing to offer advice. He was like some of the national reformers who had class, education, power, and arrogance and told the West that Easterners were better interpreters of the message of Jesus than were Western Christians: "The words of Jesus have been lost to the nations of the West, the only way of restoring the 'Spirit' or the true meaning of the words of the Bible is to secure their interpretation by 'able ministers' from the East *who are now living, and on whom the effulgence of His grace has been shed.*"[107] He was in the business of reminding the West that there were many Christs or jnanis and "able ministers of the New Testament" among them. Their collective task was to "restore to Western nations the 'Key of Knowledge' and interpret truly the teachings of Jesus, and the earlier Sages of Judaea!" They also should be devoted to rescuing "seekers from the perils of atheism and materialism, and leading them to God."[108] Ramanathan saw his task as telling the West that the finest teachings of Indian jnanis are all found in the works of Judean jnanis. The same Hindu doctrine of the inner improvement of the indi-

vidual, "training the mind to prefer the needs of the spirit to the crav-
ings of the flesh," had been brought to Westerners by Jesus.[109] To remind
Christians that similar ideas are found in their scriptures, Ramanathan pointed to the Lamentations: "Let us search and try our ways, and
turn again to the LORD" (3.40). What the West needed to do was to
recover the truth of the jnani, through a proper reading of their own
shastras and by "imbibing sound doctrine from the living lips of evangelists and apostles of God."[110]

Ramanathan, a person who vehemently opposed conversion of his
own people, was not averse to converting the West to his idea of Hinduism. He urged Christians to recover the true meaning of the message of Jesus, which, in his reconfiguration, was nothing but the Saiva
tenets. For him, one of the common features of the Saiva and Christian traditions is their portrayal of an ideal, spiritual world beyond
our material one. In projecting such a concern with the spiritual
realm, he characterized these traditions as an undifferentiated set of
beliefs. Implicitly, what Ramanathan's Jesus offered was a Saiva form of
the Gospel, and the notion that the future of the West depended on recovering this Saivized kerygma in their own scriptures and traditions.
Without being overly aggressive, his depiction of Jesus is infused with
exclusive tendencies.

For Ramanathan, what was important was the practical life of a
Christian. His message to his Christian audience was to stay clear of
speculative Christian theology and focus on the experience of grace, or,
as he keeps reminding them, to realize Christhood within themselves.
He was all along clear about Christianity as a system of doctrine, and
Christhood as the inward principle.

Like the Hindu reformers of the time, Ramanathan subscribed to the
stock picture of Victorian Christianity as being tainted with industrialization, which had left people depersonalized. As a result, the West
had become materialistic, mechanical, secular, and soulless. Such cari-
catures are telling comments on the superficial and flimsy nature of
Western accomplishments. For him, the increasing disintegration of
the society was due to the technological hubris of the West and its ap-
petite for modern gadgets. He attacked the West for its desire for
material goods but not for its colonial impulses or its cultural control.

The overproduction of material goods, in his view, had alienated socie-
ties from their traditional roots and created a false chasm between life
and religion. He was not totally against industrial enterprise. What
bothered him was the West's obsession with new scientific appliances.
His solution was to turn to the pre-industrial East, where the spiritual
values of humanity were still preserved. For him, the greatness of India
was that it maintained this neat harmony between the spiritual and
the material, which had so far spared it from the fate that had befallen
the Babylonian, Phoenician, Egyptian, Greek, and Roman civilizations,
among others. He reminded his Western audience that Indian civilization had thrived all these years because it had retained a healthy balance
between materiality and spirituality. He maintained that the East had
the right ideals and ethical conduct needed for the "ripening" of the
soul in an industrialized age. The enduring value of Indian civilization
was that, in spite of its worldly advancement, its arts and architectur-
ally marvelous marble palaces, it had not forgotten the impermanence
of material progress, whereas the West did not know how to untangle
itself from worldly desires and attachment to material possessions that
are bound to perish. The sages of India had proclaimed the importance
of "rearing the spirit with utmost care" as the *greatest work of life on
earth*."[111] Ramanathan was convinced that only Indian spirituality could
restore the harmony between material desire and one's inner strength.

At the same time, Ramanathan differed from his Indian counterparts. Whereas most of the Indian reformers belonged to the Vaishnava tradition and reinvented the Sanskrit Vedanta as the solution to
the ills of the West, Ramanathan was a Saivite. In trying to promote a
Tamil spiritually expounded by the Saiva saints, he offered a philosophy
based on Saiva theology. He told his American addressees: "We call our
religion the way to Siva or *Saiva marga*. It is the worship of one Lord of
all nations, who is all Peace and all Power, for that is the meaning of
Siva."[112] The Saiva Siddhanta that Ramanathan advocated differs from
the Advaita Vedantic position of the Hindu reformers, especially that
of Radhakrishnan, whom we will encounter later.[113]

The conceptualization of Jesus as one of the Hindu avataras (literally "descent," but an incarnation of a deity on earth) features persistently in the writings of the Hindu reformers, but the notion of avatara

is barely mentioned in Ramanathan's writings. Perhaps this is because, being a Saivite, he would not have given much significance to incarnation. In Saivism, avataras play a subsidiary and smaller role. There are incidents where Siva was supposed to have taken human form, but these are all limited and brief. Vaishnavism, by contrast, accords importance to avataras. Most of the Hindu reformers, especially Radhakrishnan, belonged to the advaita tradition and invested greatly in the idea of incarnation.

Ramanathan, however, the only interpreter at that time who had written a full-blown commentary on Saint John's Gospel, a Gospel that is easily related to notions of avatar, gave little importance to incarnation. He interpreted "the word made flesh" (John 1.14) not as an incarnational affirmation, but as a "manifestation" or "enfleshment" of spirit for spiritually weaker people. He regarded the translation of this verse as erroneous and offered his own: "the Word appeared in flesh." The event being described, in his view, had little do with the person of Jesus or with the coming of Christ; in his rendering, it is shorn of any of the markers associated with incarnation. It was not a public event enacted in the theater of history but instead a private event to assess whether a person was ripe for discipleship. It was the gradual liberation of a person from the "captivity of darkness."[114] Ramanathan's Johannine Jesus even speaks of "freedom from incarnation."[115] When Jesus is described as an avatara, the focus is on what he did, but when he is described as a guru, as Ramanathan tends to do, the primary concern is his teaching.

In another respect, Ramanathan was manifestly different from the contemporaneous Hindu rehabilitators. Although Ramanathan's line of argument was persistently simple—to trace affinities between Saiva spirituality and the Christian message embedded in biblical writings—he did not insist on the supremacy of Saivism, nor did he view it as a decadent tradition needing repair and spiritual reinforcement, as the missionaries and orientalizers insisted. He was not advancing Saivism as a solution to the West, which had lost its soul to "selfish mercantile principles and the worship of wealth."[116] Although Ramanathan claimed that "only one [i.e., Saivism] at the present day is able to impart a full knowledge of those principles and practices which result in the actual attainment of God," he was not claiming a superior status for Saivism.[117] For him, it mattered "little whence knowledge of the doctrines was derived," whether "principles are to be viewed as Judaic or Hellenic or Hellenistico-Judaic," or whether these principles are proclaimed by Jesus or any other sanctified souls.[118] Instead this is a clear case of a siddhantin, who while permitting a place for all religions in the world, holds fast to the claim that Saivism is the "highest and final stage before release." As V. Paranjoti notes, while not obliterating the differences among the religions, a "Siddhantin accommodates them all in the category of religious enterprise that rises in spiral fashion up to the apex of his own 'end of ends.'"[119]

Unlike those Indian thinkers who portrayed and privileged India as *punyabhumi,* the blessed land with spiritual resources to save the world, Ramanathan did not impose any such geographically specific restrictions on salvation: "It matters not in what land or sphere of society a man is born if in humble spirit he acts up to the faith he was born in."[120] Human beings, in his view, have the ability to move to a "higher form of faith" until their thoughts are centered in God. For him, the sanctified souls are everywhere in the world. The sacred teachings are likewise not confined to Indian holy books. He told his Western bhaktas that God teaches through "other agencies" such as parents at home, teachers at school, pastors, evangelists, and the apostles of God. These are the people who are imbibed with love and who bring "discernment unto truth."[121]

Ramanathan invests Indian jnanis with a mythical quality. For him, it is the jnanis who "stand for the highest and most sacred ideas of Indian civilization—all that is finest, noblest, and purest in it. They are the efflorescence of the life of the nation as a whole."[122] They transcend all religious barriers and treat every religious adherent in the same way. All go to them when seeking wisdom. They are portrayed as ideal; the finest, noblest people; the antithesis of the puritanical Victorian preachers. Jesus was such a jnani. Ramanathan magnified the role of jnanis in the disciple's self-realization without mentioning how some jnanis could be authoritarian and manipulative. He overlooks another weakness as well: jnanis are good at inculcating spirituality but not at creating equality and social justice.

Like most of the reformers, Ramanathan embodied some contradictions. He persistently told Christians that their religion did not "consist in words, professions, and ceremonies but in heartfelt longing for the imperishable substrate of all things," then went on to renovate the temple his father had built in Colombo.[123] He also made sure that the two schools he built in Jaffna had temples on their campuses. His claim that the authority for revelation is not an infallible book, or an infallible institution, but one's inner light, looks hollow when he himself encouraged temple rituals. He dismissed submission to an external authority but then insisted on an inward illumination that is possible only through a guru. The high ideal he advocated for Christians, that the highest and best form of worship be neither a visual nor a mental act, but a purely spiritual act, seems hardly to apply to all Hindus.

Ramanathan belonged to the long line of Hindu scholars whose faith in their religious tradition remained staunch and undeviating even as they appreciated the value of the Gospel. The Christianity that they constructed looked much like a variant form of Hinduism. Within the colonial context, Hindus were being forced to defend their culture and religion. Ramanathan did so by utilizing subversively Western methods and approaches. What looked like Westernization was often a means of reining in the West, sometimes by neutralizing its potency, and at times by presenting the cherished Gospel of the West as a cheap imitation of Hindu ideals. Ramanathan was more than happy to be an erudite sage of the East. His spirituality was basically mystical, meditative, and nondoctrinal. He placed great emphasis on the individual's inner development. The salvation that Ramanathan's Jesus announced was not a public story in which the poor and oppressed were rescued from their misery, but a private transaction between God and individuals—individuals who were spiritually fit to receive the message.

Ramanathan's language of spiritual self-discovery seemed to offer a transcendental alternative to the Christian West, which was burdened with antiquated rituals and doctrines. He ended up employing abstruse conceptions from Indian spirituality or Indian wisdom. His work is therefore full of enigmatic, vague, metaphysical oversimplifications. He elevated Indian spirituality to a lofty and idealistic plane but, in doing so, prevented discussions about its vile and ugly side. The open and all-embracing Hinduism he projected to the West could be intolerant: for example, in the sixteenth century, the Hindu King Cankill I killed nearly seven hundred Roman Catholic converts in Ramanathan's own beloved Jaffna. More worryingly, he reduced Saivism to an irrational mysticism. His message offered a spiritual vision of India that was nothing but a celebratory return to and a replica of the Western ideal of a static, timeless, spiritual East.

Writing at the same time, Surendra Kumar Datta, an Indian Christian who advocated Christian missions in India in his book *The Desire of India*, commented that the "nearest approach to a distinctively Indian interpretation of Christ had come from a non-Christian sect, the Brahmo Samaj."[124] Although Ramanathan was never part of this Indian reform movement, his Christological articulations were certainly distinctive. He and other Hindus, like Rammohun Roy and Keshab Chunder Sen, set the tone and template for Indian Christian theology. For all the radical and creative posturing of current Indian Christology, its content, parameter, and methodology have not changed appreciably since these Hindus first began to articulate how to integrate this *mleccha* (foreigner) Jesus into the Indian philosophical and religious framework.

4

The Nonexistent Jesus

A t the turn of the twentieth century, a brief and muted debate about the myth of the historical Jesus occurred in the West, mainly at the outer edges of Western biblical scholarship. Some scholars insisted that the historical Jesus never existed but was an invention of the Christian church. The inspiration for this denial of the historical Jesus came from two newly emerging fields of study: the critical approach to the Bible, and the History of Religions School. Once critical methods began to be applied vigorously to the Gospels, it became perhaps inevitable that the historicity of Jesus would be called into question—and the comparative study of religions, encouraged by the History of Religions School, would further undermine Christian claims of the distinctiveness of its message. The mythical parallels to Christian ideas and the prevalence of redeemer myths, blood sacrifices, and divine visitations in Near and Far East religions, identified in the works of Hermann Gunkel, E. B. Taylor, and James Frazer, led scholars to surmise that Christianity might have been a product of the countless mysterious religions that had been widespread in the Roman world.

The purpose of this chapter is neither to determine who conceived the idea that the historical Jesus never existed, nor to analyze the impact or ill effects of the Western versions of this claim, but to draw attention to a similar debate in twentieth-century colonial India that went largely unnoticed in the West. Arthur Drews, a pioneer and an inspiration for many of the doubters, in his preface to *The Christ Myth*, mentions a whole list of Western scholars from Germany, England, the United States, France, Holland, Italy, and Poland who propounded the nonhistoricity of Jesus, but he fails to refer to the Indians involved, especially Thakur Kahan Chandra Varma, whose work went through twelve editions.[1]

The two Indians who spearheaded the denial of the existence of Jesus were Chandra Varma and Dhirendranath Chowdhuri. Details are scanty about these two men. Both belonged to Hindu reform movements that were very active in colonial India. Varma was part of the Arya Samaj. His *Christ a Myth: Historicity of Christ,* which first appeared in 1903, attracted considerable attention in the form of a robust rebuttal from missionaries.[2] J. N. Farquhar of the London Missionary Society led the Protestant defense, which was included in subsequent editions of Varma's book, while the Roman Catholic refutation came from a Jesuit named A. Lebeau.[3] Chowdhuri was a member and a propagandist for Sadharan Brahmo Samaj, a splinter group of the Brahmo Samaj. Chowdhuri's *In Search of Jesus Christ,* a tome more than four hundred pages long, aimed to demolish the historical Jesus. These two men latched onto some of the insights of the Western Jesus-myth writings, enlarged them, tailored them to suit their purpose, and in the process massively overplayed them in their own battles against missionaries. Both had a simple objective: to attack the historicity of Jesus and confute claims for the supremacy of the Christian message. Although both had a cantankerous attitude toward Christ and Christianity, and to some extent used the same sources, there is no evidence that Chowdhuri knew Varma's work, which preceded his.

Varma and Chowdhuri had three interrelated hermeneutical purposes. First, their overwhelming intention was—to use the words of Varma—to prove that a "person like Christ ha[d] never lived."[4] Chowdhuri had a similar mission, to establish that "there [was] no such historical person as Jesus Christ."[5] Chowdhuri claimed that there were Jesuses and Christs but all were "mythical amalgamations."[6] Both Varma and Chowdhuri set out to try to trace how the suffering, dying, and rising servant of God depicted in the prophetic writings, and the astral and mythological speculations of the Gnostic sects, were transferred to a historical figure like Jesus. For Chowdhuri, the personal and communal experiences of the early Christian communities played a decisive role in transforming an abstract, speculative figure into a living, historical personality—in other words, in turning many mythical Jesuses into a single historical one. In this endeavor, the two scholars, unlike most engaged in the contemporary Western quest for the historical Jesus, did not start with the Gospels. They sought to "reconstruct the life of Jesus from the pre-Christian Old Testament instead of waiting till the post-Christian second century when the New Testament was completed."[7]

Their second aim was to challenge the supremacy of the Christian gospel. Both of their books were written in the context of a persistent, toxic missionary onslaught on Hinduism and India, and an insultingly patronizing attitude toward idolatry and polytheism by the Indian reform movements. During this period, Farquhar accused the Arya Samajists of a false interpretation of the Vedas, predicting that the whole edifice would collapse with the introduction of biblical and the Enlightenment values. Chowdhuri reserved his ire particularly for the Centenary Forward Movement of Calcutta, which in its literature painted a picture of Indians starving for the Gospel. Its publications contained phrases like "India's heart is yearning towards Christ" and the "New Testament will bring spiritual Enlightenment to India," implying that Indians had a deep hunger for Christianity.[8]

Aligned with this was the third motive, to save Hindus from the predatory practices of missionaries who saw their sole task as the conversion of India. Varma declared that his purpose was not "to revile Christianity" but to save Hindus "from the clutches of these missionaries who play tricks like jugglers for entrapping young students and illiterate folks into their fold, for the sake of their belly."[9] He saw this as a noble cause, to rescue the susceptible Indian succumbing to missionary preaching. Chowdhuri clearly stated in the preface to his book: "If the book can wean a single soul away from the Christian Church I will deem my labour well recompensed."[10]

Negating the Narratives

A closer reading of Varma's and Chowdhuri's work reveals that there are similarities in their mission to deny the historicity of Jesus. What these two Hindu reformers set out to do is refute and throw out both the medium and the messenger. They mercilessly attack the Gospels and the Gospel writers, as well as those who associated with Jesus, such as the disciples and Jesus's family. To establish the nonexistence of Jesus, they devalue the historical content of the New Testament. They instinctively follow the axiom of the advocates of the Jesus myth: "Of the real history of Jesus but little is preserved in the Gospels."[11] Chowdhuri uses all kinds of phrases to reduce the importance of the New Testament. He calls it a "scrap of paper," a "confused mass of writings," and "spurious."[12] The New Testament, according to both men, is a contrived document containing materials from older sayings and myths and, far worse, is chock full of "misquotations and misinterpretations." They even find fault with the English version, in Chowdhuri's case calling it full of "mistranslations and errors."[13]

The New Testament, in their view, was not antique enough to befit its status as a sacred scripture. For Varma, unlike the Vedas, the New Testament was not as "antique in its origins" as the Christian church arrogantly claimed. As far as these men were concerned, scripture, religion, or revelation must date from the beginning of creation. In this respect, the Christian scriptures failed to measure up to their standard; in particular, the Gospels emerged much later, and all became canonical only after much controversy. The New Testament in general acquired its divine and canonical status very late, in 364, and even then, only by a bizarre method of voting. In Varma's view, this was not the way to accord sacred credence to a religious book.

Varma and Chowdhuri gleefully highlight internal historical, chronological, and topographical discrepancies in order to show the unreliability of the Gospels, thus negating their value. They were not the first to draw attention to such inconsistencies; both cheerfully accepted the work of literary critics of the time, who, in studying the literary features of these texts, drew attention to their style, contradictions, inconsistencies, and inaccuracies. That the Jesus Myth books drew attention to the discrepancies among the Gospels only reinforced their case. Varma spoke for both when he stated that the New Testament was "bristling with contradictions."[14] Both Varma and Chowdhuri, for instance, reproduce a list of inaccuracies in historical references surrounding the birth of Jesus. They point out that Cyrenius was not the governor of Syria when the census took place, and that Jesus was born several years after Herod's death. Chowdhuri finds fault with Luke, whom he regards as a reliable historian, accusing him of being "equally bad in his references."[15] (Indeed, Luke was not entirely correct in his historical references to the imperial census and taxation.) Chowdhuri, too, lists a long catalogue of erroneous information in the Gospels, including the massacre of the innocents, the friendship between Herod and Pilate (Luke 23), and the character of Pilate. He and Varma also point out that the Gospel writers were weak on geography. Not knowing the sites of the two feeding miracles, and the muddled itinerary of Jesus in the region of Tyre and the eastern shore of the Sea of Galilee, are indications to them that the Gospel writers lacked knowledge of the local landscape.

Varma and Chowdhuri sneer at the unsophisticated nature of the New Testament language. They find its Greek not as polished or sophisticated as in the writings of Xenophon, Demosthenes, and Plutarch. They argue that because the New Testament was not written in the language of the people—Aramaic, Syriac, or Chaldean—but in Greek, it must have been produced after the extinction of these languages and thus much later than the events depicted. The preponderance of Latinisms in the New Testament, too, meant that it must have been written by Romans and not by Jews. And the fact that the New Testament abounds with phrases and dialects of the Greek language, Hebraisms, foreign idioms, and compositional errors proved to Varma and Chowdhuri that it was written at a time when Greek had become corrupted and was not as "pure and elegant" as in the time of Jesus. As far as Chowdhuri was concerned, the New Testament is "so quite foreign to her genius." After their relentless criticism of the Gospels, nothing valuable or positive remains.

Along with discrediting the Gospels, Varma and Chowdhuri were equally scathing about the Jewish scriptures that Jesus grew up with.

Both disparage their historical worth, writers, and doctrines with a mixture of derision, rejection, and ridicule. For Chowdhuri, the Hebrew Bible is a "gospel of hatred, a hymn of hate from end to end."[16] Varma's method of stigmatizing the Jewish texts is to identify morally repugnant actions of the God of the Old Testament such as "Thus saith the LORD, Behold, I will raise up evil against thee out of thine own house, and I will take thy wives before thine eyes, and give them unto thy neighbour, and he shall lie with thy wives in the sight of this sun" (2 Samuel 12.11), and then to pose the question, "can a book consisting of these sayings be of divine origin?[17] For him, the Bible is a revealed text, but not through a divine being, or by divinely elected prophets. It is a "revelation of sacerdotal trickery, a revelation of the barbarous brutality of the ancient Jews, a revelation of the follies, superstitions, and prejudices to which the Hebrews were subject in days of yore." He goes further, describing the biblical revelation as "a budget of blunders, a description of crimes, a storehouse of obscene, indecent narratives, . . . indeed a revelation of the ignorance of the uncultured brains of those who compiled this curiosity."[18]

Aligned to this defamation of the Hebrew Bible is a full-scale attack on the God of Jesus depicted in the Gospels. They scoff at the "Father" of Jesus with a view to sowing doubt about the moral impeccability of the God so passionately proclaimed by Jesus. Varma accuses the God of the Hebrew Bible of having a "temper" and being "violent and irascible."[19] Divine weakness and vulnerability are evident in Jacob's struggle with God (Genesis 32). Another example of the Hebrew God's helplessness is the inability to drive away the inhabitants of the valley because they had superior chariots of iron (Judges 1.9). This is the God who hands over women to men to be prostituted (2 Samuel 12.7–8); sanctions war, slavery, and piracy; commands people to seek revenge for the mistakes committed by earlier generations; and encourages incest. The God of Jesus is seen as one who lacks compassion, for example, in the Parable of the Friend at Night and in the Parable of the Unjust Judge, where God is portrayed as a "lower order of the culture than what is claimed for the New Testament." For Chowdhuri, the God of Jesus is a "tribal God, located in a temple," able to be appeased only by "abominable sacrificial offerings."[20]

Like the message, the messengers are severely criticized. The Gospel writers are described as essentially "simple superstitious people" who had no "spiritual cultures." The Gospels were written by "mixed hands." The authors were not actual witnesses to the events they were describing, and were writing much later; thus they were essentially "myth makers" who failed to separate fact from fiction. Chowdhuri enumerates a hundred cases where they had "modified the texts, added, altered, revised and cancelled [them]." It was they who had "fabricate[d the] historicity" of Jesus. If we can't trust them with details, asked Chowdhuri, "in what can we trust them?" Chowdhuri claimed that none of the Gospels had been written by the persons whose names appear as authors; the authorship of these books had instead been "foisted on some known persons" to fit in with their personalities, "supposed or real."[21] Strangely, the two men made the case for the Gospels being the first celebrity endorsement in history.

Next Varma and Chowdhuri presented as unhistorical and worthless those who were around Jesus, especially his disciples. Chowdhuri found the disciples of Jesus more "mythical than real." There is no evidence of a single reference to Jesus's words and deeds in their preaching. His disciples never proclaimed the rabbi to be a carpenter, nor, in his view, did they show any personal knowledge of him or speak of him as a friend. His followers, such as Peter, John, and Paul, knew "nothing of his human qualities."[22] These disciples were thus useless for any "apostolic purpose." Jesus clearly made hardly any impression on them given their atrocious behavior. One deceived him, another disowned him, and the rest were asleep when Jesus was passing through the most critical time of his life. Their actions, or inactions, stood in contrast with what the disciples of the Buddha did for their master. This desertion and denial, in Chowdhuri's view, points to the "non-historical character" of these disciples. They had nothing to do with the actual life of Jesus; instead "they are an imaginary part of an imaginary drama."[23] Chowdhuri taunted the missionaries as to why there was no mention of Jesus's teaching in the epistles, the Book of Revelation, and works by the Patristic apologists.

The two men also named and shamed the family of Jesus. They persistently portrayed the ancestors of Jesus as people of moral disrepute.

Varma listed all the biblical figures who had a tainted past: Abraham was incestuous, Jacob and Solomon were polygamists, and David and Bathsheba were an "unspeakable pair." Varma accused Jesus of selecting his ancestry from the "most disreputable of all families." He could not imagine that the "saviour of the world who had specially got himself fleshed and humanised to purify mankind, would have crept through such a sewer as the ancestry of Mary." For Varma, Jesus was a "God of the lowest possible tastes and instincts."[24]

Maligning the Messiah

The supreme aim of Varma and Chowdhuri was to damage the reputation of Jesus himself. They achieved this in a number of ways. To begin, they called into question all the events related to the historical Jesus, starting with his birth. Chowdhuri claimed that Jesus was born neither in Bethlehem like a mythical Christ, nor at Nazareth, like a historical Christ, but was conjured up in the "hearts of the pious."[25] It was the pious who "manufactured" a living picture of Jesus and "read it into the gospels." Chowdhuri summarily dismisses much of the attention paid to the death of Jesus as simply setting the seal on his Messiahship. Quoting the passage from Deuteronomy "for anyone hung on a tree is under God's curse" (21.23), he claimed that a Messiah cannot die "an ignominious death," and that the idea of a crucified Messiah is not in keeping with the concept. Even Paul's Jesus, who is identified with the death and Resurrection, was "symbolical—an allegory reconciling the world with God." For Chowdhuri, the Resurrection is not a man risen from the dead, but the "rise of monotheism to conquer the world . . . symbolically so represented."[26]

To prove the ahistoricity of Jesus, these Hindu thinkers rehearse stock arguments prevalent at that time. One is the absence of the message of Jesus in Paul; another the absence of any reference to the historical Jesus in Jewish and Roman writings. Restating the argument of the Jesus Myth propounders, Chowdhuri and Varma claim that there is no evidence of the life, work, or teaching of Jesus in Paul's letters. Paul knew "no Man Jesus" since nowhere in his writings does he mention Jesus of Nazareth. The two men reckon that the historical Jesus takes a somewhat secondary place in Paul's writings. Citing many Western scholars to support his claim, including Wrede, Chowdhuri points out that the important teachings of Jesus, such as the "fatherly goodness of God, love of neighbour, fulfilment of the law, emphasis on meekness and mercy, warning against any desire of worldly goods—all these are conspicuous in Paul by their absence."[27] The message that Paul preaches did not come directly from the historical Jesus, but was revealed to him mysteriously "from within." To augment his case, Chowdhuri quotes the very words of Paul: "But I certify you, brethren, that the gospel which was preached of me is not after man. For I neither received it of man, neither was I taught it, but by the revelation of Jesus Christ" (Galatians 1.11, 12). The deification of Jesus, Chowdhuri argued, was started by people who had not seen or known him personally. It was Paul who first mooted this idea of transforming this mythical person into a God. He was followed by the authors of the Epistle to the Hebrews and the Gospel of Saint John, who were separated from Jesus by an even "greater distance of time and space."[28]

Varma and Chowdhuri then exploit the contradictory picture of Jesus in the Gospels to attack him as an unbalanced personality. He is portrayed as both a jolly diner, a winebibber, and as a puritan encouraging people to live a life of poverty and make themselves eunuchs for the sake of the kingdom. Invoking Drews, Chowdhuri claims that such irreconcilable contradictions of Jesus prove that "several persons, and not only one, are behind them."[29] The implication is that Jesus is not a single, consistent person but includes several personalities with unstable tendencies.

Varma and Chowdhuri follow this up by undervaluing Jesus as unoriginal and uninventive. Chowdhuri quotes with much glee Wrede's claim that Jesus is not the proprietor of his own words: "not a single word of Jesus has been preserved and . . . everything has been put into his mouth."[30] The message of Jesus, they claim, is an updated composite from various religious traditions: whatever Jesus taught as a distinctive Christian message was already prevalent in the older religions of Egypt, Mesopotamia, and Persia. The Indian Krishna and the Buddha contributed to the evolution of Christianity, too. Chowdhuri, with a Himalayan confidence, asserted that the "discourses attributed to Jesus Christ possess not a shade of idealism that was not current coin of the day, or had not found expression in ages before."[31] The ethical teachings of Jesus, for example, had been gathered from various sources. Chowdhuri found that there was nothing new in the command to love your enemies—which is supposed to be the supreme teaching of Jesus. This saying, he reminds the readers, was as old as the Vedas: "May all beings regard me with the eye of a friend. May I regard all beings with the eye of a friend" (Yajur Veda 35.18). Even this admirable teaching about love was not spoken in a "lovable and winning manner" by Jesus, but uttered "dictatorially, with an air of superiority."[32] The Golden Rule, too, has parallels in China and India. Chowdhuri pointed out that Laozi had not only laid down the Golden Rule, but also proclaimed a set of six maxims that clearly resembled the Beatitudes. At best what the Beatitudes promise is compensation—do something and you will be rewarded. In contrast, Jesus's teaching on forgiveness is "not at par" with the Buddha's. Similarly, Jesus, in his view, had failed to rise to the lofty moral standards of the Buddha. For instance, Jesus was found wanting in his attitude toward slavery—"the plague spot of human society"—whereas half a millennium before the Christian era, slave dealing had been forbidden by the Buddha.

Another unique teaching of Jesus that came under severe scrutiny is the idea of the Fatherhood of God. This concept, Chowdhuri stressed, was not a "Christian virtue." He accused Christian authors of their "blissful ignorance" of this notion in other traditions. The study of comparative religion has "utterly demolished" any such Christian claim. He affirmed that the fatherhood of God was as old as the Rig Veda: "Did not the Rishi approach his God and rely on him not only as 'thou art Father but thou Mother'"? More importantly, rishis did not approach God in a "dry emotionless mood but in the exuberance of feelings." For Chowdhuri, the Christian version of the fatherhood of God smacked of "sexual anthropomorphism." Moreover, it was a stumbling block to a higher conception of God that the Hindu philosophical tradition cherishes: "it is not a woman, it is not a man, nor is it neuter."[33]

Another tactic these Hindu reformers used to bring down Jesus for their readers was to ridicule Christian doctrines that defined the uniqueness of Jesus. Employing the words of the rationalist Walter Jekyll, Varma made fun of the doctrine of Incarnation: "While the Second Person of the trinity is in heaven with the First Person, the Third Person is alleged to have had intercourse with the Virgin Mary, and the resultant birth is the Second Person."[34] The cross was stripped of its sacrificial character and regarded as an egoistic, selfish act on the part of Jesus, whereas the death of Socrates was of the "purest kind" and suffered in a "homely fashion."[35] Chowdhuri dismissed the Resurrection as a "stop gap for the failure of the Messianic mission." The event was not about a man risen from the dead, but about the "rise of monotheism to conquer the world." Similarly, the teachings of Jesus about the last days were dismissed as the dream of a dreamer who had no practical message to offer, and his future appearances were disregarded as the vision of an "insane" person (as Adolf Harnack and Alfred Loisy have branded him).[36] The life hereafter promised by Christianity was seen as "monotonous and derogatory," with endless shouts of halleluiahs and no desire to fathom the greater mysteries of life.

Another ploy of these Hindu reformers is to present Jesus and his message as lacking universal appeal. Jesus is described as someone with only limited, local vision, and unlike the Eastern faiths such as Hinduism and Buddhism, his message is criticized for having no provision for salvation or universal relevance. Chowdhuri was severely critical about the supposed provincial nature of Jesus. In his writings, the Gospel Jesus comes across as a "narrow tribal patriot."[37] He was not the noblest and highest personality in history, but restricted in comparison with the great Eastern and Greek thinkers. Jesus was not "an exemplar" because he was a "narrow minded ignorant Jew," "too narrow and too uncultured even for the first century." Nothing in the Gospels suggests to Chowdhuri that the mental outlook of Jesus "extended beyond his own nation." The supreme example of Jesus's inward-looking attitude is found in the statement recorded in Matthew: "I am not sent but unto the lost sheep of the house of Israel" (15.24).

According to the perception of these reformers, this is a Jesus who refuses to do any charitable acts for those who were outside the Jewish circle because he thought himself as sent only to the house of Israel. His disparaging remarks about the Gentiles, such as "after all these things do the Gentiles seek," or "and when ye pray, use not vain repetitions, as the heathens do," are seen as flagrant examples of his arrogance toward the peoples of other nations. For Chowdhuri, it is "criminal to speak contemptuously" of the Gentiles, and such an attitude shows a touch of racism in Jesus.[38] Chowdhuri also notes that there is an underlying assumption among Jesus and his followers that they belonged to a higher human race. Chowdhuri resents such a notion and points out that historically it cannot be proved that Jews were "spiritually higher than the Hindus." In his writing, he affirms vehemently that the Hindu-Buddhist Gentile nations were "overwhelmingly superior to that of the Jews."[39]

Another device that these two Hindu men resort to is pointing out the striking discrepancies between the preaching of Jesus and its enactment by his followers, especially the institutional churches. A convenient weapon in the hands of the colonized is to expose the deep division between the highly ethical words of Jesus and the dastardly deeds of the colonialists. Varma provides a lengthy list of atrocities done in the name of Christ by the church. The church had been harmless when it had no power, but when it gained authority and control, it became "vindictive and revengeful." It spread its influence through harassment, enticement, and dreadful methods. His examples include the Spanish inquisition, the conquest of Latin America, and the forceful conversion of Indians during British colonial rule. Varma's damning conclusion: "Christians as a class are at least not better than the members of any other religious sects."[40] He wrote that "the charm in Christianity" existed only in "words, and never practically in this world of temptations." Chowdhuri asserted that the "precepts and life of Jesus are outrageously opposed to each other" and are the inevitable "result of their being fabricated by different hands."[41] Calls to resist evil were "positively flouted." Chowdhuri sarcastically asked, too, whether it was not ridiculous to talk about love, mercy, and humility as distinctive aspects of the Christian message while at the same time "committing 99 percent of mankind to hell-fire."[42]

The two writers also mitigated the uniqueness of Jesus by seeking parallels in other religious traditions. Varma claimed that the Gospel account of the Annunciation was borrowed from Egypt, where imagery of the goddess Isis holding the divine child Horus was chiseled on the walls of the temples of Luxor before the Jewish scriptures were written.

The Temptation of Jesus, in Chowdhuri's view, was also not a unique event; Zoroaster, too, was tempted when he was thirty. He drew attention to the parallel temptation story in the Katha Upanishad that goes back to the Vedic period, involving Nachiketa, son of the sage Vājashravasa, and Yama, the God of death.

The "curious" similarity of the names of Krishna and Christ have prompted some European orientalists like Louis Jacolliot to suggest that the legends surrounding Krishna might have been a prototype for those concerning Christ.[43] There are striking similarities between these stories: the massacre of the innocents at the birth of these infants, the visiting of wise men, the family moving to pay a tax, and so on. Varma latched on to this idea and embellished it by writing that it was the Brahmins who went to Egypt and carried the stories of Krishna, which in turn supplied the background material for the life and work of Jesus. Varma even went on to note, without providing any convincing evidence, that Philo, the Jewish historian, confirmed that Krishna had provided resources for Jesus. Chowdhuri, however, who was quick to find archetypes for Jesus in any ancient tradition, was surprisingly reluctant to endorse the Krishna connection. He admitted that he was not an orientalist and had "no axe to grind by establishing the priority of the Krishna cult."[44]

For Chowdhuri, the influence of Buddhism on Christianity was an "acknowledged fact."[45] He based this on the work of the orientalists who drew attention to the trade routes connecting India and the Mediterranean world. Buddhist temples in Persia that had scenes from the life of the Buddha sculpted on them further strengthened his belief that Buddhism had influenced the biblical world. The availability of translated Buddhist scriptures during that early era reinforced the idea that as an older creed Buddhism had "stuff to lend."[46] In making his argument, Chowdhuri uncritically appropriated the often contentious claims of Albert J. Edmunds and Arthur Lillie. Based on the work of Lillie, Chowdhuri identified a number of parallels in the life of the Gospel Jesus and the Buddha. Among those similarities listed are the washing of the feet of the disciples, the story of the widow's mite, the compassion toward the women caught in adultery (as the Christian version of the Buddhist story of Ambapali, the courtesan, who became a follower of the Buddha), and the penitent thief whom Jesus converted (which is traced to the conversion of the robber Angulimala by the Buddha). In all these doings, the Buddha's actions seem to be superior and humane. For instance, the no-strings-attached Buddhist version of the washing of the feet is seen as morally more nuanced than the one in the Gospel narrative. Buddha's advice that "whoever wants to wait upon should wait upon the soul" is undemanding and devoid of any compensation or consequences, whereas Jesus's utterance in a similar context is couched in a language of "promise of reward and punishment."[47]

Indeed, most of the parables of Jesus that these reformers traced to the Buddha are found to be better nuanced in the Buddhist original than in the Gospel reproduction. The reconciliation of the younger son with the father in the Prodigal Son story, in Chowdhuri's reckoning, is "far more scientific" in the Buddhist version. The Parable of the Laid-up Treasure found in the Gospel, too, is found to easily lend itself to an other-worldly interpretation, whereas the same parable in the Buddha's teaching is deemed much more refined and as having a clear differentiation between worldly and spiritual treasures.

Chowdhuri also makes an extraordinary claim that "not only ideas but the very texts of the Buddhist Scriptures" were "incorporated in the Gospels and the Evangelists did not make a secret of it."[48] Drawing on of the work of Edmunds, he cites two examples, both from the Fourth Gospel: "He that believeth on me, as the scripture hath said, out of his belly shall flow rivers of living water" (John 7.38); and the "multitude therefore answered him, We have heard out of the law that Christ abided for ever" (John 12.34). For both of these Johannine statements, Chowdhuri provides the Buddhist equivalent: "From his lower body proceeds a torrent of water," and "if he so should wish, the Tathagato could remain [on earth] for the eon." Chowdhuri is convinced of Edmunds's conclusion that the Buddhist text was the source of both quotations from John since the Buddhist texts were fairly well known at that time: "the Buddhist canon . . . in the first Christian century was most wide spread of all Sacred Codes."[49]

In the estimation of these two Hindu reformers, Jesus has nothing special to offer. They made their case for his insignificance by seeking spurious and often unsubstantiated parallels between his teachings and those of other ancient masters. Jesus in this rendering is reduced chiefly to a reworking of Paul's crucified son of God.[50] His use of the parables to describe the Kingdom of God is a strategy to conceal the fact that there is no new message to announce. In his characteristic bluntness, Chowdhuri put it thus: "Consequently, this non-existent preacher had nothing to preach."[51]

A Palestinian Palimpsest

Both Varma and Chowdhuri became convinced that the Jesus one confronts in the Gospels was not a divinized human person as the Christian church claims but a craftily constructed humanized God. The human Jesus, in their view, was manufactured out of Near Eastern and Far Eastern materials. In other words, Jesus was not an earthly figure, but the Gospel writers historicized him. Chowdhuri, in declaring that the "historic Jesus did not exist," explained that Jesus was as historical as the Hindu Gods: "Jesus is God historicized as Indra, Varnuna or Vishnu of Hindu mythology." His is a "composite character, but its elements have been gathered from all directions." Chowdhuri was unequivocal in his claim that there was "no such historical person as Jesus Christ." He firmly believed that there was "no historical evidence as to the existence of a personal Christ" but that "around a historical person legends grew up." Chowdhuri wrote: "The founder of historical Christianity is not any historical Jesus but the idea of a coming Christ." For Chowdhuri, the Gospel Jesus was a "manufacture, pure and simple." He was "fabricated from ancient scriptures," a "mythical amalgamation," a "construction." Stated strongly, for Chowdhuri, Jesus was the classic *"embodiment of the special traits of all the great saints and prophets, Jew and Gentile."* Chowdhuri held the view that the historical Jesus was not a prerequisite for the Gospel narrative. He claimed that a "historical Jesus would be a dream." Jesus's activities—including suffering, dying, and rising again—were not sufficient proof of his "historical personality."[52]

For his part, Varma uses the internal disputes among the early followers of Jesus to question the historical existence of Jesus. He cites Paul's First Letter to the Corinthians, where Paul refers to people who doubted the corporeal existence of Christ and his risen status. Such misgivings about the historical Jesus, especially at these early stages of Christianity, played neatly into the hands of Varma's claims.

Both Chowdhuri and Varma asserted that the historical person of Jesus was largely manufactured by non-Jewish, pro-Roman writers who, in order to "conciliate the Romans," deliberately concealed the political Messiah and substituted a "universal," "denationalized Jesus," proclaimer of a purely spiritual Kingdom. The actual Jesus, in their view, was put to death by the Jewish priests. The Gospel Jesus was instead a "misconstrued" figure based on the misunderstanding of the prophesies of the Hebrew prophets, prophecies that were about a Messiah who was supposed to have rescued the Jews from the oppression of the Gentiles. When this did not happen, the Jews rejected him and non-Jewish people took over the idea. The result: the trials and tribulations of the Jewish people increased at the hands of their non-Jewish contemporaries.

As in the case of all Jesus deniers, Varma and Chowdhuri use as proof a list of Jewish and Roman writers of the first century who failed to mention the historical Jesus in their work. As Varma put it, Jesus was "unnoticed" by writers "living near upon the times." If the birth and death of Jesus were such public and prominent events, asked Varma, why is there no record of their dates? Varma lists an array of writers such as Josephus, Tacitus, Seneca, and Plutarch who must have had access to some information about the historical Jesus but register "no allusion to him or any act of the Roman government respecting him." His contention was that if such "public and conspicuous events" as the Crucifixion went unreported in the writings of these historians, "Christ never lived and if he did exist, he was not the personage represented in the Gospels."[53] Even when there are references, the Jesus deniers tended to dismiss them as later interpolations or to refer to the legend rather than to the actual person. Chowdhuri, for instance, rejects a single reference to Jesus in the works of the Jewish historian Josephus as an insertion added later—in keeping with complaints by other advocates of the Jesus Myth.

Echoing the views of the Jesus deniers of the time, these two men believed that Christianity emerged in a cosmopolitan atmosphere where popular figures such as Plato's Just One or the image of the Stoic sage could have easily supplied the model for the Gospel Jesus. Chowdhuri's contention is that the proto-Christian period is "rich in personalities," but there is "no iota of proof that Jesus was one of them." Based on the work of Drews, Chowdhuri identifies a number of prototypes for Jesus such as Job, a just man who, like Jesus, was tempted by Satan, suffered unbearable suffering and disgrace, but was subsequently restored to his earlier status. Another prototype for the "divine life of Jesus" depicted in the Gospel, in Chowdhuri's view, could be the Suffering Servant of "Isaiah of the prophetic fame." The Gospel depiction of the sufferings of Jesus, including his death and the Resurrection; his concern for the oppressed and the weak; his gentleness; his submission to God; his miraculous power; his teaching in parables; and his lack of shame or other response to the abuse unleashed by his enemies are all drawn from Isaiah. Chowdhuri dismisses the idea of Jesus as God's anointed being the friend of the poor and downtrodden as Bolshevism "pure and simple."[54]

Both men argued that the elements of a Christology were already available without pointing to a particular Christ. What was needed was a personality to whom these characteristics could be attached. So when the Christ came, he came "not as an actual agent" who fulfilled prophetical predictions, in their view, but was made to match existing expectations. He was seen as the "logical finale" in an atmosphere surcharged with messianic ideals.[55] The imagination of the early followers played a "supreme part in turning the gospel-Jesus into the very Christ." In other words, the church created this "sublime figure of Christ" not from the memories of Jesus but from the second-century experience of the church. To buttress his argument, Chowdhuri uses quotations from Joseph Estlin Carpenter and Otto Pfleiderer. The Jesus depicted in the Gospels was an "afterthought," a response to the "exigencies of the situation," which in turn required the image of a human being. Consequently, in spite of his being identified as "the God of the very God," Jesus shares the "full ignorance and superstitious of the time that made him so."[56] Both Varma and Chowdhuri were relentless in arguing that the biography of Jesus from birth to death was written beforehand in the scriptures by those who held the key to the mysteries. He was manufactured out of myths and prophecies by the Christ-makers, though Chowdhuri does not give any clue as to who these Christ-makers were.

Chowdhuri even advised the missionaries that they should give up the historical Jesus and concentrate on "symbolic interpretation," which is the "secret which will make facts of Christianity intelligible."[57] He told them that instead of the flesh-and-blood Jesus, a figurative and allegorical Jesus would have more appeal—and might help to clear up some awkward elements of Christianity. In this way Chowdhuri alleged that the miracles could be explained intelligently. For example, the Gadarene Demoniac could be interpreted as the pagan who gives up worshipping many gods for one; and the man with a withered hand could be taken as a representative of a reinvigorated Judaism. Similarly, the words of Jesus to his mother—"Woman! who art thou, what have I to do with thee"—might sound rude if they are taken literally. Interpreted symbolically, the mother stands for "the old Jewish order" from which Jesus was distancing himself. (Chowdhuri wouldn't have noticed the hint of anti-Semitism in that remark.)

For both of our authors, Christianity had pagan and mythical beginnings. It sprang from pre-Christian cults in which the celebration of a crucifixion and the eating of a sacramental meal were central. Varma maintained that Christianity "originated from an eclectic religion of the Egyptians."[58] Chowdhuri, for his part, stated that Christianity is a "heretical form of Judaism and not a new religion." Instead of declaring a new faith, Paul affirmed his belief in the law and the prophets: "all things which are according to the law and which are written in the prophets."[59] There is not a "single tenet or idea which is not borrowed from older creeds and cults," Chowdhuri argued. The person of Jesus was "thrust upon the world as a brand-new revelation under the grandiloquent title the New Testament."[60]

Following Drews, Chowdhuri believed that everything about Jesus had a mythical character and therefore there was no need to assume that a historical Jesus ever existed. Christianity could have been developed without Jesus (though certainly not without Paul). Chowdhuri claims that to preach Christ, knowledge of the historical Jesus was not necessarily important. He cites the case of Apollos, the learned Alexandrian, who spoke with fervor and taught accurately about Jesus without knowing the so-called historical Jesus (Acts 18.24–25). If there is no historical Jesus, will people lose anything? Chowdhuri asked. His answer was that virtues like "nobility," "devotion," and "love" were prevalent in the world before the historical Jesus propagated them, and would continue to be "secure" and cherished "in the higher human nature" even after the image of Jesus had vanished from people's collective imagination.[61]

A Cobbled-Together Messiah

"Hate as well as love can write a life of Jesus and the greatest of them are written with hate," wrote Albert Schweitzer.[62] He went on to explain that "hate" in this connection meant not the hate of the person of Jesus, but hate of the supernatural halo that the faith of the church had given him. In the case of Varma and Chowdhuri, it was the sheer disgust with the Christian mission, its insulting attitude to Hinduism, and its predatory nature that inspired their venomous appraisal of the life of Jesus.

The Jesus debate that originated in the West, and was transferred to India, challenged primarily the liberal theology that, according to Jesus deniers, had reduced religion to a cult of personality and instead promoted monism, German idealism, and rationalism. Arthur Drews, on whom Chowdhuri was heavily dependent, was a believer in discarding Judaism and Christianity because of their relatively recent entrance and for their advocacy of dualism. Drews campaigned for a renewal of faith anchored in monism and German idealism. For him, true religion could not be reduced to an intense worship of one person, even if that person was the historical Jesus. Drews's quarrel was with the Protestant liberal theologians who had made the "personal life of Jesus" the "essential element of Christianity!"[63] His chief target was the adaptation of the Great Man Theory of history promoted by the Romanticism of the nineteenth century. The attack he and others launched on portrayals of Jesus as the "representative of the noblest individuality" or the "incarnation of the modern ideal of personality" was seized upon by these thinkers to validate their own Hindu agenda.

Varma and Chowdhuri were feisty discussants in matters of biblical criticism. Both seem familiar with the critical biblical scholarship of mid- and late-nineteenth-century Europe, consulting most of the Western writers who supported their cause. They were like toddlers let loose in a sweet shop, overwhelmed by a range of anti-Jesus options, and so grabbing anything that suited their hermeneutical purpose. They studied serious work from David Strauss to Albert Schweitzer, political thinkers like Tom Paine, and popular novelists like Jerome K. Jerome to prove their destructive cause. Both consistently looked for authoritative support and approval. What they claimed as audacious was often based on an uncritical appropriation of Western anti-Jesus writings. Their work comprised endless juxtapositions of Western authors that congested and constrained their argument. Their relentless citations overlooked and underplayed the Western context in which these debates originated and were vigorously contested.

Varma and Chowdhuri wrote with confidence and passion, but their ideas were derived mainly from a small group of rationalists and free thinkers who were outside of Christian orthodoxy and rarely engaged with the mainstream. A great deal of Chowdhuri's interpretative DNA was predictably owed to Arthur Drews and J. M. Robertson. He and Varma did not make clear the historical context and hermeneutical presuppositions of the Western works they relied on so heavily. Often the internal critique of Christian thinkers was summoned to augment their anti-Jesus arguments. They repeated the stock arguments found in the works of the Jesus deniers—that the Gospels and the Letters of Paul have little historical purchase in establishing the existence of the earthly Jesus; that there are no references to Jesus in the secular history and literature of the period; that the Christian Gospel is a conglomeration of various myths and rituals of the ancient world, including characteristics of savior figures who predated Jesus and were known for suffering, dying, and rising again; and that Paul, who had hardly any dealing with the terrestrial Jesus, fashioned a Christ who was attractive to all humanity.

Varma and Chowdhuri were not the first writers to study textual discrepancies in the Gospel. Source criticism, which was a potent tool at that time, had exposed the contradictions in the Gospel narratives. But scholars who employed this criticism argued that these discrepancies did not necessarily prove the nonexistence of the historical Jesus. These incongruities instead enabled them to seek out and reconstruct the oral forms of expression behind the written texts—a task that Varma and Chowdhuri failed to pursue, although both came from a tradition that paid much attention to the oral form of truth.

The tone of Varma's and Chowdhuri's writing is often bad-tempered and castigatory, and occasionally sarcastic. In denigrating the "other" they were Donald Trumps before Donald Trump. In making fun of the infant Jesus, Varma mockingly asked whether the baby Jesus did "mewl and puke in his nurse's arm?" Was he "suckled by his mother, or brought up on the bottle?" Did he "play at marbles and make mud pies?"[64] Both men blame Christian theologians for being cowards, more interested in safeguarding their reputation and that of the Christian church than searching for the truth. Chowdhuri told them that their Christian training got the "better of their erudition."[65] He was particularly harsh toward Estlin Carpenter, the Unitarian minister, calling him an apologist who was concerned more with the "integrity of the character" of his hero Jesus than with the historical accuracy of stories about him.[66]

The implicit message that runs through their writings is that Hinduism is superior to the white man's religion and is uncontaminated by outside influences. Varma made it clear that the Vedic religion is eternal and did not contradict the laws of nature. It was the religion of Krishna, Rama, Patanjali, and the Buddha. He urged Indians to believe in this "ancestral religion" and be saved. There was no doubt in Varma's mind that, because the Hindu dharma remained uncontaminated by foreign influences, it was the "only religion" that had been that disclosed to humankind for its "good and salvation."[67] Chowdhuri likewise argued that unlike the Gospel message, the Bhakti Dharma had an "independent origin and natural growth," whereas the teaching of Jesus was a "construction of the propagandists."[68] Citing Max Müller for support, he promoted the Bhakti Dharma, an indigenous belief system dating back to the Upanishadic age and untouched by Christianity, as a panacea for the world's problems. He further haughtily announced that Hinduism was so advanced that his Christian compatriots "could learn at its feet for centuries." Mother India was crying herself hoarse inviting the world to learn: "Child, sit at my feet."[69]

Even before the members of the Jesus Seminar made it fashionable to look at the first five hundred years of literary production in examining the life and times of Jesus and the early church, Varma and Chowdhuri, in keeping with the practice of the Jesus Myth expounders, went beyond the fixed canon and investigated the whole gamut of early Christian literature. Chowdhuri accorded undifferentiated authority to both the canonical and the apocryphal Gospels. He questioned the idea of giving "greater credit" to the canonical Gospels, which he thought was an "absurd" notion that imputed some mysterious intuitive power to those who had selected them. As far as he was concerned, both the canonical and noncanonical Gospels were "equally factual and fictitious."[70] Varma, too, looked favorably on the noncanonical Gospels. He found them essentially of the "same character as those in the four Gospels" and claimed that the Gospel of the Infancy of Jesus was as "accurate as those in the New Testament."[71]

Chowdhuri went further and agitated for an expanded religious landscape to study nascent Christianity. (He was not the first Indian to do so; K. M. Banjera and Keshub Chunder Sen had preceded him.) Castigating the European scholars who worked within a narrow Jewish-Hellenistic framework, Chowdhuri accused them of being "bounded by the Euphrates."[72] He wanted to enlarge scholars' understanding of the source and origins of the biblical religions, both Judaism and Christianity, beyond the Mediterranean world. His contention was that the books of the New Testament could not be "explained by the books of the Hebrews, the Greeks and the Romans." He explained: "our pond no longer is the Mediterranean but the Pacific Ocean."[73]

Varma's and Chowdhuri's plea to look beyond ancient and Near Eastern sources for inspiration and insights for the Gospels and for the personality of Jesus was not based on a desire to seek textual resemblances or historical connections between the Mediterranean world and India, or to work out a hospitable comparative exegesis. Rather, it was based on a desire to impose a universalistic spirituality revolving around a Hindu notion of spiritual self-realization, which they believed could be found within each religion and was attainable by every person. Yet in spite of this Hindu-centric spiritual nationalism, the issue that Chowdhuri and other Indians raised at that time about enlarging the spiritual influences of Jesus away from the biblical milieu has some relevance today, for much of current Western biblical scholarship on Jesus is tightly tethered to Hebraic and Hellenistic sources and there is a reluctance to see beyond them.

In focusing their attack more on the historicity of Jesus than on his precepts, Varma and Chowdhuri shifted the debate from his spiritual nature, character, and the importance of his teachings to the historical narratives surrounding his life. Their target was the historical, flesh-and-blood, terrestrial Jesus as portrayed in the Gospels and the New Testament writings. These two Indians questioned the very usefulness of Jesus and the historical veracity of his existence at a time when academic efforts had been made to loosen Jesus from what Schweitzer called the "stony rocks of ecclesiastical doctrine," and untether him from traditional Christological statements fraught with Greek metaphysical terms—to instead make him a great man to emulate and a good teacher to follow.

There are contradictions in Chowdhuri's approach. On the one hand, he reprimands the Gospel writers for the diversity in form and content of their various narratives, but on the other hand, he concedes that a harmonized, single view would have been hard to achieve because these writers drew their ideal pictures from "their personal culture and social environment." Chowdhuri called Schweitzer a "bleeding heart" because he believed in the historicity of Jesus, but he did not hesitate to cite with much satisfaction Schweitzer's advocacy for a Jesus "spiritually risen within men."[74]

There is a wanton recklessness in these writers' casual connections between Jesus and other Eastern religious figures like Buddha and Krishna. Many of the Buddhist-Christian, Jesus-Krishna parallels that they advocate are extremely tenuous and impressionistic. The range of textual connections they cite are largely imaginary, and they read the texts with their preconceived notions rather than recognizing what the texts really permit. For instance, the Katha Upanishad story that Chowdhuri used as the model for the Temptation accounts is impossibly far-fetched. Even a cursory reading of the Vedic narrative will show that this story is not about temptation, but about asking for boons. Even if these borrowings were substantiated, they do not lead to the conclusions that Varma and Chowdhuri would have liked to espouse and endorse. There are, in other words, willful vandalistic tendencies in their writings.

Both Varma and Chowdhuri made much of a problem that they saw as purely a creation of Christian theology—the insistence on the historical nature of the faith. This unique claim of Christianity came under their heavy fire and scrutiny. For both, depending on historical evidence was "rather a dangerous principle."[75] In his clash with Farquhar, Varma told him that even if it were proved that the Buddha or Kalidasa, the supposed author of the Raghuvaṃśa (the stories related to the Rahgu dynasty), did not exist, the value of their work would not be affected. The historicity of Kalidasa was not essential for enjoying the Raghuvaṃśa, whereas the authority of the Gospel rested not "on its own merits but on the historicity of Christ." As he wrote, "Do away with Kalidasa, the world could read Raghuvamsa. Do away with Christ, nobody or but few would attach any special importance to it. The Gospel, then, would be a most ordinary thing."[76] Varma was very firm in declaring the uselessness of a historically rooted faith. In his deliberations with Farquhar, Varma communicated to him condescendingly that "a single historical fact, like the life and death of a man Jesus, could not in any sense be made a ground for faith. In religion, the individual avoids history: he shakes it off, to live his own life."[77]

Both Varma and Chowdhuri benefited from the evangelical Christianity of the time and deployed effectively its methods and tactics both to discredit the Christian Gospel and to enhance and establish the superiority of the Aryan faith over it. Just like the Christian evangelicals, the Arya Samaj came up with a set of criteria for evaluating the religion of the missionaries and their texts. A sacred text, religion, or revelation (1) must originate from the beginning of creation, which placed the Vedas above the Bible, (2) should perpetuate general principles and not a specific personality (thereby ruling out all historical religions), (3) should not exhibit any internal discrepancies, and (4) should obey the rule of nature and not be dependent on miracles.[78] On all these counts, they claimed that the Vedic religion passed with flying colors, whereas Christianity was found deficient and adulterated.

"What do we find in him?" Chowdhuri asked rhetorically about Jesus, answering that Jesus could not be "offered as an example to any decent set of men in the 20th century for their imitation."[79] Jesus was found to be wanting at the personal, social, political, and homiletical levels. He was seen as an anti-family person, whereas the Buddha is presented as a person who extolled duty toward parents and siblings. Chowdhuri also found Jesus useless as far as the Indian political struggle was concerned. He criticized Jesus's discouragement of the subject people's engagement in political struggle, and he considered the enigmatic injunction of Jesus—give to Caesar what is Caesar's—a deterrent. As a communicator, too, Jesus was a failure in Chowdhuri's eyes. He failed to explain what the Kingdom of God was, intentionally making it "unintelligent to the multitude," and he held back information about the very message that he sent his disciples to announce.[80] Varma was blunter in his assessment. For him, the "so-called Christ is a myth." He conveniently summoned the words of Strauss: "The Jesus of History is simply a problem and a problem cannot be the object of faith."[81] Jesus, in both men's view, was a total failure. After three years of strenuous efforts, Jesus had hardly made any impression on a "single person."[82]

Just as the colonialists denied India any significant history in order to construct their own vision as an aid to subjugation, these two reformers denied the existence of a historical Jesus for the advancement of their Hindu-centric view of India. Their methodology was a combination of a highly exaggerated and mythologized version of India, a blind veneration for Indian religious figures like Krishna and Buddha, and heavily twisted readings of the sacred scriptures, especially the Christian Bible. Chowdhuri and Varma were fine examples of Thomas Macaulay's notion of "a learned native" who was "familiar with the poetry of Milton, the metaphysics of Locke, and the physics of Newton." They went even further, mastering Western theologies and the nuances of biblical interpretation. Macaulay, in his famous "Minute on Education," envisaged that this class of Indians who were well-versed in Western philosophy, science, and literature would act as interpreters between their own people and their white masters.[83] He could not have anticipated that their fine Western learning would one day be metastasized into an unremitting Hindu nationalism. What we see here in the work of Varma and Chowdhuri is the reverse of Macaulay's expectation. Instead of interpreting the West to the East, they became interpreters of the West to the West. Their impressive scholarship was turned not only against the English, but also against the iconic figure of Jesus Christ, whose words were often exploited to endorse their imperial endeavors.

5

A Jaffna Man's Jesus

During British colonial rule in India, a number of American evan-gelical preachers frequented the subcontinent. Perhaps the best-known among them was Stanley Jones (1884–1973), and before him George F. Pentecost (1842–1920), who led evangelical campaigns in Ma-dras, now Chennai. On a February evening in 1892 in a hot tent where these meetings were held, a Jaffna boy was listening to the stirring mes-sage of the American preacher who emphasized the sinful nature of human beings and the salvation offered by Jesus Christ. After the sermon, as was customary at these revival meetings, there was the altar call. Pentecost urged those who had decided to accept Jesus to come forward, and he started to sing Charlotte Elliott's hymn, "Just as I Am without One Plea." One of those who answered the call and went up to accept Pentecost's blessing was that Jaffna boy, C. T. Alahasundram (1873–1941), who subsequently reverted to his paternal grandfather's name, becoming Francis Kingsbury. Later, Kingsbury recalled that the day he had decided to follow Jesus was the day Hindus celebrated the Maha Sivaratri—the day on which Siva, one of the Hindu Gods, not only married Parvati but also saved the world by consuming poison. The im-plicit meaning of that message was that one savior was exchanged for another—a reading reinforced by a comment in the preface to his trans-lated work on the Saiva saints. Referring to Siva taking the poison to save the world, Kingsbury noted: "There is a link here, small but real, with the Christian teaching of God as ready to suffer for the sake of humbler beings."[1] Kingsbury's attitude toward Hinduism was that of Paul toward Judaism. Casting himself as a latter-day Paul, Kingsbury rephrased the famous Pauline words in Galatians: "I advanced in the religion of my ancestors beyond many of mine own age among my country men, being more exceedingly zealous for the traditions of my fathers."[2]

Kingsbury was the son of C. W. Thamotharampillai, a renowned Tamil scholar who is credited with recovering ancient Tamil classics that otherwise would have been lost. Although from Sri Lanka, both father and son pursued successful careers in Southern India. Apart from what Kingsbury has written about his conversion in *How I Became a Christian*, there is little information on his life, nor any account of how his theological views changed so considerably over the years, from being a conservative to a liberal.[3] More disappointingly, there is no clue as to what led him to produce his version of the life of Jesus.[4]

This initially staunch Hindu's conversion story has all the clichés attached to such a transference of faith: a strict Hindu upbringing, which involved receiving *diksa,* an initiation into ceremonial Saivism; a deep reverence for Hindu sastras; an innate hatred of Christians; continual teasing at a missionary school for being an idolater, devil worshipper, and heathen; a gradual disenchantment with Hinduism's rituals and philosophy; a vigorous reading of the Bible; exposure to rational thinking through magazines like the *Indian Social Reformer;* a vulnerable spiritual state of limbo; an enticement by evangelical preaching; an eventual embrace of Christianity, and inevitable opposition from the family, in his case his father. Interestingly, his father's hostility was based not on religious but on social grounds. Kingsbury recalled later that his father, who "recognized salvation through other religions," was forbidden to "have a Christian in his house" because of the social stigma attached to such conversions.[5] It took Kingsbury a year to prepare for his baptism.

Kingsbury's books on Jesus, central to our task here, were preceded by the well-received translation of Saiva Thevaram (devotional poetry) entitled *Hymns of the Tamil Saivite Saints.*[6] His first foray into the life

of Jesus was the introductory *Jesus of Nazareth: His Life and Teaching,*
in which he depicted Jesus as a hesitant Messiah divested of his divinity.[7]
A decade later he went on to produce a larger, much more exegetically
informative but still theologically contentious *Life of Jesus,* which had a
foreword by the Jewish scholar C. G. Montefiore.[8] Montefiore wrote
a guarded appreciation, saying that Kingsbury had "produced not only
a clear and simple book, but a brave one."[9] A further and final volume
on Jesus, in Tamil, appeared in 1939, two years before Kingsbury's
death.[10] There he took more liberties with the Gospel narratives, in-
dulged in some historical fantasizing, and sprinkled the text with
choice quotations from the Saiva saints. In this Tamil narration, the
chapters are called *paddalam*—episodes—as in the Ramayana, the heroic story of Rama, as if to indicate to his readers that Jesus was a religious figure in the line of the great Hindu Gods.

Seeking Jesus in the Synoptic Gospels

Kingsbury, in his introduction to his early *Jesus of Nazareth,* makes it
clear that he was writing from the point of view of liberal Christianity,
which he suspected would not be appreciated by traditionalists. His
purpose was to help ordinary readers know the truth about Jesus. There
is also a secondary interest: to make available recent Western scholarship on Jesus in an accessible form and at an affordable price.

Kingsbury saw his task as producing a "purified edition" of the Gospel,
and was even bold enough to describe his life of Jesus as "this Gospel,"
calling himself "compiler"—the very term he used for the Gospel
writers—and so claiming a legitimacy and competency like theirs.
This drive came from a conviction that had been drilled into him by his
brother, that, as a Jaffna boy, he ought to know the Bible better than
others. Such boastful claims were dropped in his later works. He envisaged his hermeneutical enterprise as a kind of "truth jihad": "In the interest of truth—religious as well as historical—it is necessary to try to
disentangle the historical from the unhistorical and to make the Jesus
of History shine in his own glory and not with any false halo which later
generations of Christians may have cast around his person."[11] His aim
was to present all that was historical in the life of Jesus chronologically

in "one book," leaving out later accretions, but he conceded that such a task might not always be achievable. He was audacious enough to claim that "wherever a true story or the actual saying seems to have been altered" by the Gospel writers, he did not hesitate to "restore it" to what he thought was "most likely to be historical."[12] So the correction was offered not by textually analyzing the Gospel narratives, but by basing them on his theological instincts.

Kingsbury was ruthless in omitting key events surrounding Jesus that he believed were later additions and of no historical value. Examples of Kingsbury's textual stripping include the nativity stories and any references to Jesus's Davidic ancestry. A notable case was where he left out the words of the blind man—"Jesus, Son of David, have mercy on me!" The baptism of Jesus, too, is recounted in a matter-of-fact manner; he states simply that Jesus was baptized by John the Baptist. (Kingsbury's choice of the words that Jesus heard at his baptism and his explanation of them is interesting; I shall return to this later.) He also dispenses with the additional conversation between Jesus and John the Baptist recorded in Matthew, presumably on the ground that it had no historical basis, but had been inserted later to satisfy embarrassing problems that the early church faced, such as, why was Jesus baptized by John the Baptist, and who was the greater, John or Jesus?

Kingsbury removed the elaborate Temptation accounts found in Luke and Matthew, staying instead with the minimalist Markan recollection, which does not mention what the temptations were. It is intriguing that Kingsbury treated the Temptation not as a preparation for Jesus's vocation, but like any other ethical problem a person might face in life. Kingsbury reckoned that the Temptation was not a single event that happened in the wilderness, but was an ongoing process throughout the earthly life of Jesus. In his Tamil version, he universalized the Temptation of Jesus and informed his readers that it was similar to that which the Buddha faced. Kingsbury also left out the Transfiguration account from his version. This might be due to his aversion for supernatural events, which was further fueled by his doubt about the Resurrection, to which this event might allude.

He also discarded all the "fulfillment citations" that played a significant part in Matthew. In Kingsbury's view, this hermeneutical device was employed by the early Christians to demonstrate that Jesus had successfully accomplished what the Old Testament prophecies foretold, and so God's plan for human salvation had reached its full realization in Jesus. In other words, according to Kingsbury, the early church had matched carefully selected prophecies with the story of Jesus in order to make a strong case for Jesus being the promised Messiah, and as proof that Israel's history had been building up to the arrival of Jesus. Kingsbury omitted these fulfillment passages because they had been used by Matthew to meet the theological demands of his communities. He left out another Gospel segment—Jesus explaining the parables to his disciples—on the same grounds that it arose out of the needs of the early church.

Kingsbury's reconstruction of Jesus was characterized by a basic mistrust in the Gospel records, although he conceded that his life of Jesus was based on the first three Gospels. This skeptical tone was in total contrast to what he enthusiastically endorsed in his conversion narrative: "I am satisfied with the evidences for the genuineness and the truthfulness of the four Gospels."[13] Nevertheless, he gave no historical credibility to the Gospel writers. The compilers of the Gospels arranged the material "not always chronologically" but "topically."[14] Not one of the canonical Gospels, not even Mark, Kingsbury remarked, was "absolutely accurate."[15] Among the Synoptic Gospels, he gave some credence to Mark as the "earliest and the most historical"—a view that was the default position among the liberal biblical critics of the time.[16] Interestingly, it was the Gospel of Mark that Pentecost sent Kingsbury soon after his conversion.

The Gospel of Mark, Kingsbury noted with confidence, was more about the sayings of Jesus than about his "doings and sufferings," as was commonly said of the first Gospel, Matthew. Probably to compensate for Mark's omission of the sayings of Jesus, Kingsbury listed a series of them at the end of his three volumes. Reflecting the prevailing liberal consensus and showing an awareness of the dominant source-criticism of the time, Kingsbury reiterated that Luke was based on Mark and the now lost Q, the supposed textual source for Luke and Matthew. Kingsbury credited Luke with recording some of the "most beautiful" parables of Jesus. He also acknowledged that Q contained many sayings of

Jesus but doubted its historical value, though he also pointed out that a saying or an incident was "not necessarily true" simply because it was found in Q. While acknowledging that Matthew remained one of the sources for his life of Jesus, Kingsbury conceded that it contained, like the other Gospels, sayings that were dated later than the time of Jesus. (This did not prevent Kingsbury from including Matthew's Parable of the Laborers in the Vineyard, however.) And finally, in keeping with the scholarly trend at that time, he dismissed the Fourth Gospel, John, as unhistorical and more of a theological work.

Kingsbury made the Gospel writers look like eclectic textual scroungers who felt perfectly free to pick and choose materials that were available to them, loosely arranging them thematically and not necessarily in historical order. He claimed that when it suited the Gospel writers, they did not hesitate to "alter or even to amplify both the incidents and the sayings."[17] For instance, the Sermon on the Mount was not "*one* sermon." As an account of a single event, it was untrustworthy, in part because it was not delivered as one discourse in a solitary location but dispensed at a range of venues and at various times. Kingsbury also claimed that the Sermon of the Mount contained several sayings that were later than Jesus, but he did not bother to identify these. Of the two versions, he regarded Luke's as original compared to Matthew's recollection.

Kingsbury's life of Jesus largely followed Mark's chronology. Jesus's birthplace was identified as Nazareth, where he spent his first thirty years. He contended that we know little of Jesus's childhood and youth, though we do know that Jesus made Capernaum his headquarters for his Galilean ministry. Kingsbury was doubtful of Jesus's formal education. In the Tamil version, he conjectured that the young Jesus must have learned at home, in the synagogue, and by observing nature. Jesus was thirty years old when he started to preach, and his ministry lasted three years, of which two were spent in Galilee. According to Kingsbury's account, his preaching in Galilee attracted both fame and fury in equal measure. His amazing claims and his fraternization with sinners, tax-collectors, and disreputable women were shocking to the local community. As a result, he and his disciples moved to Gentile territory. Peter's confession at Caesarea Philippi was the decisive moment, and from there, Jesus moved on to Jerusalem. The entry into Jerusalem and the Temple cleansing initially proved successful. Then the crowd, the religious leaders, and the temple traders whose commercial interest he threatened turned against him. Kingsbury's Jesus seemed to alienate everyone. But he remained a true pharisaic Jew, as was confirmed in his summary of the twofold command of love. His answer to Pilate allowed him to be presented as a blasphemer, rebel, and usurper.

In Kingsbury's rendering, Jesus had misgivings about his mission and did not encourage armed rebellion; instead he persuaded people to repent. Jesus doubted the idea of establishing a kingdom in the fashion of David, and he seemed unsure of himself. He did not go to Jerusalem with the "intention of being put to death." Indeed, his prayers at Gethsemane the night before his death, his cry of despair from the cross, clearly indicate that if possible, he would have "escaped death honourably" and "preferred to live." What made him to go to Jerusalem? Kingsbury thought that Jesus even then "hoped for the best," anticipating "release by divine intervention."[18] The Sanhedrin (council) did not believe him to be the Messiah, and Pilate put him to death for "misleading" the people. Kingsbury's story of Jesus ended there. Kingsbury's Jesus died not in a "highly charged apocalyptic context" as many biblical scholars claim, but as a person who was deceived by God and disillusioned with his appointed role.

Jesus without a Halo

The Jesus that emerges in Kingsbury's construal is one who continued the work of John the Baptist, urging repentance and announcing national independence to the Jews—a subversive message that led to the death of both men. In Kingsbury's presentation, Jesus is not the divine human being of traditional orthodoxy, but simply a human being like any other, and one who was tempted like anyone else. At other times, Kingsbury sees him as "a poet, an artist."[19] This Jesus considered himself a prophet—"an inspired teacher of religion and morality," the one "who reveals God's will; or a guru."[20] It is interesting that this was exactly the position that Kingsbury held before his conversion: "Jesus was a great *Guru* like Śaṅkarāchārya or Buddha, and was worthy of our respect as such, that he himself never claimed to be God, and that if Christians worshipped him as God, it was nothing but hero-worship, for which Jesus was not responsible."[21] In other words, Kingsbury's Jesus represented a full hermeneutical reversal for Kingsbury himself, and was certainly not Schweitzer's Jesus, who acted out his own apocalyptic expectations.

Kingsbury's Jesus preached the Gospel of God, not a message about faith in oneself. This was a Jesus who was keen to make an impression on his hearers, so he spoke in aphorisms and parables. His preaching method was uncomplicated and intended for the simple folk of Palestine. It was characterized by concrete language and not complicated with philosophical ideas or abstract imagery. For instance, instead of the Leviticus injunction "Do not harbour a spirit of revenge in your heart," Kingsbury claimed that Jesus came up with "If a man strikes you on one cheek, turn to him the other also." Kingsbury immediately added a caveat, saying that no one who heard this should be "silly enough" to take it literally. Kingsley's Jesus also believed in the use of weapons for self-defense as was evident in his question to his disciples before his arrest: "Have you swords?" This Jesus teaches "non-resistance," and "not passive resistance."[22] One can see unacknowledged echoes here of Gandhi, whose ideas were gaining popularity then.

In keeping with a liberal project of the time, Kingsbury deliteralized the words of Jesus. For instance, he explained that when Jesus said that he would destroy the Temple, he was trying to convey a religious truth: that when the Jews realized that God must be worshipped in truth and spirit, the Temple would become redundant and be discarded.

Kingsbury's Jesus comes across as a highly prejudiced person who firmly believed that the Jews were the chosen people. His narrow Jewishness comes through clearly in his dealings with and attitude toward the Gentiles. His reluctance to acknowledge that Gentiles like the Centurion were capable of faith, his reduction of the Syrophoenician woman to the status of a dog, and his disparaging words about the material things the Gentiles seek such as clothes and food, were all seen as examples of "how little" Jesus knew of the Gentiles. It was this Syrophoenician who showed Jesus that Gentiles were also human beings like the Jews—a curious case of the evangelizer being evangelized.

Kingsley recognized the agency of the woman in radicalizing Jesus before feminists hailed her biting back talk. It was through this encounter that Kingsbury claimed that Jesus overcame his cultural superiority and became "Jesus the Man."[23] Even after this change of heart, however, Jesus did not come across as a person with a universal interest. He could not preach to the outside world because the substance of his preaching would have meant nothing to the Gentiles. He limited his preaching to Israel and did not assign his disciples the task of teaching worldwide. Kingsbury's lives of Jesus did not contain the famous risen Christ sending forth his disciples. Resonating with the widespread view of the form critics, Kingsbury dismissed the missionary command found in Matthew 28.19 as *"not historical"* and regarded its present form as "not earlier than the fourth century."[24]

This is a Jesus who neither consciously opts for the poor nor outrightly condemns wealth and riches as evil. Kingsbury's Jesus does not seem to censure the amassing of wealth itself as long as it is distributed to the disadvantaged, thus vindicating the initial accumulation. Jesus, Kingsbury claimed, did not ask the rich man to give up all his wealth. The fault with the rich man was that he trusted "too much" in his wealth. Kingsbury reflected the conventional liberal position that all human beings are equal before God. His inference was that Jesus never advocated that wealth meant hell or that poverty ensured paradise. Kingsbury himself posed a rhetorical question, and answered it: "Does Jesus mean all rich men will go to hell and that all beggars will go to heaven? No."[25] He castigated contemporary commentators who were "erring on the other side," that is, taking the side of the poor, reminding them that, as in the days of Jesus, what was denounced was the "abundance of the things" one possessed.[26] The fault of the rich man was his unwillingness to share his wealth. Kingsbury's implied message was that poverty was not a condition for discipleship. It appeared that standing up for the marginalized was not a moral imperative for Kingsbury's Jesus.

The Jesus of Kingsbury was not the mighty miracle worker that some conservatives might have made him out to be. Kingsbury interpreted the miracles as "signs," "wonders," and "powers" performed by Jesus not on his own authority and command, but at the behest of God.

Sometimes Kingsbury rationalized the miracles: for instance, the feeding miracle is interpreted as people sharing the food they had with them. Sometimes too he minimized the severity of an illness. The blind are not all born blind, but are recovering their temporary loss of vision. He dismissed all nature miracles outright, but he was not always true to his liberal credentials. With all his apparent skepticism, he did not rule out all the healing miracles because modern psychology could account "for most, if not for all" of them.[27] One such was the healing of people possessed by demons, which he interpreted as "insane or demented persons being restored to reason" by Jesus. This was a Jesus who took for granted the "primitive" beliefs of the time. Kingsbury conceded that demon possession was an "article of faith" in Palestine, and that Jesus and his contemporaries believed in such a practice, but, he added, this did not mean that his followers in the twentieth century should accept it as true. Although demon possession was prevalent in colonial Ceylon, Kingsbury was unequivocal about his stance: "I do not believe in demon-possession or demoniacs."[28]

Kingsbury's Jesus was also not the new Manu or Moses. He was not the new ethical legislator who came to replace the earlier ones. He did not encourage people to break the law. His ethical teachings were not relevant to the modern day. Jesus basically labored among simple folks nineteen hundred years ago, and, therefore, his moral precepts were ill-suited to the twentieth century's complex civilization and culture. His moral rulings are situation-specific, bound by time and place: "Again, we must remember that Jesus' injunction to a particular man or class of men, even supposing that the injunction was sound, is not to be regarded as of universal application for all time." Kingsbury even invoked Julius Wellhausen to bolster his claim, citing the German's observation that one cannot use the commands of Jesus as a "solution of any of our own difficulties."[29] Commenting on Jesus's prohibition of divorce, Kingsbury wrote that Jesus was projecting "an ideal marriage" and that it was "silly to bring him down to the level of a legislator." He even challenged this ruling of Jesus and went on to say that there are cases where divorce may be "perfectly right."[30]

Having doubted the ongoing relevance of the ethical message of Jesus, Kingsbury identified two ways of dealing with it. One was to appropriate it literally, especially the injunctions in the Sermon on the Mount, without watering down those maxims to a "lower level." This he dismissed in his customarily sneering fashion, for a reason that will be evident in what follows. The other was to disregard it as irrelevant to modern society. Kingsbury's contention was that Jesus's teachings were not about the duties of a citizen toward the state or how nations should behave in international affairs. He reckoned that it would be absurd if any modern society or government or nation applied Jesus's teaching to contemporary problems. Kingsbury's Jesus directed his followers toward an internal and personal service of love and did not urge the community to show compassion toward the lost and the hopeless. Jesus was more concerned with an individual's relation to his neighbor than with his or her efforts to promote social justice. Kingsbury envisaged a Jesus who was not a lawgiver promulgating rules but a prophet concerned with individual people and their principles. In his conversion account, Kingsbury remarked that while Hinduism and Judaism catered to nations and national concerns, "Christianity maintains that each individual is an end in himself," and he went on to argue that the "responsibility of every individual is emphasized in Christianity in a manner altogether unknown in Hinduism."[31] Jesus's teachings were not about public life, or citizens' responsibilities, but about good neighborliness. It was the individuals who needed support and succor, so Jesus stressed the importance of people rather than laws.

The New Testament writers' tendency to ignore state or societal problems is customarily explained in terms of the future arrival of the Kingdom, but in Kingsbury's view the true reason lay in Jesus's individualism, that is, the relationship of the individual to God eclipses national and familial relationships. To address the world's ills, Kingsbury came out with a vague idea of first being imbued with "the spirit of Jesus" and then "all problems, private and public, will solve themselves."[32] For Kingsbury's Jesus, the ethical demand is more of an inner, internal prompting than something to do with societal deeds. Kingsbury reduced Jesus's moral ethics to individualism.

The Jesus that emerges from Kingsbury's writings is a complex figure. On the one hand, Kingsbury praises him as a "genius" for bringing together the two commandments found in the Law of Moses—"You shall love Yahweh your God with all your heart, and with all your soul, and with all your might," and "You shall love your neighbour as yourself." But on the other hand, Jesus comes across as a hardhearted and unforgiving personality. A conspicuously offensive example of this is Jesus's words to the man who wanted to bury his father—"Leave the dead to bury their own dead." In Kingsbury's view, this was "heartless."[33]

Jesus is portrayed as "too conscientious to think he was good." He not only makes discourteous remarks about the Gentiles but also has no qualms about preaching rewards and punishments. While emphasizing God's love, goodness, and compassion, this Jesus, disturbingly, does not hesitate to talk about election and rejection, and rewards and punishments. Jesus gives the impression of backing the case for the final destruction of the wicked, with the burning of the darnel in the Wheat and the Darnel parable seen by Kingsbury as indicative of the ultimate destruction of evil. A notable case of apparent support for the election of some and rejection of others is found in the words of Jesus to his disciples—"Your names are written in heaven."

Kingsbury was uncomfortable with Jesus's statement implying that there was a specific sin, namely blaspheming against the Holy Spirit, that would not be forgiven. With the inherent confidence of an upper-class Jaffna man, he thus corrects these bleak theological pronouncements of Jesus, saying that there is no eternal hell and that God has the capacity to forgive people: "There is no sin that a man cannot give up; and when a man gives up sin, God will forgive. There can be no eternal hell."[34] The presumption is that in matters of last-day judgment Jesus was not always right: Kingsbury, the modern-day compiler of the Gospels, knows better.

Invoking the then-prevalent idea among liberal biographers of Jesus, Kingsbury projected a Jesus who did not show any interest in religion or in its institutionalized forms. His contention was that the religion of Jesus became a religion about Jesus only after the Resurrection—Jesus's intention was not to start a religion, which came about only due to the work of the disciples and Paul. True, Jesus had an inner circle and a group of people around him, but he never thought of separating them from the rest of Jewish society and organizing them into a well-knit structure. In his characteristic manner, Kingsbury dismissed Jesus's words—"You are Peter and upon this rock I will build my church"—as not from Jesus but from an "ecclesiastical saying" dated later than Jesus.

Even if Jesus had intended to establish a church, Kingsbury wrote, his purpose was not to start a formal religion but to initiate a spiritual one. Jesus found that those who were around him professed to be religious but their religion was "formal . . . and merely ritual." Instead, he offered a counterexperience that was "spiritual, moral, personal." What follows from the Sermon on the Mount is that religion is about "*positive* goodness" and is "never content with merely shunning evil." Again, in the words of Kingsbury: "Doing good and not merely keeping from wrongdoing is religion, according to Jesus."[35] Jesus envisaged the reign of God and not a structured religion. Christianity emerged as a religion only after his death.

Similarly, Kingsbury dismisses the two sacraments that strengthen the power of the institutionalized church—baptism and the Lord's Supper (or Eucharist)—as not being instituted by Jesus. He specifies that Mark and Luke are silent about baptism as a rite; it is mentioned only in Matthew, whose account is not historical. The baptism that was part of the Matthean missionary command, Kingsbury alleged, has been inserted to fit with the Trinitarian formula. In any case, the text in its present form is not from earlier than the fourth century. As regards the Last Supper, the Gospels record Jesus participating in it, but there is no indication that it should be repeated. Kingsbury attributed this practice to Paul (1 Corinthians 11.23–25). He contended that Jesus, who insisted on the spirituality of religion, would not have started or encouraged such showy ritual practices.

The picture of the Messiah that Kingsbury sketched is a bit confusing. His Jesus never publicly acknowledges or claims his appointed role. His Jesus is not the one who is stirred by apocalyptic expectations, but is a less-confident, cautious, confused, and dithering Messiah who continually modifies his ideas, or, as Kingsbury sympathetically put it: "Jesus was growing intellectually all the time, and . . . at times he changed his views."[36] Jesus did not begin his ministry thinking that he was the expected Messiah. The words heard at the baptism are traditionally held up as a sign of the early public acknowledgment of his messianic call, but Kingsbury disputes this interpretation. He characterizes this occasion as a private one in which Jesus embarks on God's service, and, more importantly, he strips it of any uniqueness or exclusivity. Instead he describes this baptismal rite as "an experience of many a man who whole-heartedly and once and for all has dedicated himself to the service of God."[37] Kingsbury's choice of words at the baptism is suggestive of his thinking. In his first portrayal, *Jesus of Nazareth*, he included Matthew's version: "This is my beloved Son, in whom I am well pleased," which was a public announcement. But in his second biography, the *Life of Jesus*, he replaced it with Mark's "You are my son," which was a personal and private communication. In the Tamil version, Kingsbury is even more audacious. He tells his readers that the events surrounding the baptism—heaven opening, the spirit of God descending like a dove, and the hearing of the voice—were not open to or witnessed by the public, but experienced by Jesus alone. Kingsbury challenges the orthodox explanation that the words heard at the baptism signaled the messianic call. For Kingsbury, this is not about messiahship but about Jesus's awareness of his role as a spiritual son. In the Tamil version, without providing any historical evidence, Kingsbury advanced the view that the idea of sonship and messianic tendencies were kindled in Jesus through the teachings of his parents, teachers, and his own intuitive observations about the flora and fauna of Galilee. It is only at the end of his Galilean ministry that Jesus "began to cherish the belief that he was the Messiah-elect"—a belief for which he paid "dearly." Kingsbury's Jesus may have reluctantly taken upon himself the Jewish messianic hope, but he often questioned this choice. What must have influenced his decision, according to Kingsbury, was the "futility of attempting to lead his people against the Romans."[38] Another reason for Jesus's reluctance, in his view, could have been that Jesus characterized himself as someone like John the Baptist and envisaged his mission as preparing people for God's reign.

In Kingsbury's vision, the Kingdom of God envisaged by Jesus is perceived as present and future, political and spiritual. The nature of the Kingdom, however, is unclear. On the one hand, he maintained that it was "spiritual and moral," and on the other, he saw it as political and revolutionary. For Kingsbury, the reign of God meant "*always* a political rule, that was to bring national independence to the Jews." Jesus was projected as a Messiah whose task was to deliver Israel and restore its national pride. His claim to be the King of the Jews was deemed to be a political act, and it was for this reason that Jesus was put to death by Pilate. At the same time, as indicated earlier, this was the same Jesus who saw that resistance to Roman rule was a pointless exercise.

The realization of the reign of God was also uncertain in Kingsbury's view. Like John the Baptist, Jesus looked forward to the sudden "advent of the messianic or political kingdom" that would "overthrow the existing world order," but at the same time he believed in the "slow, gradual coming of the moral, spiritual Kingdom of God" described in the Parable of the Seed Growing in Secret.[39] Kingsbury was not sure whether Jesus himself was conscious of this discrepancy. His readers must also have been confused as to where Kingsbury's own opinion lay—whether the reign of God was present and political, or future and spiritual. Their bewilderment must have been further complicated by Kingsbury's intriguing statement that "history has shown that the advent of an eschatological or Messianic reign was an idle dream never to be realized."[40] It seemed that only personal morality and decency counted in the Kingdom. There is no question of this Kingdom incorporating the Gentile world.

The life and work of Jesus in Kingsbury's narration comes to an end with his death and burial. In all his writings, the Resurrection, the central event and the very basis of the Christian faith, is ominously left out. Kingsbury's narrative ends with Joseph of Arimathea asking for the body and Kingsbury's unemotional observation: "Pilate gave him the corpse." The body was taken and buried by Joseph of Arimathea. The whereabouts of the grave, Kingsbury maintained, had not been identified as yet. And only women witnessed the event: there was no mention of any male disciples being present. The twelve had already left after the arrest, except for Peter, who stayed behind but at a distance. The women who were bold enough to be present were Mary Magdalene and Mary, the mother of James and Joses.

In completing his account of Jesus with the burial, Kingsbury also informed his readers that what happened afterward was the beginning of Christianity, another story and not his present concern. The appearances of the risen Jesus in Kingsbury's reckoning were circulated after

Jesus's death, by Paul, whose earliest account can be found in his Epistle to the Corinthians. Even these accounts, Kingsbury was keen to point out, did not suggest any physical resurrection. Paul himself was "emphatic" that the resurrected body was "spiritual."[41] Because Paul was neither a Galilean nor a Jerusalemite but a Roman and a Hellenist, Kingsbury considered these stories as part of neither the Galilean nor the Jerusalem traditions. Moreover, Kingsbury claimed that Jesus neither believed in individual or universal Resurrection nor taught about it. In line with his skepticism about the Resurrection, Kingsbury dismissed or explained away any references to Resurrection in the Gospels. The rising of the little daughter of Jairus, in Mark, is discounted as lacking evidence that the little girl was dead, "so there is no rising from the dead."[42] Kingsbury minimizes the significance of the discussion between the Sadducees and Jesus, too, as a conversation about life after death rather than about physical Resurrection. Similarly, the Transfiguration scene and the ensuing discussion among the disciples about the "rising again from the dead" is unceremoniously omitted from Kingsbury's retelling. Interestingly, this was the same Kingsbury who three decades previously had unambiguously declared after his conversion: "I am satisfied with the historical evidence for the resurrection of Jesus."[43]

Kingsbury admits that it is difficult to decide after nineteen hundred years whether the Resurrection was an objective or subjective event. But he conceded that those who had the vision "sincerely believed in their objectivity."[44] Kingsbury identified himself with the standard liberal position of the time. The Resurrection, for him, was not an event that happened in the life of Jesus, but an event that changed and empowered the lives of the distraught disciples. The origin of the church could not be accounted for unless something had happened to the "runaway disciples," who changed into the "brave heroes that they proved to be."[45] Kingsbury reassures his readers that many of the theologians of the day "mean by *resurrection* nothing more than *personal immortality*."[46]

Putting Kingsbury in His Place

Kingsbury's works describing the lives of Jesus resemble that of Tatian's second-century *Diatessaron*—they were an attempt to produce a single, uncomplicated narrative of Jesus by deleting duplications, legendary items, later accretions, and whatever else seemed incompatible with Kingsbury's way of thinking. The harmonized format was an endeavor to discover the self-consciousness of Jesus and his innermost life, which had been obscured by the needs of the early church. Kingsbury was not the first from the Indian subcontinent to produce a harmonized version of the Gospel. That honor goes to Rammohun Roy, whose *Precepts of Jesus* came out in 1820, sixty years before the first modern version, W. G. Rushbrooke's *Synopticon.* Inevitably, Roy and Kingsbury faced the ire of the missionaries. Roy, being a Hindu, escaped excommunication, but he experienced the heavy weight of evangelical bombardment from the Baptist missionary Joshua Marshman.[47] Kingsbury, however, a Christian, was forced to leave the church.

Kingsbury's life of Jesus was written in imitation of the Western portrayals of Jesus, which most of his readers would not have had access to. His construals of Jesus differed from those of earlier generations of converts. While the Christologies of Nilakantha Sastri Goreh (1825–1895, baptized Nehemiah Goreh) and Sadhu Sundar Singh (1889–1929) were a mere replication of established Western conservative thinking, and took an obsessive apologetical tone, Kingsbury's work represented a liberal, humanistic portrayal of Jesus's life that was relatively new to South Asian readers. His work also differed from that of another group of Indian thinkers. The deep Christological reflections of converts like H. A. Krishnapillai (1827–1900) and Narayan Vaman Tilak (1861–1919) lifted Jesus out of his surroundings and drew heavily on Indian *bhakti* (devotional tradition) to illuminate him. Their work was not steeped in or shaped by the latest Western theology, as in the case of Kingsbury. He was stuck with the Gospel narratives, and focused on biblical images, and so tried to frame Jesus within his Jewish environment. Unlike those Indian converts who struggled with what Chenchiah called a "double bondage"—"dogmatic Christianity and the traditions of Hinduism"—Kingsbury did not seek a Jesus in relation to the inexhaustible riches of Hinduism, but mechanically followed the twentieth-century liberal program of appealing directly to Jesus himself, against later church dogma.[48] He was trying to unearth a Jesus who was already interpreted in the pages of the Gospel rather than finding him behind the layers of tradition, as the historical critics of the time tended to do.

While Indian contemporaries of Kingsbury like P. Chenchiah and Chakkaria were inclined to describe aspects of Jesus's life yet never ventured a full-scale biography, Kingsbury was bold enough to come up with one. Kingsbury's bibliography shows that, in creating it, he depended more on the British biblical scholars of the time than on the German ones. This was not unusual for a self-confessed "indiscriminate admirer of English."[49] He mentions only two German thinkers, Joseph Klausner and Adolf Harnack; the rest are all standard British biographers of the time on whose work Kingsbury closely relied.[50] English-based depictions of the lives of Jesus thrived during this mistakenly called "no-biography period." These British biographies of Jesus did not have elaborate technical notes but utilized judiciously the results of German scholarship in order to strengthen the religious feelings and perceptions of ordinary churchgoers and the Christian public. Kingsbury's writings demonstrate that he was fairly well informed about the shades and subtleties of Western historical scholarship and the hermeneutical principles that undergirded it, but he employed them in a very unobtrusive manner in his writings.

Sadly, Kingsbury did not break any new ground, nor did he perceptively change the agenda of the Jesus-quest enterprise. His English-language lives of Jesus follow and reiterate both good and unsatisfactory aspects of the liberal biographies of Jesus. He could have been more adventurous and imaginative, like the Hindu thinkers we encounter in this volume, but he remained broadly within the dry Western liberal tradition.

His Tamil presentation of Jesus, however, is more exploratory and slightly more exciting than the dull, routine liberal Jesus found in his English writings. His English Jesus could have been written by any Western academic or cleric of the time, but in the Tamil version, he is more daring, filling in details missing in the Gospels with a bit of historical fantasy. For instance, even as he casts doubt on the historical authenticity of the Gospels, he does not hesitate to inform his readers— without providing any evidence—that the young Jesus's early education came from his parents and his own personal observation of nature.

More interestingly, Kingsbury's Tamil version is interspersed with quotations drawn from the Tamil saints and sacred texts, which he uses to explain and to illuminate biblical narratives. Commenting on "And why beholdest thou the mote that is in thy brother's eye, but considerest not the beam that is in thine own eye?" for instance, Kingsbury quotes three couplets from the Thirukkural, a comprehensive Tamil "manual of ethics, polity and love" that dates back probably to the sixth century.[51] One such couplet is "His failings will be found and shown, Who makes another's failings known" (Thirukkural 186). When Jesus came out with a baffling claim, "Who is my mother, and who are my brothers?" Kingsbury linked this to a verse of a ninth-century Saiva poet adored by Saivites, Manikkavasakar: "I don't want the kith and kin; Nor do I want the town (of influence); Nor want the fame." Similarly, when Jesus said a prophet had no honor in his country, Kingsbury cited from the same Saiva saint: "I ask not kin, nor name, nor place, Nor learned men's society." He also provided historical examples from Indian history to explain Gospel incidents. For example, Jesus's retreat from Galilee to Tyre and Sidon when he feared that Herod might be after him is likened to Ramanuja (the Vaishnavite philosopher and teacher) leaving the Chola Kingdom ruled by a Saivite king and seeking refuge in the princely state of Mysore.

Kingsbury's intertextual comparisons—between the Gospels and the Tamil scriptures—may impress the casual reader, but a closer inspection of the relevant passages may reveal no common elements in them. Sometimes texts sound the same in their splendid separate situations, but when read in their respective contexts they reveal dissimilarity rather than resemblance. For example, when commenting on the utterance of Jesus "Who is my mother, and who are my brothers?" Kingsbury cites a similar saying from Manikkavasagar's *Tiruvasagam* that came out of Siddhanta philosophy and emphasizes worldly detachment and the soul's love for God. Jesus, however, was trying to redefine family beyond original and immediate family ties and forge a new kinship among those who do the will of God. These apparent textual agreements and rough similarities result in exaggerated and unrealistic claims.

The Tamil Jesus of Kingsbury speaks chaste and classical Tamil, which is refreshing compared to the Sanskrit-saturated Tamil Bible of the British and Foreign Bible Society, to which his Tamil readers were accustomed. While Kingsbury modernized the language in his English lives of Jesus, omitting the Authorized Version's archaic "thee's" and "thou's," his employment of *centamil* (beautiful or fine Tamil) would have distanced his Jesus from the ordinary folks of Jaffna.

In these writings, Kingsbury kept away from the vigorous indigenization that was taking place in India and Ceylon. At a time when Indian Christian thinkers were trying to claim Jesus as a man of the East, Kingsbury did not make any regional or ethnic claim, nor did he embellish Jesus's story with Eastern imagery in order to establish his relevancy. Concepts such as Jesus as the Avatara were gaining popularity and were enthusiastically advocated by Indian theologians like V. Chakkarai (*Jesus the Avatar*, 1926) and A. J. Appasamy (*Christianity as Bhakti Mārga: A Study of the Johannine Doctrine of Love*, 1926). But Kingsbury, like his fellow Jaffna Tamil Ramanathan, showed hardly any interest in such a conception. The nearest that he came to using an Indian concept was when he called Jesus a guru, but he did not attempt to situate Jesus within the Saiva Siddhanta system as Ramanathan did. Essentially he perceived Jesus as a Jew who "believed in the Jewish scriptures" and as someone who thought of himself as the last in a line of Jewish prophets who hoped that his message would be heard.[52] For Kingsbury, the thinking and personality of Jesus belonged within the Jewish sage tradition, not, as the scholarly consensus went, within an apocalyptic milieu. In another sense, too, Kingsbury vehemently differed from these Indian theologians. For emerging theologians at that time like Chenchiah, Chakkarai, and Appasamy, a deep personal and direct experience of the risen Christ was vital to their spiritual nourishment and theological articulation. Kingsbury, by contrast, discounted the Resurrection accounts as not part of the Gospel story but as a concoction of the early church. For him, the wisdom of Jesus was critical.

Kingsbury distanced himself from another theological trend that was sweeping across India at that time, namely, that God was in some unknown ways preparing the hearts and minds of Hindus through their rishis and their scriptures to receive the Christian revelation. This idea was emerging as a potential vehicle for making the Gospel relevant to India. Kingsbury knew very well two of the exponents of this theory,

William Miller of Madras Christian College and J. N. Farquhar, the lit-erary secretary of the Young Men's Christian Association, Calcutta. Soon after Kingsbury decided to become a Christian and walked out of his father's home, it was Miller who took him under his wing and "promised unconditionally to give . . . [him] a sound education."[53] Miller was the one who mooted the idea of "Jesus the fulfiller," an idea that, according to his biographer O. Kandaswami Chetty, had become "more familiar, and more agreeable to the minds of Christians in Southern India."[54] This was later picked up and made into a potent theological template by Farquhar, the editor of the Heritage of India Series under whose banner Kingsbury had brought his translation of the Tamil Saiva saints. Kingsbury did not bother to interact with or pursue the proposal that Hindus had been prepared to accept Jesus as the fulfillment of Vedic expectations.

Historical portrayals of Jesus's life, though often touted as objective, are intimate, intuitive, and emotional affairs. Jesus's life story has been enlisted for various political and national causes, varying from vali-dating the Victorian values of British colonialists to supporting the National Socialists' Aryan agenda, to promoting Christianity via Hindu reformers. (The liberationist Jesus, who championed the marginalized and women, came later.) Kingsbury's Jesus, however, remains distant and detached from any ideological cause, and worse, is dull. This is not a story of a daring, decisive, energetic, messianic leader, but one of a dithering, effete, unsubstantial Jesus expounding the case for an inner spirituality and self-realization. This was a time of political upheaval and self-conscious nationalism in both India and in Sri Lanka, but Kingsbury's Jesus shows no interest in such secular affairs; instead, fearing failure, he does not even engage with his occupying power—the Romans. He appears on earth independent of the religious history of his people, and does not help to realize their eschatological hopes. Al-though he stands within the Jewish tradition and re-echoes its wisdom, he does not show any universal interest or unusual originality; he does not preach any new dharma or satya. Given the current impatience with a culture- and gender-free Jesus, and the penchant for ideologically slanted and situationally specific portrayals, it is difficult to feel any at-traction toward Kingsbury's detached and aloof Jesus. His simple, good, compassionate, self-giving man divested of his divine status must have upset both innately conservative Jaffna Christians and the inherently evangelical missionaries of the time. Most Jaffna Christians, who often honored the name of Jesus with a bowed head, would have been appalled at the way Jesus was hauled before the headmaster, Kingsbury, to be corrected, molded, and absolved by him. Reminiscing about his conversion, Kingsbury wrote: "In Jesus I have the ideal I need for life."[55] The interesting next question is whether anyone answered the altar call for Kingsbury's colorless and inoffensive Jesus much as Kingsbury himself had responded to the revival preacher's Jesus all those years earlier.

6

Jesus as a Jain Tirthankara

At the outset, it is worth mentioning three remarkable facts about Manilal Parekh, the subject of this chapter. First, he was a rare Jain who embraced Christianity while remaining true to his own tradition, infusing his newly found faith with his rich heritage. His story is rare because he made the surprising move from atheistic Jainism to theistic Christianity.

Second, Parekh was inspired to convert not by missionary propaganda, but by writings on Jesus by fellow Hindus, in particular by the recruiter-in-chief Keshub Chunder Sen (1838–1884), a towering figure of the time.[1] Pandita Ramabai (1858–1922), who championed the cause of women and brought out her own translation of the Marathi Bible; the Bengali Brahmabandhab Upadhyay (1861–1907), who pursued a vigorous Hindu-Christian synthesis; and a Tamil Brahmin, Mahadeva Iyer (1868–1922), from South India, were three examples of converts inspired by reading or listening to Sen's lectures or writings. To this list, one could add Manilal Parekh (1885–1967), who confessed in his autobiography that Sen took "control of my whole life" and had become his spiritual father and guru.[2] As this chapter will demonstrate, however, Parekh was not a blind follower of the master.

A third factor was his troubled and tortured relationship with the institutional church. Parekh opted for baptism, which he regarded as a purely spiritual sacrament, demonstrating a new discipleship to Christ. But he felt strongly that the word "convert" should be dropped because it had come to mean some sort of perversion. More worryingly, for the caste-conscious Parekh, the church was depressingly overcrowded with untouchables and adivasis. He wanted to maintain his high-caste status, claiming that the main aim of Jesus was to change the "life of the individual from sinfulness to Godliness." He urged that "the new disciples be kept in their homes" and remain within their "respective communities."[3] The Hindu idea of *swadharmagraha* (insistence on the religion of one's birth) provided him with the hermeneutical ploy to maintain his caste status even after conversion. He bemoaned the fact that conversion for higher-caste people meant "social submergence and ecclesiastical bondage."[4]

Like other high-caste converts of the time, Parekh maintained a safe distance from denominational Christianity, which he found to be controlled by missionary demands. He also disliked the ecclesiastical differences espoused by missionaries. These divisions, he claimed, came out of a European context and so should not be imposed in India. His stint with the Anglican church did not last long. He was disenchanted with its Western style and its imperialistic and materialistic manifestations. He found that Western churches had become a secularized civic community and were "intoxicated with pride of race, culture, creed, and empire," rather than a spiritual fellowship.[5] He cut himself off from all churches and missions but remained committed to Jesus, calling himself a Hindu disciple of Christ.

Parekh's byline says that he was a religious teacher and an author. He was a prolific writer and his specialty was biographies. He produced life histories not only of Raja Rammohun Roy and Keshub Chunder Sen, prominent personalities in the Brahmo Samaj, a Hindu reform movement, but also of modern Hindu saints like Swami Narayana and Vallabhacharya.[6] His personal profiles of ancient preachers included one on Zoroaster.[7] The last in his line of life stories was on Jesus. *A Hindu's Portrait of Jesus Christ: A Gospel of God's Free Gift of His Sonship* is more than five hundred pages long.[8] Its message: if a Hindu could hold on to Jesus in the manner Parekh had done, there would be no need for Hindus to become Christians. Parekh fully expected Christians "not to like the book."[9]

An explanation is needed here of Parekh's use of the word Hindu, which he uses throughout his writings. He found that the term had become too narrow and the people of India had become victims of this restricted definition. He claimed that the term Hindu did not have a scriptural or semi-scriptural reference that limited it to identifying a religion. He thus redefined it as a cultural or spiritual descriptor for all those who live in Hindustan as Hindus. He made the term inclusive in that Muslims or Christians had the right to apply it to themselves.[10] This is a far cry from the current Hindutva understanding of the phrase, which is restrictive and sectarian. His incorporation of all Indians under one umbrella expression comes from Parekh's feeling of equal respect for all religions, as found in the Hindu concept of *sambhava*.[11]

Jesus Was Oriental, Not a Despot

Like Sen and his erstwhile colleagues of the Brahmo Samaj before him, Parekh set out to rescue Jesus, who had become the "king of the white races" and enmeshed in Western imperial ambitions. In his autobiographical sketch, Parekh declared that his aim was to "separate the pure Christianity of Jesus Christ from the accretions that had grown upon it during the last nineteen hundred years."[12] Whereas Western scholars were keen on weaning Jesus away from doctrinal entanglements, Parekh was determined to pry Jesus away from the clutches of imperial attitudes. His interpretative aim was to cleanse Christ, who had been hailed as a "Europeanized Kaiser of Christendom."[13] Parekh was convinced that Christianity had become tainted with "absolutely unessential and even anti-Christian elements such as Western civilization, European culture and foreign imperialism, whether Portuguese, as in the time of Robert de Nobili, or British as in our times."[14] He thus took upon himself the mission of sanitizing a Christianity that came "loaded" with British, Dutch, French, and Portuguese civilization, culture, and imperialism. He identified five imperialist realms associated with Christianity—"religious, racial, cultural, economic and political."[15] Parekh was not an anti-colonial agitator like J. C. Kumarappa, a rare Christian who joined Gandhi in his independence struggle.[16] Parekh stood aloof from the national life during the agitation for independence, and from post-independent India when active nation-building was encouraged. Unlike Gandhi, he desisted from using religion for political purposes. He was yearning for spiritual meaning not in public life, but in private. It was not only the identification of Jesus with colonial power and privilege and with Europe's aggressive civilization that troubled Parekh, but also the "un-Hindu and even anti-Hindu" way he was presented in India.[17] He saw his task as making Jesus suitable and intelligible to Indian spirituality.

In line with most of the Hindus identified here, Parekh located Jesus in "his true oriental setting," thus removing him from traditional Jewish and Hellenistic habitats.[18] While his mentor, Sen, placed Jesus within a large assembly of religious personages that included Moses and Elijah, and Eastern thinkers like Sakhya Muni, Confucius, and Zoroaster, Parekh drew parallels between the lives life of Jesus and twentieth-century Hindu saints such as Swami Narayana (1781–1830).[19]

When writing the biography of Swami Narayana, Parekh found much common ground between Vaishnava and the Christian faith and even greater similarities between Jesus and the Swami. He claimed that the Swami was the only Hindu teacher who offered "the closest of parallel to Jesus in his life and work."[20] The "speed, urgency and energy" found in the life and work of the Swami resembled that of the work of Jesus recorded in the Gospel of Mark.[21] The supernatural and wonderful power that was seen in the life and work of Jesus could be seen in Swami Narayana's life as well. Parekh does not provide any detailed account of the similarities between these religious men; instead he describes their superficial likenesses. Like Jesus, the Swami never worked miracles on a mass scale. The ministry of one man lasted thirty years, whereas the other only a little longer. Both men attained the fullness of yoga, which only a couple of people had achieved in the past millennium. Parekh mentioned a parable of the Swami that resembled the Parable of the Dishonest Servant. Both had disciples who were jealous and showed dissension. Neither was a social revolutionary. While working for the salvation of the people, there is nothing to suggest that either man's message was intended to "subvert the Hindu social order."[22] And both respected temporal powers, with Parekh claiming that when Jesus said "Render unto Caesar the things that are Caesar's," he spoke for the Swami as well.

These comparative efforts may not sustain a closer scrutiny. Parekh largely asserted his case without giving due weight to a textual study of the teachings of Jesus and Swami Narayana. He placed exaggerated importance on parallels and similarities, often forgetting that in the history of religions, diversity and differences are more significant than straightforward parallels. Pointing out mere similarities is not enough. Such similarities have to be demonstrated textually, which Parekh's work sadly failed to do.

Jesus as a Jina (Conqueror of All Passions)

Although Parekh claimed, with characteristic oriental humility, that he had "no proper knowledge of the New Testament," his writings show that he was familiar with the source analysis approach that was in vogue at that time. Like most liberal contemporary interpreters, he was skeptical about the historical value of Saint John's Gospel. He claimed that "as history it has limitations." His Jesus was largely drawn from the Synoptic Gospels, even though he had some doubts about their historical reliability. He regarded them as the "working of the pious imagination of the devotees of Jesus."[23]

Parekh had no doubt that Jesus was a historical figure and that the accounts of him were as authentic as those for other figures about whom he had written. He admitted there were serious differences among the Gospels about the way they narrated the story of Jesus. This did not surprise him because the same was true of the life stories of Krishna, Zoroaster, and the Buddha. He reconciled these differences by distinguishing between the Jesus of history, whose story he claimed could be found in the Synoptic Gospels, and the Christ of experience, which is described in the Gospel of John.

Parekh resisted the then-popular hermeneutical practice of linking Jesus with Hindu avataras—a convenient, but lazy, approach used both by Hindu reformers and Indian Christians to make Jesus an Eastern figure. He also differed in another way. While Jesus searchers of the day emphasized the ethical teaching of Jesus, he considered the life and personality of Jesus as "far more important than his teaching, and in this lay the origin of the Gospels."[24] He cited Mark's Gospel as an example of a work that gives importance "to the incidents in the life of Jesus and he rarely gives the teaching as such except what came incidentally in the course of the life itself."[25] In his autobiographical sketch, Parekh remarked that he was attracted by "the marvellous charm of the personality of Jesus Christ"—a near Sen-like description of which his master would have been proud.[26]

Perhaps not surprisingly, Parekh dismissed the Virgin Birth as irrelevant and not essential to "any true scheme of salvation." He granted that miraculous intervention was possible for God but that there was no need for God to do this. His view was that Hindus would be more enthralled by the story of Jesus's life, teaching, and death than by the idea of his being born of a virgin, which would have "no attraction" for them; they would have treated it as a "pious myth." In his analysis, the belief in the Virgin Birth in the early church owed its existence to three factors—the prevalent stories about the birth of the Greek heroes, the prophecy of Isaiah, and the doctrine of original sin. He also suspected that the idea could have come from the women who were close to Jesus and who wished to "idealize Mary."[27] The cult of Mary could have grown especially among the Roman Catholics, in order to rectify the Protestant notion of the overpowering fatherly image of God. Unlike some of the Indians studied here, he did not subscribe to the view that the infancy narratives were influenced by Hindu myths.

Parekh found Jesus to be a "supreme Yogi," but not in the Hindu sense, since he acknowledged that Jesus had not known or followed any method of Hindu yoga. Instead it was Jesus's self-surrendering devotion—his complete yielding that led to his communion with God, which is the "goal of all yoga"—that made him a yogi.[28] The secret of his attainment was traced to his abstinence, his long prayers, and his fasting, especially his forty-day fast, when he was in contact with the "infinite reservoir of spiritual power" and came to be endowed with authority to work miracles as well as to announce the Kingdom.[29] For

Parekh, Jesus was the one who had attained both *atmajnana*—"realization of soul, considered by the Hindus as of very great importance"—and *atmanistha*, that is, faith in his being a spirit, the foundation of all spirituality.[30] Such a framing of Jesus within Hindu thought patterns, Parekh thought, would naturally be attractive to Hindus. This led him to declare that to be Hindu was to be a "true disciple of Christ, and to be a true disciple of Christ meant to be a more Hindu and not less."[31]

These words echo those of earlier high-caste Hindu converts who were deeply conscious that their Hindu background was more of an advantage than a hindrance in exercising their newly found discipleship in Christ. One of those converts was Brahmabandhab Upadhyay, who wrote that "all that is noblest and best in the Hindu character is developed in us by the genial inspiration of the perfect Narahari (God-man), our pattern and guide. The more we love him, the more we love our country, the more proud we become of our past glory."[32] A similar sentiment was expressed by Pandipeddi Chenchiah, who regarded Hinduism as his "spiritual mother" and had discovered "the supreme value of Christ, not in spite of Hinduism but because Hinduism has taught him to discern spiritual greatness."[33]

What was appealing to Parekh as a Jain was the self-denying aspect of Jesus's teaching and the embodiment of it in his life. Jesus's renunciation of wealth, home, and family, in Parekh's reckoning, identified him as a sanyasin or a fakir. Such teaching and lifestyle were "so revolutionary" that Jesus's own disciples found it difficult to emulate. The Sermon on the Mount, the Beatitudes, and the Counsels of Perfection (chastity, obedience, poverty) appealed to Jains as well.[34] Parekh claimed that Jain *sadhus* and *sadhavis* (monks and nuns) were the true practitioners of the self-sacrifice and austerity preached by Jesus.

Another feature of Jesus that was attractive to Parekh was his God-consciousness. Most Indian thinkers treat the Johannine verse "I and the father are one" as the apotheosis of Jesus's God consciousness. Parekh instead chose a verse found only in Luke, repeated several times in the third Gospel—"rejoicing in the Holy Spirit." He declared confidently that if the saying was true, this must have been one of the "greatest ever uttered by man."[35] Parekh interpreted "being in spirit" as a kind of "trance or semi trance, a sort of *Samadhi*" during which Jesus arose from his ordinary human awareness and "spoke from a plane which was divine."[36] While "he was in spirit," his own consciousness was overtaken by the divine consciousness and overwhelmed by the love that removed all barriers between him and God and between him and humankind. This was the mark of "spiritual oneness with God." It was during such times that Jesus uttered things that he would not have done otherwise. It was in such life-transforming moments that the ministry of Jesus changed from a "purely national and Jewish one to universal."[37] It was here that, for the "first time," a new relationship between God and a human being was forged and expressed in the term Fatherhood of God, which was the "greatest spiritual possession of mankind" since the time of Jesus.[38] In all of this, Parekh made use of the conventional Hindu idea of spirituality, which strongly believed that human beings were meant for union with God. He claimed that to be a Christian meant to share this consciousness with Jesus, and that this spiritual relationship was the Kingdom of God. This experience was not exclusive to Christians, but available to all "whosoever have this consciousness."[39]

The divinity of Jesus, his status as the unique son of God, proved be a thorny issue for Indian interpreters, including Parekh. Resonating with the majority Hindu view, Parekh was reluctant to accord a divine status to Jesus. Sen, who showed intense warmth toward Jesus, regarded him only as "the Father's begotten Son, a child, a creature."[40] He was unequivocal about Jesus's status and role: "Christ never said, I am God. He never proclaimed himself the Infinite Father, the Unbegotten Eternal Spirit. He was simply the Logos, an emanation from the Creator; he was born and begotten. He came to do the Father's will, not his."[41] Parekh conceded that the father and son were believed to be one, but he argued that Jesus was "never looked upon as the Father" but always remained the son; in this way, he became the "Elder brother of men."[42] This sonship was deeply ingrained in the consciousness of Jesus—he felt himself to be the Son of God as no one before him had. What Jesus established, Parekh believed, was a filial relationship with God that was moral and spiritual and not related to the metaphysical theories that had emerged over the years. The moral union of the father and son is not particularly original to Parekh. For a generation of Indian Christians, A. J. Appasamy challenged both the Chalcedonian understanding of the metaphysical union of the father and the son and the advaitic union in a nondualist sense. Employing the bhakti tradition, he popularized the notion of the union as a moral and functional one.[43] Parekh's assessment was that it would have been the "rankest of blasphemies" to treat Jesus as God or his equal. The idea of the preexistence of Jesus and coexistence with the father were all "after-thoughts superimposed upon his filial consciousness."[44] In Jesus's view, God alone is Good, as exemplified by his answer to the young man: "Why dost thou call me good?" He suggested that Jesus would have even been content to be called rabbi.[45]

Jesus is portrayed as the person who reaffirms once again the idea of friendship with God, a notion that formed an integral part of Bhāgavata Dharma—the religion of personal theism—which Parekh put forward as a counternarrative to Advaita Vedanta, which most Indians favored at that time. One of the striking features of the Bhāgavata Dharma is the realization of the idea of warm and loving friendship between Krishna, an incarnation of God, and Arjuna, a humble but heroic disciple. Parekh found such kinds of friendship advocated by Jesus. In the Fourth Gospel, Jesus "delights" in calling his immediate disciples "friends." In this Gospel, Jesus taught them some of the "deepest truths of the spiritual life," including that the principal aim of the spiritual life was to work for the regeneration of human being and make them friends of God.[46] Parekh regarded this companionship as the proper "communion of saints."[47]

The Kingdom of God as a Spiritual Realm

The Kingdom that Jesus preached about was somewhat "akin to that of *moksha,* emancipation held by great Aryan teachers of India." This Kingdom was not about national deliverance but "conceived individualistically." Such a view was "altogether new as far as the Jews were concerned." For them, the overthrowing of the Roman empire was part of Kingdom thinking. But Jesus was "dead politically." Basically, he did not identify with the political aspiration of the Jews or associate himself with a materialistic idea of the Kingdom. He described the coming of the Kingdom not with portrayals of national heroes of the resistance, but with images of agriculture such as the "sowing of seed" and "growing of corn," which must have mystified his listeners. The Kingdom was "something deeply, profoundly, personal." In Parekh's view, Jesus's apolitical vision of the Kingdom was much more "original" than that of Socrates, Laozi, Mahavira, and the Buddha, because those thinkers lived in a much more sophisticated metaphysical and philosophical age, whereas the time of Jesus was marked by apocalyptic thinking.[48] It was from John that Jesus drew the spiritual character of the Kingdom. For both, repentance was the sole criteria for entrance. In such a Kingdom, the Jews had no privileged place of their own unless they had repented of their sins.

Parekh's aversion to a political Kingdom had to do with his portrayal of Jesus as an apolitical figure. Again, he painted essentially a spiritual rather than secular or political Jesus. Jesus's appeal is intensely personal rather than collective. Jesus did not entertain any idea of political messianism, which he regarded as a "positive evil, a temptation of the devil."[49] His sole aim was to work to redeem humankind from "pain and suffering."[50] Jesus never wanted to create a socialist or communist state. His appeal was made to individuals or to the "body of regenerated individuals who constituted the Kingdom of God."[51] Parekh claimed in his biography of Vallabhacharya that the "real history of the Hindus does not lie in the secular realm much as in the spiritual," and as such, the new Kingdom that Jesus envisioned was spiritual rather than secular.[52] He firmly advocated that Christianity should remain true to its earlier call to Mokṣa Dharma (a salvific and a spiritual religion) rather than the Constantinian Samāj Dharma (a social religion).

In Jesus's mind, the Kingdom meant loving obedience of human beings to the will of God. This, in Parekh's view, was the "original meaning of the idea of the Hindu Bhakti, which meant not only loving God but serving him." The goal of the Kingdom preached by Jesus was to be "perfect as your father in heaven is perfect." The Kingdom of God and the worldly kingdom were "incommensurate." One stood for all the glory, power, and honor of the world, whereas the other stood for genuine service to God. These were hostile to each other and they must ever

remain so. No other religious leader than Jesus had realized this division: when Jesus told his followers that no one could serve both mammon and God, he was demonstrating his "peculiar glory."[53]

But the Kingdom that Jesus spoke of lacked something: an impetus from India. Like the Hindu reformers of the time, Parekh did not hesitate to advocate the infusion of Hindu spirituality to vitalize the Kingdom, in a kind of reversal of the fulfillment theory advocated by some missionaries. It was not Christianity but Hinduism that complemented and purified the foreign faith. Parekh wrote triumphantly: it is "only when the spiritual heritage of the Hindu race, this ancient and most intensely religious race, is brought into the Kingdom of Christ that the kingdom will reveal its richest treasures of truth."[54]

Parekh also castigated Christians for identifying the Kingdom of God with the church. Such an identification was an "evil of the first magnitude."[55] It also provided those who were not Christians an example of "manifold imperialism."[56] By connecting the Kingdom with Christianity, the Western churches were falling into the very temptation that Jesus had avoided in his battles with Satan—seeking a worldly kingdom. This atrocious association by Christians was a sin that went against Jesus and made his death pointless.

Crucifixion as Self-Immolation for the Sake of Others

As with most Indian reformers, Parekh found the key events surrounding the life of Jesus unappealing. He attributed the death of Jesus to the loss of the sympathy of the crowd and a connivance by the Jewish religious authorities. The crowd that gathered in Jerusalem realized that he was not the Messiah of their expectations, and this view was encouraged by the Sadducees, the Pharisees, the Scribes, and even the Herodians. These Jewish leaders looked upon Jesus as a "disturber of peace" and judged him and his work as a "serious menace" to the security and the prosperity of the nation.[57] Jesus's triumphal entry into Jerusalem, the messianic fervor he inspired, the cleansing of the Temple, his teachings which ran "counter to popular beliefs and traditions," and his denunciatory remarks about the established religious leaders were sufficient reasons for the "forfeiture of Jesus' life."[58] The Zealots,

who would have been his natural allies, found him "spoiling their cause" because he simply excited the crowd without doing anything. Parekh thus took the conventional view that the "Jewish leaders, without perhaps a single exception, were united in condemning Jesus."[59] Interestingly, Parekh absolved the Roman authorities of any involvement in his death. He claimed that Pilate was wrongly blamed for it, and that Herod did not take Jesus seriously, instead simply mocking his royal claims.

Parekh's interpretation of Jesus's experience on the cross is truly unique and indigenous. It is buried in an article that he wrote nearly thirty years before he published his Jesus book, which sadly pursues a very traditional biblical exegesis.[60] In that article, he was more culturally adventurous than his mentor, Sen, who simply replicated the traditional belief about the cross event as one of ultimate self-sacrifice, a worthy example to be imitated by Indians for their self-regeneration: "I hold up to you the cross on which Jesus died. May his example so influence you, that you may be prepared to offer even your blood, if need be, for the regeneration of your country!"[61]

Rather than using redemptive images from the Hebrew Scriptures or from the church tradition, Parekh interpreted events on the cross from the perspective of Jainism and made Jesus into almost something of a Jain *Tirthankara*, a revealer of Jain spiritual truth. He believed that the Jain doctrine of *ahimsa* (nonkilling or nonviolence) was a preparation for accepting the work of Christ on the cross. Parekh wrote of the cross experience as the manifestation of *swahimsa*, which is the "immolation of the self for the good of others" which goes beyond *ahimsa*. On the cross, Jesus won the "greatest and final victory over Himself and the world and became a veritable Jina (i.e. conqueror, from which term we have the word Jaina)." According to the Jain tradition, a true teacher should pass through such "trials and sufferings" and prove "victorious over and through them." Jesus showed "remarkable forbearance and forgiveness" on the cross, which "confirmed his authority as the teacher."[62] He did not stop with words such as "love ye one another as I have loved you" or "there is no greater love than this, that a man lay down his life for his friends."[63] Instead he went beyond the "furtherest extent in teaching and practicing love, so much so that it became *swahimsa* in

him."[64] In this action of Jesus lay the "advance of the Christian religion over others." Parekh claimed that the cross would not have had any "value and significance" if Jesus had been "assured in his mind that he would rise on the third day." Such an assurance would have taken the "sting from the cross and made his crucifixion a thing of secondary importance."[65] His death, a "supreme tragedy," would have been "reduced to a poor comedy if he knew that he would rise again on the third day."[66] Parekh criticized the Christian church for not "mastering the higher lesson of *swahmisa*," and for instead envisioning this event as having imperial overtones.[67]

Parekh, who is quick to see discernible points of contact with other traditions, is unusually reticent about seeking parallels in history for the death of Jesus. He does not make any facile comparisons with previous martyrs and saints. There are elements of tragedy in the deaths of Socrates, Joan of Arc, and the martyrdom of Ali Hussein, but in his view they are of a "slender kind" and do not match the moral and physical agony that Jesus underwent. Their deaths "wholly" lacked a sacrificial element, or what Christians called the Passion. What made the death of Jesus special and different was that an insignificant man from a backward nation like Palestine, born and raised in a very poor household without any proper education and with a brief public ministry, was able to turn the cross, "a symbol of shame," into the "greatest symbol of self-sacrifice and even glory."[68] Parekh's verdict was that "this is a drama and a tragedy, the like of which cannot be found anywhere else in the history of the world."[69] The cross for him was the "greatest miracle performed by God himself on our Globe."[70]

Replicating the findings of the source criticism of the time, Parekh found the Resurrection accounts in the Gospels and in the Letters of Paul full of "many discrepancies and inconsistencies," and so determined that it was difficult to ascertain the full truth of the event. He attributed these disagreements to a time when the Gospel writers and Paul were living on "a plane of life where chronology and time were of no account." Parekh also questions the words of Jesus at Caesarea Philippi, when he told the disciples that he would be killed and rise again in three days. Parekh dismissed the third day as an "afterthought" and claimed that even if Jesus had predicted his Resurrection, he would have spoken in general terms. In contradicting the claim that John's Gospel was historically spurious, he declared the Resurrection accounts in the Fourth Gospel to be "nearer the truth than any other." Among the events related to the Resurrection that Parekh counted as historical in the Fourth Gospel were the manifestation of the risen Jesus to Mary and to the beloved disciple, the appearance of Jesus on the Sea of Tiberius, Jesus guiding the disciples to fill the nets with fishes and the interchange between Jesus and Peter, and the reestablishment of Peter. He did not doubt that Jesus appeared to the disciples individually and in groups more than once. Parekh believed these accounts to be true because John's Gospel was almost "auto-biographical."[71]

Parekh comes up with his own idea of the Resurrection, which had shades of Paul in it. While his guru, Sen, treated the Resurrection as a subjective, ongoing event and urged his audience not to search for the risen Christ in the earthly grave but in their own hearts, Parekh regarded it as an objective, physical, and historical event. He preferred to call the post-Easter manifestations of Jesus not part of the Resurrection but "appearances," that is, not subjective visions or hallucinations but "actual facts witnessed by the ordinary consciousness" of the disciples. These manifestations, for Parekh, were similar to Swami Narayana appearing to his devotees. His contention was that Jesus appeared not in the physical body in which he was raised but in the "spiritual" one, as Paul termed it, and which Hindus spoke of as *sukshma sharira,* or subtle body. The physical body, *sthula sharira,* "remained where it was." He found the "risen Christ more humane" than the flesh-and-blood historical Jesus. The risen Christ ate with his disciples and even made a banquet for them. He did not rebuke the disciples for their recent "grievous lack of faith" and did everything possible, in a "most gentle manner," to reestablish faith in him. He brought together severely disillusioned and shocked disciples and bound them together in a deep companionship. He showed concern about his disciples and entrusted them to Peter. Moreover, he gave his disciples his spirit, thus becoming their "soul, individually and collectively." This union of souls was the "new creation, the creation of the Divine Family, with God as the Father, Jesus as the Elder Brother," and all who were reborn in Jesus as sons and daughters of God. As he sharply put it, the "true resurrection of Jesus" had been "the greatest instrument in the rising of Humanity to what may well be called Divine Humanity."[72] One can detect here hints of Sen's idea of Christ as coming to establish the Divine Humanity at the end of the process of Creation.[73]

Carnivorous Christ, Planet-Unfriendly Palestinian

Parekh was not always captivated by Jesus, although he writes of him warmly. He found him to be a narrow villager from Palestine, unaware of other cultures and peoples, with a "mental horizon" according to Parekh, "confined entirely to the Jewish world."[74] He also seemed to share in the Jewish masculine mentality, as Parekh illustrates by referring to the significant omission of the role of the mother in the Parable of the Prodigal Son.

Jesus's narrow view meant that he was oblivious to the presence of the Greeks and completely ignored the Romans. Parekh wondered whether Jesus was even aware that the Romans were occupying his country. Even with the Greeks, some of whom wished to see him, there was no indication of him encountering them face to face. It was his disciples who conveyed the wishes of the Greeks. Indeed, Jesus not only avoided the Greeks but also spoke enigmatically about the Son of Man being lifted up and drawing all unto himself. Parekh also lamented that there was a total absence of any parables or aphorisms drawn by Jesus from the cultural world of the Greeks or the Romans.

Parekh found Jesus to be restricted to the "extremely narrow sphere of purely Jewish life and thought" and so "even more parochial" than the many of the Pharisees and Sadducees of his time.[75] Jesus's mission, too, was confined to Jews only, as shown by his words to the Canaanite woman. Parekh dismissed outright the idea that Jesus in his silent years had visited India and learned spiritual truth. His wisdom and understanding of life was instead drawn from a limited pool of human teachers, the scriptures of his nation, the oral traditions about the great Jewish figures like Daniel—and the lessons taught by Mother Nature. Unlike Paul, Jesus seemed to believe that nature was not groaning under the curse of God, but throbbing with life and God's love, which took care of even insignificant creatures such as sparrows or a blade of grass.

The lilies, birds, and flocks of sheep and goats were what provided materials for Jesus's parables. In these creatures, Jesus saw God's power "unalloyed with any human element."[76]

Parekh was not at all enamored by the miracles of Jesus. "The miracles, including even the resurrection, have very little meaning" for Indians, and "these do not add an iota to his moral and spiritual greatness in their eyes."[77] The highest teachers, in his view, preach salvation and any petition made to them for better health or wealth is nothing but a "favour."[78] Parekh referred to Hindu and Muslim healers performing miracles, and pointed out that these healers were not new prophets with a new message. Where Jesus differed from these healers was that for him, miracles were "secondary" and his message was of "primary importance."[79] Jesus's power to perform miracles was not limited to himself, but could be achieved by all human beings through the practice of yoga.

In spite of the rich nature-imagery in the teaching of Jesus, Parekh found a lack of reverence and respect for the ecosystem in the Gospel Jesus. He totally disapproved of and was appalled at his anti-ecological behavior. His criticism was based on the Jain understanding of *ahimsa*, which means not hurting or causing harm to any part of nature, as exemplified by the words of the founder of the faith, Mahavira: "You are that which you wish to harm." Parekh finds fault with Jesus for cursing and venting his anger on a tree. This incident, in his view, showed Jesus as not only "truly human," but also "unreasonable and unnecessarily petulant."[80] As a Jain who believed that not only animals but even trees had life, Parekh found this action by a person who was distinctly more than a prophet to be not "proper." Jesus's meat-eating habit also did not endear him to Parekh. To "many earnest Jains," that Jesus gave fish to the people and took both fish and meat himself posed a "real difficulty in their acceptance of him as the perfect Teacher."[81] He was also not happy about the action of Jesus that resulted in the drowning of pigs in the lake. This deed was proof that Jesus did not raise "himself above the moral standards of his time."[82] And Parekh believed the miraculous catch at the Lake of Gennesaret, where so many fishes were unnecessarily killed, was a "breach of the law of *ahimsa*."[83] Although the miracle demonstrated the power of Jesus over nature, such a miracle would not "commend itself to those who consider all life sacred."[84] These actions of Jesus, in Parekh's view, indicated his lack of compassion for the well-being of all creatures and his failure to recognize the sacredness of all life. He attributed Jesus's anti-nature and meat-eating stance to his not being in "advance of his time."[85] His regret was that Jesus, or for that matter Christianity, had failed to address the sacredness of the created order. In contrast, Swami Naryana had a "deep love for nature" and was "sensitive to all the beauties of nature." Even the wild roars of panthers and lions "evoked in him only a note of appreciation."[86] Obviously, the Westernized and meat-eating Christian community did not appeal to Parekh's Jainist beliefs, which held in reverence every form of life, including animals and plants.

A Jain Follower Acknowledges Jesus

Parekh had no qualms in publicly acknowledging the exceptional and matchless character of Jesus. While Varma, Chowdhuri, and even Gandhi questioned the claim advanced by missionaries that the superior ethics of Jesus would help to advance the national life, Parekh was actually highlighting the spiritual wealth that Jesus could bring to India. In his view, the teaching of Jesus went further than that of the Jains and the Buddhists. The difference lay in Jesus's "active love" for all, even for one's enemies. The Buddhists propounded the idea of *maitri*, compassion, but maitri could not be compared to Christian love (*agape*). Commenting on Jesus's teaching on alms-giving, fasting, and prayer, Parekh made it clear that "Here Jesus goes certainly beyond both Mahavira and Buddha, who are the only two among the great teachers of the world with whom he can be compared."[87] He also contended that there was no match for the parables of Jesus. Although the Hindu mind had been inundated with wise sayings and aphorisms, it had created few parables that had caught the imagination of the world and become "universal." Hindu literature was rich in *drishtants*, but these illustrations were not the same as the parables; in particular, they lacked the "outstanding merit as to rivet the attention" of readers.[88]

In Parekh's evaluation, Jesus exceeds in another respect: "No other prophet or teacher, has turned so instinctively to the poor and the despised, the outcaste and the sinner, as he, and this constitutes the uniqueness of his life and work." The Jesus of Parekh had "instinctive and deep sympathy for the poor and profound knowledge of their difficulties, their sorrows and joys," which were only made possible because of his "personal experience."[89] The "lasting glory of Jesus" was to contrast poverty and wealth in sharp terms, and, in doing so, he alone among the prophets of the world stirred the conscience of humankind, leading to the rise of Christian socialism and Christian communism. Parekh was quick to add that Jesus never had the intention of establishing a socialist state. His appeal was spiritual and restricted to individuals. According to Parekh, "much of the romance of his life and work lies in this."[90]

Parekh concedes that although God has been worshipped in India in different forms, "it has fallen to the lot of Jesus alone to manifest in his life and teach and engraft on the others the relationship with God as the Father." He hails Jesus as the "Exemplar" and also the "Encrafter of this relationship." So many prophets and messengers had risen before Jesus, but "no one had entered into such loving and intimate personal relationship with God as Jesus did." Even Zoroaster, who thought of God as a friend, limited this experience to "loftiest moments only." What Parekh wrote about the death of Jesus had the "proportions of a world-tragedy" and "proved itself in course of time to be the greatest moral and spiritual dynamic of history."[91]

Parekh's assessment of Jesus's significance is unlike that offered by even the most ardent Hindu admirers of Jesus. In this respect, his approval and admiration for Christ stands in contrast to those ethical evaluations of Jesus offered by the Indian reformers. For while Vivekananda, Radhakrishnan, and Gandhi endorsed his greatness, they cautiously stayed clear of stressing his unmatched moral merit. The most Gandhi could say was that "his death on the cross was a great example to the world, but that there was anything like a mysterious or miraculous virtue in it, my heart could not accept."[92]

Unlike Varma and Chowdhuri, who perceived Jesus as an intruder and an irritant, Parekh saw him as an ideal example. He did not view Jesus as an alien who had come to dominate India in the garb of a political religious conqueror, but as a "prophet of God of the highest order, who with his unique ethical teaching and still more unique life of love and self-sacrifice became an if not the exemplar of life for all."[93] It was Parekh's understanding of Hindu swadharmagraha that enabled him to accommodate Jesus and other prophets not as prophets of foreign religion but as "God's own messengers."[94] What he objected to was the Christ that was being propagated in the mission field and the one who was identified with Christendom.

Parekh's Work in a Larger Context

Parekh's Jesus book came out in 1953, the same year as the New Quest for Jesus was launched in the West. His book was a reaffirmation of the Old Quest, missing completely the No Quest phase spearheaded by Rudolf Bultmann, which emphasized not the historical Jesus but the kerygmatic Christ. Parekh, an avid reader and follower of Western theology, showed no sign of being aware of this debate. One can, however, see hints of Albert Schweitzer's thinking in Parekh's work. Like Schweitzer, Parekh argued for an apocalyptic Jesus who expected God to bring the world to an imminent end. Parekh ticked off those Western theologians who "explained away" the apocalyptic content, which for him was the core of the teachings of Jesus. In Parekh's retelling, Jesus was convinced that the end was near and that a "new world or new heaven or new earth" was about to be ushered in. The famines, earthquakes, and wars that Jesus spoke of were signs of the coming disaster and the new dawn.

Parekh did not mindlessly repeat Schweitzer's ideas. He differed from the German in two ways. First, instead of imagining the redeemer being the Son of Man, Parekh expected kingly warrior-figures such as Rama or Krishna to redeem the world on behalf of God. (Jesus, too, was portrayed as such a warrior in the line of King David.) The second difference relates to when the expected Son of Man does not materialize. Schweitzer's Jesus realized that he had to take on the role of the suffering servant that Isaiah spoke of, and anticipated that his death on the cross would compel God to intervene, whereas Parekh's Jesus voluntarily offered himself to be sacrificed in order to jolt God into a response. On the delayed apocalyptic end, Parekh explained that the course of history was long, God was not in a hurry, and it would take millions of years to fulfill God's purpose. Here, Parekh found recourse in the Bhagavad Gita. The Gita gives "hope that just when things look their darkest, the dawn is not far off. God's special providence is most active when there is greatest need for it."[95]

As with Schweitzer, so for Parekh, the everlasting power of Jesus was not found solely in the historical man from Galilee but also in the spiritual Jesus for whom the believers acquire a mysterious affection. Schweitzer wrote: "The truth is, it is not Jesus as historically known, but Jesus as spiritually arisen within men, who is significant for our time and can help it. Not the historical Jesus, but the spirit which goes forth from Him and in the spirits of men strives for new influence and rule, is that which overcomes the world."[96] Parekh echoed this view, though he dressed his highly spiritual Jesus in saffron robes. While Schweitzer was moving in what Sen contemptuously called "eternally . . . your narrow groove," Parekh was trying to place Jesus within the assembly of the Eastern masters.

Parekh is credited with producing the last profile of the historical Jesus in the mold of the Old Quest before the dawn of the New Quest. If the first attempt at a historical Jesus in this period was by a Hindu, Raja Rammohun Roy, the last was by a Jain. Later attempts at portraying the historical Jesus, especially by Indian Christians, were renowned for their crisp summaries of various Christologies rather than for a serious search for the person and historical context of Jesus. M. M. Thomas's *The Acknowledged Christ of the Indian Renaissance* and Michael Amaladoss's *The Asian Jesus* are examples of this confessional approach.[97] These colonial projects endeavor to unearth the hidden and unacknowledged Jesus in both classical and contemporary Hinduism. The authors' imperial intentions are clear: they start from the premise that indigenous cultural resources belong not to the local people but to Christ. It was the colonizing imagination of Paul, who propagated a vision of the entire world being created through Christ and for him, that provided these writers with their theological rationale. Indians, and other peoples of Asia, had to wait another quarter century for a proper account of the historical Jesus, Shūsaku Endō's *A Life of Jesus*, which is discussed in detail in Chapter 9.[98]

Parekh's book came out at a time when the newly independent Indian Republic was engaged in five-year plans involving development, rapid industrialization, and social upliftment of the people. It was also the time of Nehruvian socialism, which, among other things, advocated the ideals of collective action, public ownership, and sustainable development. Amid these communal and political changes, Parekh's Jesus looked like an unworldly sage, uninterested in the specific needs of the nation. His Jesus does not move among and suffer for the people; instead this one-dimensional spiritualized Jesus was concerned only with individual salvation and looked remote and detached. When the consciousness of the nation was gripped by the poverty of the millions, the God-consciousness of Parekh's Jesus appeared hollow, a utopian ideal, and worse, uncaring.

Parekh had the habit of extolling the virtues of Jesus while simultaneously undermining them. He called the Sermon on the Mount the "bhakti-sutra epitomizing gospel of devotion and love of the highest order," while at the same time declaring it to be unpractical and paradoxical.[99] What was attractive about the Sermon on the Mount was its world-renouncing aspect, its emphasis on selflessness, and its stress on disinterested love, or as Parekh called it, *nishkama* love. And although Parekh praised Jesus's active love, his austere lifestyle, and his dislike of fame and honor, he weakened Jesus's significance by claiming that the ethical precepts found in the Sermon on the Mount were not exceptionally new. Not only did they belong to the "common stock of the world's spiritual wisdom"; they also had already been explicated by Mahavira and the Buddha, as well as Buddhist and Jain monks, and in his view nuns were nearer than others in practicing the teachings of Jesus.[100] He even questioned whether the sermon was originally delivered by Jesus, since he felt that Jesus would not have presented himself as another lawgiver in the mold of Moses. The discrepancies among the Gospel accounts led him to believe that the Sermon on the Mount was a "jumble of precepts given at different times and to different groups."[101] The nature of the Sermon leads Parekh to wonder, too, whether Jesus could have given these teachings "indiscriminately to all."[102] He felt they would have been wasted on the Jews—like throwing pearls before the swine.

Unlike the Hindu reformers featured in this volume, who used the Vedanta as the universal religion that subsumed all other faiths, Parekh offered bhakti as the universal faith. He wrote in a testimonial tone: "Here is the universal religion of *bhakti* whose centre is Christ, which draws on the experience of great *bhaktas* of many traditions, to which I myself can testify by experience." He replaced one Hindu idea with another as the example by which to judge all religions. He wrote:

> As I see it, all religions which believe in God can be counted as *Bhāgavata dharma*. For if we hold that whoever believes in Bhagavān and worship him is a Bhāgavat, we can surely say with conviction that all religions which believe in God are merely different forms of one *Bhāgavata dharma*. In this way, I include in it Christianity, Judaism, Islam, Zoroastrianism and all the religions which believe one God.[103]

Parekh was indifferent to the Advaita of Shankara, whose abstract and impersonal ideas were espoused by Swami Vivekananda and later by Radhakrishnan. He dismissed the Vedanta of the Hindu reformers as the "religious nationalism of the Hindus" that had intensified the "religious, racial and national pride of the Aryan people of this land"— prescient words for Modi's India.[104]

Parekh's writings have conspicuous flaws of theological and political incorrectness. He could not rise above the habitual anti-Semitism entrenched in the writings of the Hindu reformers. His description of the Jews as a people of "severe mental strain" is illustrative of his thinking. He could also be accused of "Occidentalism," or stereotyping the West. His writings are peppered with prejudices about and unflattering images of Western society, including his claim that the Aryans of the West would not be able to realize bhakti, the highest form of Hinduism, because they were "too intellectual and colour conscious" and lacked humility, the essence of bhakti.[105] In the context of the muscular Christianity expounded by the missionaries, the affirmation of Indian spiritual genius, even if this assertion led to nauseatingly overinflated claims for the indigenous culture, is understandable and even excusable. But once this self-affirmation has been established, to continue to rehearse it excessively is to risk turning it into a slogan of neo-nationalism and triumphalism. At times Parekh comes across like the character in the BBC comedy *Goodness, Gracious Me,* who claims every idea and every invention as Indian. He even discerned personal bhakti in the Gathas of Zoroaster (Gospel of Zoroaster), acknowledging at the same time that the Gathas were the "earliest and one of the noblest revelations granted to man by God." His intention of collapsing everything into Hinduism is evident when he classifies the Gathas as the "Fifth Veda" and the "Crown of Vedas."[106]

Although Parekh greatly admired Sen, he did not uncritically appropriate his master's constructions of Jesus. Parekh found his work "most inconsistent" with no "coherent system of thought."[107] He also accused Sen of yielding "too much ground to pantheism."[108] In Parekh's view, his "heart was always in advance of his head," and he was "never at his best in philosophic speculation."[109] Parekh also found that his erroneous understanding of the doctrine of the Trinity was due to remnants of Unitarianism that colored his thinking.

Finally, apart from a brief foray into the traditions of Jainism, Parekh's portrayal of Jesus was lackluster. Whereas Sen made Jesus an oriental and Asiatic, all Parekh could do was to perceive him as Son of Man—a title, Parekh claimed, that Jesus intentionally chose in order to identify himself with the ideas of Ezekiel and Daniel. Parekh could not emulate Sen's enthusiastic tone and flamboyant language. While Sen could write lyrically of Jesus as "My Christ, my sweet Christ, the brightest jewel of my heart, the necklace of my soul, for twenty years have I cherished him in this my miserable heart," Parekh could come up with only the now-clichéd description of Jesus as a "prophet, priest, poet of the simple and the little, the meek and the humble, the forlorn and the despised."[110] Sen taught directly, devotionally, emotionally, and enthusiastically about Jesus. Although Parekh claimed that he was moved by Jesus's "marvellous charm," he couldn't match such vivid language as Sen's "sweet angel of the East" nor his guru's descriptive imagery.[111] Unlike Sen, there is a reluctance to be totally gripped by Jesus, whom Parekh admired enormously. Had he written the book soon after his baptism, when he was still in awe of Jesus without his subsequent bitter encounters with the Indian church—which he found not only "positively anti-national but anti-Hindu"—Parekh almost certainly would have come up with a more intimate Jesus. As it was, while Sen made Jesus local and particular, almost like the person next door, in Parekh's construal Jesus remained undemonstrative and detached. Yet Parekh's Jesus was still a person who achieved the highest divine consciousness and a teacher who instilled such high spiritual ideals in others—a Jesus whose teachings left the individual feeling warm and spiritually exhilarated rather than socially discomforted and challenged.

7

An Upanishadic Mystic

When one mentions the name Sarvepalli Radhakrishnan (1885–1975), a hyphenated term invariably comes to mind: statesman-philosopher. Radhakrishnan was one of the most influential Hindu thinkers, dominating twentieth-century Indian religious discourse. He sought to portray, protect, and promote Hinduism—which he variously termed Vedanta, the religion of the spirit, and *santana dharma* (eternal religion)—and to turn a "very complex" tradition into a "subtly unified mass of religious thought and realization."[1] In his re-visioning, Hinduism became an evolving and all absorbing democratic faith that soaked up everything from magic to animism, and that embodied the "principle of liberty, equality, and fraternity."[2] More pertinently, he reframed Hinduism as a "comprehensive charity instead of a fanatic faith."[3]

Radhakrishnan's faith in Hinduism was "aroused by the enterprise and eloquence of Swami Vivekananda," and his rise to prominence began as a graduate student, when in his master's thesis he challenged that the Vedanta had no ethical value.[4] The rest of his career, especially his prodigious writings, his intimate acquaintance with both Western and Eastern philosophical and religious traditions, his appointment to various prestigious chairs both in India and England, and his subsequent elevation to the presidency of the Republic of India, are all well recorded and analyzed elsewhere, so need not detain us here.[5]

Radhakrishnan never worked directly or at length on the subject of Jesus, but in his various writings he did touch on the topic, leaving an impressive iconoclastic portrayal that offered a counternarrative to those pictures of Jesus presented by missionaries in colonial India.

Like most of the Hindu reformers studied here, it was "the Challenge of Christian critics" that, Radhakrishnan later recalled, "impelled" him "to make a study of Hinduism and find out what is living and what is dead in it."[6] He was trained in a scholarly tradition that encouraged him to conceal any sentimentality, nevertheless he reminisced in his auto-biographical essays that his pride as a Hindu had been "deeply hurt by the treatment accorded to Hinduism in missionary institutions."[7] Their mischaracterization of Hinduism profoundly "disturbed" the "tradi-tional props on which I leaned."[8] What "annoyed" him most was that Christian missionaries who called themselves truly religious "could treat as subjects for derision doctrines others held in deepest rever-ence."[9] He was charitable enough to dismiss this "unfortunate practice" as having "little support in the teaching or example of Jesus," attrib-uting this disrespectful attitude instead to Jesus's later followers.[10]

Placing the Palestinian in a Non-Jewish Palestine

For Radhakrishnan, what was attractive about Jesus, more than his eth-ical precepts or his austere living, was his ability to awaken an aware-ness of the divine in oneself. He routinely cites two sayings of Jesus—the "Kingdom of Heaven is within you," and "Be ye therefore perfect as your heavenly father is also perfect"—as pointing not only to the divine po-tential hidden in everyone, but also to the possibility of realizing the divine within oneself, an idea unacceptable to Christians.

Like liberal Christian theologians of the time, he distinguished between the "pure and simple teaching of Jesus" and current Western Christianity.[11] The former, according to him, was about "love and sym-pathy, tolerance and inwardness," whereas the latter was about "definite creeds and absolutist dogmatism, with its consequence of intolerance, exclusiveness and confusion of piety with patriotism."[12] He reprimanded the ecclesiastical authorities for creating a dogmatic and institutional edifice around Jesus: "Though Jesus paid little attention to organization, elaborate ecclesiastical structures have emerged from his teaching."[13] Jesus, in his view, gave us a "simple code" but subsequent doctrinal development had "obscured the divine simplicity of Jesus' personality."[14] Jesus also detested dogma and never encouraged metaphysical and theological complications—complications that led to "a good deal of casuistry, intolerance, and obscurantism."[15] What Jesus asked for instead was a "broken and contrite heart."[16]

Unlike the reformer Keshub Chunder Sen, who was prone to emotional outbursts about Jesus, Radhakrishnan envisaged Jesus in less lyrical terms. He saw him as a mixed character composed of two religious traditions, Jewish and Eastern, standing side by side, neither controlling the other. In Jesus, Radhakrishnan found messianism and exclusivism from the Jewish side, as well as universalism and passivism, which he credited as coming from the Eastern tradition. He claimed that, except for the monotheistic ideal of Jesus, his disapproval of idolatry, and his affirmation of the superiority of the Mosaic revelation, "all other elements of his system [were] those found in Hindu thought."[17]

In contrast to Varma and Chowdhuri, who were dismissive of the historical Jesus, Radhakrishnan granted his existence. Although in his spiritual re-visioning the historicity of Jesus was not particularly important, he explained, "For me, the person of Jesus is a historical fact. Christ is not a datum of history, but a judgement of history."[18] On the human Jesus, he wrote: "The life of Jesus would have no meaning for us, if he had any nonhuman elements which enabled him to reach perfection."[19] This human Jesus was inhibited by the ethos of his time: "Jesus in a number of his views, was restricted by the knowledge and outlook of his age and nation."[20] An example was his belief in demons. Radhakrishnan differentiated between the historical person Jesus and Christ. Reflecting the dialectical theology of the time, Radhakrishnan argued that this Christ was "not to be equated with the historic Jesus" and that the "manifestation of the Word in history is not limited to Jesus." Moreover, salvation is mediated through the eternal Christ and should not be "confused with the historic Jesus." Radhakrishnan summoned Kierkegaard to support his case: "History has nothing whatever to do with Christ."[21] Radhakrishnan's attitude toward the historical Jesus was similar to his approach to the historical Krishna. Although he concedes that there is "ample evidence in favour of the historicity of Krishna," he explains that "so far as the teaching of the *Bhagavadgita* is concerned, it is immaterial whether Krishna, the teacher, is a historical individual or not."[22]

Radhakrishnan's premise was that the historical Jesus did not emerge as a finished product nor did he come with a scripted role. His understanding of himself, his role in life, evolved gradually. Radhakrishnan was fond of quoting phrases such as he "grew in wisdom," "learned obedience by things which he suffered," and was made "perfect through sufferings" to underline the gradual physical and spiritual growth of Jesus. It was "through inner doubts and discords, temptations and battles" that Jesus advanced in "wisdom and stature."[23] This growth involved a move from being a staunch nationalist to becoming a broader universalist. Jesus was initially "fettered" by his Jewish upbringing and heritage and was "not able to shake himself free from the Jewish past."[24] Jesus had grown up on the pronouncements of the Hebrew prophets and believed that his people had departed from the divine purpose for which they were called, and so were in need of repentance. His first public act was to join John the Baptist in an exercise of national repentance and affirmation of faith in the coming of the Kingdom. The confirmation of the national significance of his work is found in his words to the Canaanite Woman—"It isn't right to take food away from children and feed it to dogs" (Matthew 15.26)—and in the injunctions to the disciples who were forbidden to go the Gentiles or to the Samaritans, and whom he instead urged to go "to the lost sheep of the house of Israel." That this idea of the restoration of the Kingdom to the Jews was ingrained in his followers was evident in their question to the risen Jesus: "Lord, is it at this time You are restoring the kingdom to Israel?" (Acts 1.6). But Radhakrishnan reckoned that the noblest achievement of Jesus was to escape from his "ancestral past" and to offer through his life and teaching the fundamentals of a spiritual religion that transcended Palestinianism. This was possible because, like the Indian rishis, Jesus had achieved self-realization. What Jesus underwent was not the usual process of penitence or regret but a complete change of mind and heart, the "displacement of ignorance, avidyā, by knowledge, vidyā."[25] From then on, his teachings sprang from this "transfigured consciousness" and the indwelling presence of God. This transformation led to "a new way of thinking, feeling and acting. It is a rebirth. Unless a man is born anew, he cannot see the Kingdom of God."[26] It was his comprehension of a "higher reality" that enabled Jesus to claim that his teachings were not his, but those of God who had sent him (John 7.16–18).

Another consequence of Jesus's awakening was his changed understanding of the Kingdom of God. While his contemporaries were expecting a territorial, political kingdom to come with "flaming lightning and with the appearance of the Son of Man," the newly reborn Jesus realized that the Kingdom was within oneself. Before the original Christian teaching became "organized and externalized," the Kingdom had been about "awakening from sleep through the light shed by the inner wisdom."[27] Jesus was an awakened one, like the Buddha, who taught others the way of awakening. It was this mystical experience of realizing God within himself that had enabled him to set aside "legalistic encumbrances" and sum up what was required of human beings in two old commandments: love thy God and love thy neighbor.[28] This mystic conception of the Kingdom, in Radhakrishnan's judgment, is an Indian idea, whereas the notion of a messianic Kingdom has its origin in the Palestinian tradition. He cites Rudolph Otto to strengthen his argument: "Jesus' preaching of the kingdom contains elements which are certainly not of Palestinian origin, but point definitely to connections with the Aryan and Iranian East."[29]

Radhakrishnan pictures the life of Jesus as a struggle between his inherited traditional Jewish views and the new advanced spiritual outlook into which he was awakening. In this progression, his teaching was "historically continuous with Judaism," and he was helped "considerably by his religious environment, which included Indian influences."[30] Radhakrishnan thinks that the teachings of Jesus on the Kingdom of God, eternal life, austerity, and life hereafter go beyond the Jewish tradition and "approximate to Hindu and Buddhist thought."[31] The whole complex of nationalist ideas with which Jesus had grown up—including belief in a monotheistic creed, the notion of a chosen people, a determination to aggressively defend against foreigners, and a belief in a future judgment that would culminate in a series of cataclysmic events—gave way to a cluster of ideas about the Son of Man who came not to be served but to serve, the suffering servant willing to die for others, the illusory nature of the earthly kingdom, and an emphasis on love and nonresistance. This change of perspective was attributed to the influence of "the non-Jewish currents of thought and aspiration which prevailed in his circle during his time." The thinking of Jesus must have been "shaped in the atmosphere where East and West, mystical experience and intellectual speculation, acted and reacted on each other."[32]

In Radhakrishnan's portrayal, Jesus broadened Jewish conceptions and at times even transgressed them. His universal outlook and his approach of nonresistance came into "conflict with the exclusiveness and militarism of his ancestors."[33] He was helped by the religious environment, which included Indian influences via the Essenes and the Book of Enoch. In his basic teachings about the Kingdom, renunciation, and everlasting future life, Jesus departed from traditional Jewish tenets and owed a "great deal to religious insights of the East which permeated the Jewish world in the centuries before Jesus."[34]

Unlike the Western scholarship of the time that was obsessed with the Christ of Faith, and that effectively removed Jesus from his environment, Radhakrishnan was insistent that the life and teachings of Jesus should be seen against a wider theological and cultural setting, rather than as exclusively coming from a Jewish or Greek background. He stated very boldly that the "whole life and teaching of Jesus is so distinctive that it cannot be regarded as a natural development of Jewish and Greek ideas."[35] This environment, according to Radhakrishnan, included not only Jewish, Greek, and Roman ideas, but also Buddhist and Indo-Iranian thinking. There is, of course, historical proof that Buddhism was present in Palestine a full two centuries before the birth of Christianity. Radhakrishnan claims that various ethno-religious groups of the Middle East, such as the Essenes, the Mandeans, and the Nazarenes, were "filled with its spirit." According to Radhakrishnan, John the Baptist was an Essene and his influence could be seen in Jesus's teachings; in particular Jesus's teaching about nonresistance to evil could be traced to Buddhism via the Essenes. Even Jesus's preferred title for himself, Son of Man, could have come from the Book of Enoch, which was written several centuries before the advent of Christianity and was known to the nascent Jesus movement. Based on the work of Otto, Radhakrishnan claims that of all the Christological titles, the title Son of Man, as envisaged by Enoch, could be traced to "the Aryan East" and not to any Jewish sources. Otto argues that the conflation of the Son of God who is also the Son of Man is "certainly not from Israel." Such a human being, who deals with the world and acts as a "subordinate" to an "aboriginal deity of high antiquity," is found only "among the Aryans."[36] While Otto alleges that Enoch's primitive deity is quite Indian, Radhakrishnan goes further and boldly states that the attributes of Enoch's God are found in the Upanishads. When Jesus saw himself as the Son of Man and Son of God, it was a mere continuation of an ancient Hindu tradition. Radhakrishnan's concern is to establish that the teachings of Jesus, as well as his character and personality, were not solely Jewish, as is claimed by Christian scholars, but had a broader hermeneutical base.

To illustrate further the wider provenance for Jesus, Radhakrishnan draws attention to matching events and resemblances in the lives of Buddha, Krishna, Zoroaster, and Jesus. These include the killing of babies at the birth of Krishna and Jesus. In the Indian version, at the time of Krishna's birth, Kamsa murders all his sister's children except the last one, much as Herod in the biblical story orders a massacre of children. The temptations of Jesus, too, have their matching stories in various Eastern traditions—the temptation of Naciketas by Yama, the king of death; the temptation of Buddha by Mara; and the temptation of Zarathustra by Ahriman. The words of Ahriman to Zarathustra—"if you turn away from Ahura-Mazda you shall reign over the world for a thousand years"—presage the words of Satan, who promised Jesus power over all earthly kingdoms. (I will discuss the Jesus-Buddha parallels later.)

To reinforce his point about the non-Jewish provenance of Jesus, Radhakrishnan places Jesus's teachings within a larger Asiatic context. For instance, Jesus's Parable of the Sower was taken from Buddhism. His renunciation of home and family, Radhakrishnan reckons, "is in the best tradition of India."[37] And the moral teachings of Jesus, characterized by austere detachment and rejection of worldly pleasures, had been long anticipated in the Upanishads and by the Buddha. Radhakrishnan brings in T. W. Rhys Davids, who is known as the Max Müller of Buddhism, to support his claim:

> It is not too much to say that almost the whole of the moral teaching of the Gospels, as distinct from the dogmatic teaching, will be found in Buddhist writings several centuries older than the Gospels. The moral doctrines collected together in the Sermon on the Mount . . . are found in the Pitakas.[38]

Both the Gospels and Buddhist writings contain the "same exhortations to boundless and indiscriminate giving, the same hatred of pretence, the same regard paid to the spirit above the letter of the law, the same importance attached to purity, humility, meekness, gentleness, truth and love."[39]

Similarly, there is a non-Jewish emphasis in Jesus's teaching on rebirth. The "pathway to re-birth," Radhakrishnan claimed, was to live a life of "self-control bordering on asceticism." As far as the Jewish tradition is concerned, "there is little or nothing in it of an ascetic character."[40] Besides, there was no practice of Jewish monks or nuns living detached from the world. Radhakrishnan is of the view that the "new current of other worldliness" found in Jesus, John the Baptist, and Paul could not be "accounted for by their Jewish background."[41]

Radhakrishnan's Jesus does not provide any account of the future life. He dismisses any references to an afterlife mentioned in the Parables of the Sheep and the Goats and of Dives and Lazarus as being influenced by the thinking of the time, when people believed in heaven and hell. Furthermore, Jesus did not entertain the idea of a long gap between death and judgment: Dives and Lazarus received their punishment and reward instantaneously. Jesus's words to the thief that "Today shalt thou be with me in paradise" further reinforce the idea of immediate recompense.

Radhakrishnan is not sure where to place Jesus in his deconstructed karma theory—a contentious Hindu doctrine that, in Radhakrishnan's view, was mistakenly understood as a mystical reprisal or chastisement.

In Radhakrishnan's revisionist reading, "karma is a condition not a destiny," and it is "an expression of God's will and purpose."[42] His Jesus seems to have an ambiguous attitude toward karma. On the one hand, Jesus appears to approve the Hindu law of karma. When he told the paralytic "Courage my son, your sins are forgiven," he meant that his suffering was due to past sins. Similarly, the words of Jesus to the sick man, "sin no more, lest a worse thing come unto thee," tend to indicate that Jesus had the law of karma in mind.[43] On the other hand, Radhakrishnan's Jesus gives the impression that he does not endorse the idea of reward and punishment. This is evident in his statement, "I tell you nay. He maketh his sun to rise on the evil and on the good and sendeth rain on the just and on the unjust." Radhakrishnan then leaves his readers with a puzzling sentence: "In this world there are no rewards and punishments but only consequences."[44]

Jesus: The Upanishadic Second Adam

Like all Hindu reformers, Radhakrishnan was reluctant to accept Jesus as the sole and single expression of God's revelation. In several of his writings, he made the point that out of "loyalty and devotion" Christians might claim that Jesus was the "perfect and complete" revelation, but they should not raise objections if the followers of Confucius or the Buddha "set up similar claims for their heroes."[45] For him, Jesus was, at his best, "the first born among many brethren" and the "second Adam." He treated the uniqueness claimed for Jesus as a "pious delusion" and indicated that in the history of Hinduism there were "several instances of souls who were saved, who had the experience of the oneness of 'I and my father.'"[46]

Radhakrishnan claims that the "simple story of the life and activity of Jesus is transformed into an epiphany of a heavenly being who had descended to earth and concealed himself in robes of flesh."[47] The idea of uniqueness and the one and only son of God was due to the Christian church inheriting the Semitic creed of the "jealous God" and transferring it to Christ as "the only begotten son of God, . . . [who] could not brook any rival near the throne."[48] Jesus comes across to him as a "typical Eastern Seer" who exhibited "the characteristics of intuitive realization," "non-dogmatic toleration," "insistence on non-aggressive virtues," and "universalist ethics."[49]

Finding untenable the claim of the Christians that salvation is impossible without the mediation of Jesus, Radhakrishnan cites the example of several saintly figures, including Abraham, who showed the way before the advent of Jesus. In Hinduism, every guru is a savior and at the most Jesus stands within that tradition. In some systems, like Saiva Siddhanta, God uses gurus as agents who appear out of the fullness of God's grace to help human beings to an upward ascent, a role Jesus fits perfectly. Jesus's own testimony, the philosophical truths that he preached, and the religious experience he had "demand that he should be brought into line with other great saints of God, who have not left themselves without any witness in any clime or age."[50]

The uniqueness of the historical Jesus lay in the manner in which he "gave form and substance to the dreams which had haunted his compatriots for generations, but in this he was greatly influenced by the non-Jewish currents of thought and aspiration which prevailed in his circle during his time."[51] At the time of Jesus, there was a cluster of ideas and conflicting expectations of the Messiah, some with royal overtones. Jesus did not envisage himself as one of these triumphant and all-conquering heroes who were part of God's plan to establish the Kingdom of God in history. What differentiated him was his inner realization that he must choose the will of his Father and not his own private preferences. True, Jesus had a "consciousness of mission" and thought of himself as the "inaugurator of the new kingdom" and an instrument of God's "victorious power," but these assumptions led him to choose the demanding tradition of the Son of Man, who must suffer and be delivered up into human hands to be put to death, rather than the role of enthroned Son of God.[52] Jesus must have gone through what countless Indian seers must have also endured: "an inner intuitive vision of God," when one "achieves absolute freedom and escapes from the blind servitude to ordinary experience. It is a subtle interwovenness with the realities of the spiritual world."[53] It is when one is tested that the "depths of life are revealed." Jesus's action was akin to the Hindu idea of *tapas*—a voluntary sacrifice undertaken by those who are still on the "path to perfection for the sake of self-development or welfare of the world."[54]

Radhakrishnan concedes that the "intercessory and expiative power of suffering" is common to all religions. In Judaism itself there are the examples of Moses, David, Jonah, and the Maccabean martyrs willing to give up their lives. What differentiates the death of Jesus is his inner realization that he is the "redemptive suffering servant of God." Radhakrishnan writes: "In the light of his fate, this conception seemed inwardly akin to him."[55] Radhakrishnan also advances the notion that faith in the high destiny of the human soul, which Jesus sought, is not to be found in the religions of Palestine, Greece, and Rome except in the mystic cults: "The mind of Jesus and his immediate followers on this question must have been shaped in the atmosphere where East and West, mystical experience and intellectual speculation, acted and reacted on each other."[56]

What was so special about Jesus was his asking us to bring about an inner regeneration, a "rebirth, the second birth, to become a new man."[57] Jesus was one of those who realized his latent possibilities, who was reborn to serve as an example and guide to others. In Radhakrishnan's reckoning, Jesus was implicitly replicating the central teachings of Hinduism and Buddhism. In this respect, Jesus was different from John the Baptist, who spoke of salvation through moral deeds and told us "what to *do* and not what to *be*." John the Baptist signified external piety and urged people to become better, whereas Jesus was a "man of inner understanding" who emphasized inward conversion and invited people to "become different, new."[58] John was still a man born of a woman who had not experienced rebirth. That is why the least in the Kingdom is greater than he, whereas Jesus was one who was awakened, had a second birth, and taught others the way of awakening. For Radhakrishnan, Jesus was one of those reborn, rare, and precious souls who had evolved beyond the constraints of ego and individuality into a "large impersonality," becoming, in the process, one of the "self-sacrificing exemplars." These supreme beings are no longer separate and self-centered but are instead a "vehicle of the universal spirit." More important, they do not forsake the world but throw themselves on the world and live "for its redemption." In short, these seers delight in "furthering the plan of the cosmos, in doing the will of the Father."[59]

There is another aspect of Jesus's uniqueness. Jesus struggled in deciding whether to draw from the traditional Jewish concepts he had inherited or the non-Jewish spiritual outlook and aspirations prevalent at that time. The uniqueness of Jesus was that he gradually moved away from the conventional sense of superiority offered by the Jewish tradition. For instance, his understanding of the Kingdom and the Messiah began with a combative nationalism and an inflated notion of elected status, but this gradually gave way to unassertive thinking. He changed the Jewish question, "What am I to be?" to "Who am I to be?"—the question with which Eastern religions are concerned. The aim is to be something different and to be born again. The pathway to this rebirth is not through ceremonial purity, but through self-control bordering on asceticism. The idea of austerity and self-denial, Radhakrishnan contends, is alien to the Jewish tradition. There is no concept in Judaism of nuns or monks leading a life of austerity. Jesus "enlarges and transforms" the Jewish conceptions in the light of his own personal experience. His teachings about the Kingdom of God, and his ascetic emphasis, were the sure signs that he had broken away from the foundational Jewish traditions. Though his teachings are continuous with Judaism, they did not develop from its essentials.[60]

Radhakrishnan did not see Jesus's slow change from being a Jewish nationalist to a universalist as insulting to his image. What it indicated was that Jesus was not exempted from normal human growth, understanding, and feelings. His hunger, thirst, pain, temptations, insults, beatings, and tears, in Radhakrishnan's view, gave full weight to Luke's statement that "Jesus advanced in wisdom and stature" (12.8). These experiences, though humiliating to a person like Jesus, showed that he shared the human pains and passions of his contemporaries.

Radhakrishnan was tireless in pointing out that the claim to uniqueness was made not by Jesus himself but by his disciples, and later by the church, all of whom were responsible for raising him to the rank of God. He was elevated to a status like that of Brahman, the highest Hindu deity, and credited with the powers of Brahma (creation), Vishnu (conservation), and Siva (destruction). Radhakrishnan particularly accuses Paul of making Jesus the one and only savior. Paul saw Jesus not in the flesh, but only in a vision. Radhakrishnan surmises that the person who appeared to Paul must have been one of the savior gods of the ancient Hellenistic religions through whom one could realize everlasting life. Paul, who was keen on creating a new religion, made Jesus the central figure and made a strong claim that "salvation was through Christ and Christ alone."[61]

Radhakrishnan disregarded the claims for the exclusivity of Jesus recounted in the Gospels, and for support, he quoted an array of Christian theologians—from early church theologians such as Justin, to modern theologians such as Albert Schweitzer and Karl Jaspers, to secular intellectuals like Aldous Huxley and Bertrand Russell—who questioned the "supreme saviourship" of Jesus.[62] More daringly, he claims that these dissenters did so merely "in the spirit of Hindu and Buddhist thought," which regarded Jesus as the "expression of the timeless spirit" who "transcends the confines of churches and creeds."[63] For him, "truth wears many vestures and speaks in many tongues."[64]

To sum up, Radhakrishnan did not have any qualms about Christians regarding Jesus as the "final and incomparably unique revelation of God," but he could not accept the notion that God could speak only through a single person.[65] The uniqueness claimed by Christians, in his view, was unworkable. First, it was "contrary to the love and justice of God" and went against the simple, tolerant, universal religion of Jesus.[66] Second, there "cannot be a complete manifestation of the absolute in the world of relativity."[67] Each manifestation may be perfect in its own way, but there is no absolute revelation of God. Third, because God is infinite, God's self-disclosure cannot be limited to one particular context, or one specific time in history. Therefore one has to recognize the possibility of many avataras. And fourth, Krishna, the Buddha, and Jesus are all unique in their own way and any claim of uniqueness for one is "dangerous both in its motive and consequence."[68] For Radhakrishnan, the claim to possession of a unique revealed truth is "ruinous for men" and disastrous for the world; it has led to persecution and an inquisitorial attitude regarding other faiths, and to forcing one's beliefs onto others through crusades and campaigns.

Who Does the Brahman Say That I Am?

"What do you think of Christ?" is undoubtedly one of the most important questions Radhakrishnan wrestles with. The following lengthy passage encapsulates his thinking:

> To an educated Hindu, Jesus is a supreme illustration of the growth from human origins to divine destiny. As a mystic who believes in the inner light, Jesus ignores rituals and is indifferent to legalistic piety. He is contemptuous of the righteousness of the Scribes and the Pharisees. Being other-worldly in spirit, he is indifferent to the wealth of the world and exalts poverty as one of the greatest goods. He wishes us to restrain not only our outward actions but our inner desires and carry the principle of non-attachment even into the sphere of family relationships. He is the great hero who exemplifies the noblest characteristics of manhood, the revealer of the profoundest depths in ourselves, one who brings home to us the ideal of human perfection by embodying it visibly in himself.[69]

Jesus is seen as a person who embodies the mystic joy of the Upanishadic writers. He is likened to a Rama, a Krishna, or a Buddha who appears whenever there is a "downward materialistic tendency" in order to "restore the disturbed harmony of righteousness."[70] The religion that Jesus preaches is that of faith in God as an indwelling presence—the Kingdom of God is within you. The changes in the world are not effected by the intervention of God but are part of inner progress within a human being.

The picture that emerges of Jesus in Radhakrishnan's rendering is that of "the ideal man of India," that is, not a high-minded personality of Greece, nor the courageous knight of medieval Europe, nor a scientist or a leader of industry, nor even a poet or philosopher, but a sannyasin who has no permanent abode or livelihood. This picture is akin to that of Ramanathan, for whom the ideal Indian person is the Brahma Jnani.[71] This person is free from any selfishness, has no national interests, and is above rules because he (or she) has "realized in himself the life which is the source of all rules and which is not itself subject to rules." In Radhakrishnan's words, this person is one who has "attained insight into the universal source by rigid discipline and practice of disinterested virtues, who has freed himself from the prejudices of his time and place."[72] Clarifying this further, he explains that he or she is the prototype of Siva, who has integrated with the divine. "This image," Radhakrishnan claims, has "haunted the spiritual landscape of this country from those early times till today."[73] They are the people who have gained "inward liberty" and who do not repay violence with violence but instead have tolerance and love to bear any humiliation, and are filled with peace and joy. "It is India's pride," Radhakrishnan wrote, that "she has clung fast to this ideal and produced in every generation and in every part of the country from the time of the Rsis of the Upanisads and Buddha to Ramakrisna and Gandhi, men who strove successfully to realize this ideal."[74] Jesus, in Radhakrishnan's view, is such an "ideal man." He is like the teacher of the Gita, showing a way out of the "transitoriness of things, the curse of age and death."[75]

In Radhakrishnan's portrayal, Jesus comes across as a person of a "simple faith" who spent most of his time in solitary mediation and "enjoyed only private prayer."[76] Such a depiction might fit in with his Vedantic notion of an ideal rishi who embodies and awakens God-consciousness, and proclaims "universal morality," but it does not conform to the Gospel image of Jesus, where he is seen as siding with the poor and outcast. In the canonical Gospel, Jesus of Nazareth emerges as a complex figure who sees his mission as both spiritual and political.

Censuring Christ, Rebuking the Rabbi

Just like Parekh, Radhakrishnan did not hesitate to rebuke Jesus. While he respected and admired him, he called into question some of his words and actions. Examples include Jesus's hellfire denunciation of the cities of Chorazin, Bethsaida, and Capernaum, his calling Herod the "fox," and his scolding the Pharisees, calling them vipers, liars, and hypocrites. Radhakrishnan also criticized Jesus for behaving dismissively toward the Syrophoenician woman, driving away the money changers in the Temple with a whip, cursing the fig tree, and urging his followers to sell their garments and buy swords when the right moment came. Also, Radhakrishnan found Jesus too severe toward evildoers and too stern with unrepentant sinners, finding this conduct "not quite consistent with Jesus' loving and tender disposition." More importantly, such behavior was "inconceivable in the case of a Buddha or a Gandhi."[77] To rub theological salt into the wound, Radhakrishnan referred to the words of G. Montefiore: "What one would have wished to find in the life story of Jesus would be one single incident in which Jesus actually performed a loving deed to one of his Rabbinic antagonists or enemies."[78] Radhakrishnan wonders whether this is the Jesus who asked us to forgive our fellow human beings "not seven times, but, I tell you, seventy times seven." He also censures Jesus for implicitly siding with and following the ancient laws of Moses on the issue of divorce. His contention is that any great teacher who possessed sufficient historical knowledge would not attempt to impose any law from ancient times on later generations who were unready to comprehend or appreciate them. He was quick to point out that Hindu thinkers adopted a stance toward antiquated laws of "careful tending instead of wild forcing."[79]

He also found fault with Jesus's enigmatic saying "Render unto Caesar the things that are Caesar's, and unto God the things that are God's" as an artificial division, one "permitting a double standard."[80] In Radhakrishnan's presentation, Jesus comes across not as a universal moral teacher but as a tutor who is useful to only a narrow group of people. His teachings, especially his Sermon on the Mount, are applicable only to individuals and not to sovereign states. His nonresistance was "meant only for a little flock in a hostile environment." As Radhakrishnan writes, Jesus does not "ask us to abolish the system of public law."[81] In other words, he was not a person with a grand moral design to change the world.

Past Events, Continuous Recurrences

Radhakrishnan shows little interest in the traditional Christian doctrines that were associated with Jesus, such as the Annunciation, Crucifixion, Resurrection, and Ascension. He treats them not as historically confirmable objective events but as spiritualized or inward experiences. The Annunciation is seen as the "birth of Christ in the soul"—a "beautiful experience of the soul," "a holy thing begotten within," and a "proper reconditioning of man's whole nature."[82] Similarly, he internalizes the events on the cross so that they become "significant only when we make it our own, when we undergo crucifixion"—that is, a voluntary suffering undertaken, for the welfare of others, or for the spiritual progress of one's own self.[83] As he redefined it, Jesus's experiences on the cross are "not an offence or a stumbling block" to Hindus but "a great symbol of the reality of God," and demonstrate how "love is related to self sacrifice."[84] He hastens to add that voluntary suffering for the sake of the world is not new; there have been many examples in the Eastern traditions of rishis and Buddhas who suffered for others.

The Resurrection, too, becomes an internal matter that happens in an individual's life, rather than an objective, physical phenomenon that happened in history as Christians believed. Radhakrishnan regards the events on the cross and the Resurrection not as "historical events which occurred once upon a time" but as a universal process of spiritual life that is "being continually accomplished in the souls of men."[85] For him, the Resurrection is an event that happens within oneself, "resulting in a deeper understanding of reality, and a greater love for God and man." This is the "true resurrection which lifts human life to an awareness of its own divine content and purpose."[86] The bodily Resurrection of Jesus, in his analysis, was the church's answer to the failure of the anticipated coming again of the Son of Man: "The simple story of the life and activity of Jesus was transformed into an epiphany of a heavenly being."[87] The Resurrection story is not proof of the reality of God or of human immortality, and it will not appeal to a person trained in modern science. Radhakrishnan makes clear that the Resurrection is not a "revivification of a corpse" but "the awaking of the spirit from the slumber, that which makes it capable of higher vision."[88] For him, Resurrection is a sign of attaining "security and freedom here and now," otherwise there was "no point in a resurrection."[89]

The central teaching of Jesus—the Kingdom of God—also undergoes a mystical treatment in Radhakrishnan's hands. It becomes a case of being reborn as a "wondrous new creation."[90] The Brahmaloka, or the

Kingdom of God, for Radhakrishnan, is a "revolutionary change in men's consciousness."[91] While missionaries posited the Kingdom as good political governance, he made it personality-focused. For him, the Kingdom is a "state of mind" that liberated souls possess, not a paradise on earth.[92] In his writings, Radhakrishnan frequently repeats the saying of Jesus that the Kingdom of God is within oneself. He urges that "each individual must strive to spiritualise himself so as to become a fit member of the kingdom of spirit."[93] Radhakrishnan's Jesus steers clear of the usual events that surround the Jewish expectation of the Kingdom—wonders and miracles, apocalyptic upheavals and judgment. In his vision, the Kingdom dawns without any showy display when human beings overcome their alienation and escape from their slavery to material goods. The "transformation of the cosmos" is possible only when there is the awakening of the spirit in human beings. While acknowledging that there is an element of messianism in Jesus's teaching that could be traced to Palestinian tradition, Radhakrishnan points out that "the mystic conception" of the Kingdom "is the development of the Indian idea."[94] The doctrinal concepts that Jesus preached about his birth, death, and Resurrection, and about the Kingdom of God, were all "verbalizations of intense emotional experience." They were all made historical instead of treating them as "profound inward realization."[95]

Radhakrishnan is not always true to his hermeneutical agenda of spiritualizing or internalizing all Christian doctrines. When it suits his purpose, however, he embraces these doctrines enthusiastically. For instance, the Trinity is seen as akin to the Hindu idea of three forms of God. Radhakrishnan saw the triune aspect of God as an attempt to fit Jesus within the godhead, but also as providing a correction to a one-sided view of the ultimate. God is not only an infinite power, but also the heart of love (the Son) and a living presence (the Holy Spirit). Such functions, in Radhakrishnan's view, replicate the attributes of the Hindu gods—Yahweh exercising power as Siva; the Son as the Brahma, the principle of creation; and the Holy Spirit as Vishnu, all-pervasive love. This threefold manifestation as Father, Son, and Holy Spirit, Radhakrishnan reminds his readers, "corresponds to the Vedantic formula of Brahman as *sat, cit,* and *ananda*—reality, wisdom, and joy."[96]

Incarnations, Interventions, and Irruptions (

Radhakrishnan's contention is that incarnation, whic[
tral doctrine among a few Indian Christian theol
known to Jesus and his first followers."[97] Indian Chr[
the time, spearheaded by A. J. Appasamy, employed pro
notion of avatar, both to ingratiate Christians with ind[
thinking, and more pressingly to establish Jesus as th
tion of God. Based on his reading of the Bhagavad Gita,
reenvisioned the concept of avatar in such a way tha
Christians were unsustainable. He identifies two facets
or avatar—the descent of God, and the ascent of a hum;
status of divinity. The first of these, the classical, al
Bhagavad Gita's understanding of avatars, where God int(
tory on behalf of the good when there is a struggle betw
evil. The other is the ascent of a human being into a divi
grade of life."[98] In this second understanding, the incarnat
much the conversion of Godhead into flesh as taking up
into God," which Radhakrishnan finds attractive to his he
cause.[99]

When Radhakrishnan writes of Jesus as an avatar, he is
the second aspect of incarnation as defined by him: "Jesu
ample of a man who has become God and none can say whe[
hood ends and his divinity begins. Man and God are aki[
Thou, *Tat tvam asi.*"[100] This kind of an ascent is a demonst[
human being's "spiritual resources and latent divinity." Echc
anathan, he wrote that the human body could "become an in
of divine life."[101] Therefore the divine status claimed by Krishna o
or Christ is "the common reward of all earnest spiritual se
The potential that was available to Jesus and to the countless
also available to everyone because "we are all partakers of God'
and can incarnate God's love as Jesus did."[103] "The divine sor
Christ," Radhakrishnan observes, is "at the same time the divi[
ship of every man."[104] The life of a Krishna, a Buddha, or a Je;
reminder that all can "achieve the same unity with the Absolute."[105]
nation was not a series of incidents in history but the self encoun

185

inner spirit, an inward moral and spiritual awakening. Its pur-
se is to enable us, one by one, not to become "merely Christians but
rists."[106] To bolster his argument, he cites the words of Saint Atha-
sius: "God became man that man might become God."[107]

In redefining incarnation, Radhakrishnan offered an approach that
iffered both from the Christian view and the theistic Hindu under-
tanding. While Indian Christians restricted avatarhood only to Jesus
nd proclaimed him as the final and the ultimate incarnation, he
dvocated incarnation as an ongoing event and not limited to past
istorical occurrences or a few select individuals: "Incarnation is not
a historical event which occurred two thousand years ago. It is an
event which is renewed in the life of everyone who is on the way to
the fulfilment of his destiny."[108] What he did was to open Incarnation
to all and in the process to democratize it. In Radhakrishnan's words,
not only the "historic Jesus, but the whole race will have the gifts of
incarnation."[109]

Upanishadic Kinsmen: The Buddha and Jesus

Like all Indian interpreters, Radhakrishnan easily discerned parallels
between the lives and teachings of the Buddha and Jesus. He lists the
standard similarities that have since become clichés: their miraculous
births and visitations by a venerable figure (Simeon calling on the infant
Jesus, and Asita paying homage to the baby Buddha); the temptations
they faced (Jesus by Satan, and the Buddha by Mara); their selection
of disciples and sending them out on mission; their intimate association with a woman (a courtesan called Ambapali in the case of Buddha,
and Mary Magdalene in the case of Jesus); their revolt against and
growing out of their own ceremonial and complex legalistic religions;
the performance of miracles but disproval of them as signs of divinity;
the triumphal entry into their native cities (the Buddha marching toward
Kapilavastu, and Jesus entering Jerusalem); Buddha's cousin Devadatta
doing a Judas by arranging to kill him; and the quaking of the earth
when both men died. These resemblances indicate that "Buddha and
Jesus are men of the same brotherhood."[110]

Besides the similarities surrounding the lives of these great masters, Radhakrishnan found echoes of Buddha's teachings in Jesus's preaching. Both urged their disciples to lay up for themselves a treasure that neither moth nor rust could corrupt nor thieves could steal. As pointed out earlier, Radhakrishnan believed that the ascetic and otherworldly teachings of Jesus had not been exclusive to Christianity but had been prefigured in the Upanishads and in the teachings of the Buddha.

While identifying the common features in the two religious sages, Radhakrishnan is also quick to point out that there are deep divergences beneath the resemblances. Whereas the Buddha preached a suprapersonal spirit, Jesus believed in a personal God. Although both emphasized the redemptive power of suffering, the idea of a savior dying to emancipate the world is alien to Buddha's thinking. Their attitudes toward the world were also strikingly different. Buddha thought of it as undesirable and unattractive, and Jesus believed it was sinful. Radhakrishnan found the Buddha a calmer person, good at handling the world. There was no "nervous irritability or fierce anger" in him. He faced the world with "calm and confidence" and his behavior was a "perfect expression of courtesy and good feeling with a spice of irony in it." Jesus, by contrast, was "angry with the world which will not hear him."[111]

Radhakrishnan indicates that when the Christian faith was in its formative years, Buddhism was "both settled and enterprising" and Buddhist missionaries were active in the Mediterranean world.[112] Unlike Varma and Chowdhuri, Radhakrishnan remained open on the question of Buddhist influence. Instead of questioning who borrowed from whom, Radhakrishnan attributes the resemblances to the natural religious urge of humankind. Such coincidences are a "natural outcome of the human mind," since the hopes, fears, desires, and aspirations of humankind are the "same on the banks of the Ganges as on the shores of the Lake of Galilee."[113] He also does not pay much attention to the idea that Jesus traveled to India during his missing years: to him, the question of whether the Buddha and Jesus "met in early times and one borrowed from the other is of little moment."[114] Such concurrences and correspondences, in Radhakrishnan's view, prevent any claim to uniqueness to one particular avatar or text, or to one religious tradition. The noblest type of self-sacrifice urged by both teachers might be regarded as common to all people and all ages. If both men applied similar images and illustrations, this could be due to the fact that both came from agricultural society. If these teachers both taught in parables it might be because that is the "easiest form of teaching for simple men."[115] The following quotation from Radhakrishnan goes against the jaundiced view of Varma and Chowdhuri: "Whether [the Buddha and Jesus] are historically connected or not, they are the twin expressions of one great spiritual movement."[116]

Radhakrishnan comes closer to Varma and Chowdhuri, however, when he betrays a streak of Hindu exclusivism. Ultimately, for him, the validity of any master's teachings has to be judged by the Upanishads, the personal records of the ancient rishis: "Buddha and Jesus are the earlier and later Hindu and Jewish representatives of the same upheaval of the human soul, whose typical expression we have in the Upanishads."[117]

In the hierarchy of religious figures, the Hindu reformers always placed Jesus behind Krishna and the Buddha, and Radhakrishnan was no exception. He asked whether anyone would have wished "to have the gracious and magnetic personality of the Buddha superseded by some Old Testament worthy?"[118] For him, the Buddha was the one who had attained "*brahma-bhuta*, the one who has become Brahman."[119] Jesus, for his part, was only a "first-born among many brethren," "the eldest begotten," "the first born of a new race of men," and a "new species of spiritual personality" who spread truth on earth as "instruments of the divine for the spread of the spiritual religion."[120] For Radhakrishnan, the Buddha is more appealing than Jesus because the Buddha recognized diverse ways to reach the truth, an idea that resonated with Radhakrishnan's theological agenda. Jesus's insistence on a single path to salvation, by contrast, Radhakrishnan found injurious to humankind.

What these religious figures teach us is that we can apprehend the eternal with "directness and immediacy." When the rishis of the Upanishads spoke about jnana, or the Buddha preached about the bodhi or enlightenment, or when Jesus said that the truth will make us free, they are referring "to the mode of direct spiritual apprehension of the supreme, in which the gap between truth and being is closed."[121] What the lives of the Buddha and Jesus tell us is that we can achieve a similar union with the divine. Everyone has in himself or herself the "possibility of this spiritual freedom, the essence of enlightenment, [and so] is a *bodhisattva*. The divine sonship of Christ is at the same time the divine sonship of every man."[122]

Unlike Varma and Chowdhuri, who sought out Eastern parallels with the intention of diluting the message of Jesus and making him seem unimaginative and a counterfeit, Radhakrishnan used these parallels to highlight the interconnectedness of the stories and cultures and make Jesus part of the great company of Eastern spiritual savants. As he put it, "it was from India that the beauty of Christ had sprung up."[123] More importantly, Radhakrishnan opposed vicious religious bigotry, and envisioned a multireligious India, which Varma and Chowdhuri bitterly resisted. He was keen to draw attention to the Eastern influence on Christianity in order to show that the Eastern religions like Hinduism or Buddhism were not devoid of a salvific dimension and were not inferior to biblical religion, as the missionaries had so vehemently argued.

Vedanta Rules the Waves

Often the discourse of the colonized is seen as one in which the wounded vilifies the colonizer and berates those in power. Although Radhakrishnan's seminal writings appeared at the height of the British Raj, he generally steered clear of such traditional haranguing and antagonistic critiquing of claims for a superior Western civilization. An exception was his master's thesis. In that, he derisively points out that when Europeans were eating raw animal flesh with the "greatest gusto" and when Jesus was voicing such vengeful thoughts as "the brother shall deliver up the brother to death, and the father the child," India already had "six most subtle systems of philosophy."[124] Later, he regretted his thesis as a "juvenile and rhetorical production."[125] Generally, he does not wallow in victimhood. His writings show that the cultural activities of the colonized can be very productive, often cordial, and can even unsettle the hegemonic views of the authorities.

Radhakrishnan was uneasy that despite Christianity's Eastern origins, it had been damaged by acquiring "forms characteristic of the Western mind." This change was inevitable when the "simple truths" taught by Jesus were taken over by the traditions of Caesar. When the Greek dialecticians and the Roman lawyers took over, Christian theology became logical in form. The result was that "creeds and dogmas took the place of vision and prophecy, and intricate subtleties of scholasticism displaced the simple love of God." Moreover, colonial Christianity in both its Protestant and Catholic forms had become a "religion of authority."[126] Radhakrishnan reminded the missionaries and British administrators that the "truth is that no doctrine becomes sounder, no truth truer, because it takes the aid of force." To strengthen his case that the spread of the Gospel depends on arms, he even invoked the words of the African explorer H. M. Stanley, who remarked after inspecting the original maxim gun: "What a splendid instrument for spreading Christianity and civilization among the savage races of Africa!" It was not the "pale Galilean that has conquered, but the spirit of the West," asserted Radhakrishnan.[127]

In his anxiety to challenge the West, Radhakrishnan was keen to discover some Indian indigenous characteristics that were equal to, if not superior to, those of the West. Indian spirituality provided such a convenient weapon. He emphasized spirituality and the indwelling of the divine within oneself as distinct features of the Indian mentality and in doing so he overlooked the Indian materialistic thinking explicated in the philosophies of Lokāyata and Cārvāka, which took the empirical reality of the world seriously. It is not that he was unaware of such thinking, but he saw materialistic ideation as a passing phase that had emerged at a turbulent and unsettled period in India's history and had led to such "metaphysical fancies" and "futile speculations." While conceding that Lokāyata had played a role in declaring the "spiritual independence of the individual and the rejection of the principle of authority" and dogmatism, as an ardent Vedantin he saw its true function as leading the way to the Vedanta.[128]

Just as Western orientalists like Max Müller and others routinely reminded Hindus that their pure religious tradition was safely stored in the original textual sources, Hindu thinkers like Radhakrishnan in a perverse way took it upon themselves to reverse the claim by telling Christians that the true message of Jesus was preserved in the writings of the New Testament. He told Christians that it was true of Christianity that "the water of a stream is purest at its source."[129]

Radhakrishnan's method, in another sense, resembles that of the orientalists. As with orientalists like William Jones who used the flood narratives in the Hindu Puranas to attest the historical validity and authenticity of the Genesis narratives, he used seemingly comparable words of Jesus to conform the ideals and the universal nature of the Upanishadic message. The noncanonical saying of the ascended Jesus that "Him that overcometh will I make a pillar in the temple of my God, and he shall go no more out," especially the phrase "he shall go no more out," in his view alludes to the "Hindu view that the saved soul does not return to the struggle of *samsara*."[130] Similarly, Jesus's exemplary behavior—"Who, when he was reviled, reviled not again; when he suffered, he threatened not"—is seen as endorsing *ahimsa*, the central feature of the Upanishads. The joy and peace that Jesus spoke of was nothing but the shanti or peace of which the "Hindus speak."[131] Just as for Jones the Hindu Puranas strengthened the historicity of the biblical narratives, the sayings and behavior of Jesus reinforced, for Radhakrishnan, the universality of the Upanishads.

Most of Radhakrishnan's articulations about Jesus happened at the height of the "no-biography period," when scholars, especially Germans, turned away from writing portrayals of Jesus's life. It was during this time that Radhakrishnan's *Eastern Religions and Western Thought* (1939) appeared, in which he devoted a considerable amount of space to formulating his thoughts about Jesus. While the nineteenth-century liberal theology was effectively describing Jesus in apocalyptic terms, and was trying to figure out whether he was a "rabbinic teacher" or a "messianist-apocalyptist," Radhakrishnan released him from the shackling effects of such eschatological images and carried him into the light of Vedic idealism via the eighth-century Shankara's Vedanta. Shirley Jackson Case and his Chicago School were trying to place Jesus in his socioeconomic context, but Radhakrishnan enlarged the province of the religious landscape of Jesus and nascent Christianity to include Iranian and Indian influences.

Radhakrishnan offered to the Christians a Christ divested of standard biblical characteristics, and they found fault with his Christology for playing down the principal events in Jesus's life such as the Passion and Resurrection. In defense of Radhakrishnan, it must be said that his starting point was entirely different from that of the traditional Christian perspective. He did not perceive humanity as fallen and in need of an atoning sacrifice to propitiate an angry God. Instead, for him, God is in human beings, waiting to realize "new possibilities" and help them evolve into a "higher species."[132] What were needed, in his view, were gurus who could hasten in their disciples the love of God and nurture the seed of the spirit "capable of fructifying in them."[133] To him, the divine manifestation in a human being is not an "infringement" of human personality. Rather it is the "highest possible degree of man's natural self-expression since the true nature of man is divine."[134] It was this notion of the divine residing within the human being, a notion largely unfamiliar and unknown in the West, that, he maintained, differentiated Hinduism from other religions—that "man with his sense of values is the most concrete embodiment of the divine on earth."[135] He claimed that "what is possible for a Gautama or a Jesus is possible for every human being."[136]

What biblical scholars call messianic-consciousness is God-consciousness for Radhakrishnan. Christian exegetes search the scriptures for messianic prophecies and frame Christ as fulfilling these expectations, the implication being that Jesus did not have a mind of his own but was simply co-opted into a larger divine scheme. In Radhakrishnan's construal, however, Jesus takes control of his life, convinced of his role as a Messiah, and tries to shape his life as a meek resister who puts truth above dogma, humankind above his own people, and love above force—a Messiah who advocates revolution through ascetic life and love.

Radhakrishnan's reconfiguring of Jesus is not different from what he did to the other Eastern seers like Mahavira and the Buddha, who were likewise hailed as upholders of the Upanishadic ideals. Mahavira, who played a crucial role in strengthening Jain ideas, was called the great hero not because he won great battles, but because he won the "battles of inward life" like the Upanishadic rishis. Through ascetic practices, restraint, and self-cleansing, he "raised himself to the position of a man who had attained divine status."[137] Likewise, the Buddha, far from being an innovator, was seen as a replicator of the Upanishadic teachings. What the Upanishads called Brahman, the Buddha called the Real. Buddha's protest against ritualism, and his teaching that one should free oneself from desire, were all in "the spirit of the Upanishads."[138] Radhakrishnan's Jesus was nothing but genetically identical to an Upanishadic seer or ascetic.

Although Radhakrishnan is very much at home in the liberal critique of Christianity, his understanding of it seems somewhat problematic. He paid undue respect to marginal opinions of the liberal thinkers and magnified them as the mainstream. He drew heavily on the works of a range of Christian mystics and exegetes who deviated from the majority view, and whose ideas resonated with his vision of religion and reality. He even implied, in a condescending way, that the digressive stance of these scholars was inspired by the spirit of the East, and particularly Hinduism. Interestingly, while Radhakrishnan was quite confident in handling the biblical sources, he failed to make use of the Pauline notion of *kenosis,* which would have enhanced the idea of the self-emptying of ego, one that his Vedic seers persistently espoused and demanded.

In his handling of Western sources, Radhakrishnan did not always follow academic standards. He was selective in using them. For instance, he makes use of Otto's idea of the Indo-Aryan origins for the Son of Man, which gives the impression that Otto is championing a wider religious background for Jesus and placing him in the line of Eastern masters. Otto conceded that Jesus was a "Galilean," but "certainly not typically Jewish."[139] Radhakrishnan would not have noticed the pro-Aryan streak in Otto's work. His writings emerged at a time in Germany when the identity of Jesus as a Jew was going through a severe reappraisal, and he was being made an Aryan on the basis that the eschatology that he depended on originated in ancient Aryan sources.[140] Radhakrishnan also conveniently overlooked Otto's *Mysticism: East and West,* which offered a devastating critique of Radhakrishnan's cherished *Advaita Vedanta* as a distant, morally dubious, and world-negating phenomenon, and accused Radhakrishnan's beloved Shankara of being "trivial" and of "transforming the original mystery-filled figures of the Upanishads into abstractions."[141] Shankara, in Otto's view, was not as dynamic as Radhakrishnan had portrayed him.

Unlike some of the Hindu reformers we have studied here, and the current Hindu-only-India Hindutva brigade, Radhakrishnan was conciliatory toward Christianity. He urged Indian Christians to rediscover their roots in India. He never missed the chance to remind them that their faith had emerged from the East but had got mixed up with Greek and later Western cultures. It was time, he told them, for their faith to have its "rebirth today in the heritage of India."[142] He was persistent in reminding them that the original Christian gospel, before it became dogmatized and institutionalized, was essentially Upanishadic in that it was about the awakening of the inner soul. He also threw down a challenge to the Christians: "If the Christian thinkers admit that men may have access to God and can be saved other than through the mediatorship of Jesus, the Hindu will heartily subscribe to the essential features of the religion of Jesus."[143] Instead of listening to what Radhakrishnan had to say, Indian Christians chided him for watering down what Stanley Samartha called "Christian convictions cherished and hallowed through the history of the Christian Church and in the life of the believers."[144]

Radhakrishnan's Jesus is the perfect embodiment of Upanishadic ideals, the standard that Radhakrishnan expected all religions to derive from and ultimately to refer and aspire to. Radhakrishnan's Jesus was influenced by this "Vedantic exclusivism," which was built on the idea that the Vedanta is the very core and spirit of religions. Radhakrishnan was resolute in his claim that "the Vedanta is not a religion, but religion itself in its most universal and deepest significance."[145] For him, Hinduism at its Upanishadic mystic best is the religion and Jesus was one of the rishis who personified it. As he succinctly put it: "While the experiential character of religion is emphasized in the Hindu faith, every religion at its best falls back on it."[146] It was this exclusive nature of Vedanta that Jesus was made to represent. This approach stands in contrast to that of Ramanathan, for whom the "love of God is the essence of religion."[147]

Radhakrishnan did not warm to the idea, popular at that time, that Jesus was the crown of Hinduism or fulfilled the Vedic expectations advocated by K. M. Benerjea, J. N. Farquhar, and Raymond Panikkar.[148] To Radhakrishnan, such ideas sounded the "imperialistic note that Christianity is the highest manifestation of the religious spirit; it is the moral standard for the human race while every other religion is to be judged by it."[149] While he resented such a patronizing attitude among Christians, Radhakrishnan himself was not averse to administering a similar dose of paternalism to them. Just as the missionaries found Hinduism to be imperfect and needing the Gospel to vitalize it, so Radhakrishnan reversed the process, claiming that other religions were defective and were in need of a theological correction that only Upanishadic mysticism could provide. He earnestly told Christians that to "quicken their religious aspirations," the message of Jesus required the "reinforcements" expounded in the mysticism of the Vedanta. The only way that historical religions like Christianity could "regain universality," he argued, was by "bringing them nearer the religions of India."[150] He wrote: "Hinduism absorbs everything that enters into it, . . . and raises it to a higher level. Every God accepted by Hinduism is elevated and ultimately identified with the central Reality."[151] His contention was that all religions, including Christianity, were genuine attempts at reaching the divine, but they were in various phases of progress—they were all in the process of realizing what Hindus already professed to know as dharma. The truth that the different religions were seeking was the truth first revealed to the Hindus and was to be found in the Vedanta—India's spiritual treasure, which other religions need for their survival and regeneration. The implication behind this apologetic assertion was that other religions must strive to be like the Advaita Vedanta.

The Hindu ideal he projects borders on casteism. The Brahmanical values become the universal standard to which all should aspire. He stated that that the "ideal of the Hindu dharma is to make all men Brahmins." He further claimed that "true Brahminhood represents the highest of which human nature is capable."[152] Radhakrishnan is not open and tolerant toward other faiths, as is often made out. Underneath his charitable exterior lies a confidence and pride in Upanishadic spirituality, and a belief that India is the world's spiritual home.

In colonial-postcolonial terms, Radhakrishnan can be seen as a subtle spiritual imperialist. His imperial tendency comes across when he wants to civilize other people with a nonaggressive diffusion of Hindu ideals, just as the old Hindu empires did in the past. He was an admirer of former Indian empires, whose civilizing activities extended from Western Asia to Java. He proudly claimed that even today, Japan, China, and Myanmar "look to India as their spiritual home." The Indian imperial success, or as he called it, "cultural conquest," was not due to India's religion being "old," because "her empires were great," because it "developed weapons of destruction," or because it "exercised force on a mass scale." Instead, India's "intelligent understanding of the deeper unity in the midst of all diversity," its "vision of unity in all things in God," and its "assimilative genius" made its culture and Hindu religion special. Radhakrishnan wanted other religions to absorb the spiritual intuitions, detachment, and synthesizing impulses of Hinduism. Advocating these Indian values, in his view, was not "imperialistic expansion" but the "peaceful penetration of thought and mind of peoples."[153]

In spite of his unassuming manner and tone, Radhakrishnan's colonial impulse is evident in the following words that could have come from any nineteenth-century imperialist: "There is nothing wrong in absorbing the culture of other peoples; only we must enhance, raise, and purify the elements we take over, fuse them with the best in our own," that is, with Upanishadic spirituality.[154] He was a gentle lobbyist for the Hindu cause. Where he differed from the current Hindutva propagandists was in his dislike for their aggressive and violent methods as the means for achieving Hindu superiority.

In an India that is becoming more robust in its Hindu identity, Radhakrishnan can be seen both as an ally and an alienating figure. His version of a Brahmanical mysticism that soaks up, subsumes, and systematizes everything non-Vedantic can become a profitable tool in the hands of Hindu nationalists in their attempts to propagate what the Indian academic Muthu Mohan calls Vedantic nationalism, and about which Parekh cautioned. But the nationalists' way of copying ancient Vedic truths and applying them in a literal way to the present would not find favor with Radhakrishnan. Although he advocated recuperating the spirit of the past, he was insistent that the body and the "pulse must be from the present." He was unambiguous about this hermeneutical task: "It is possible to remain faithful to the letter and yet pervert the whole spirit."[155]

Amid all his admiration for the West and Christianity and his encouragement of mutual enhancement, Radhakrishnan's underlying message is clear, even missiological. There is an unwavering belief that the future of the world depends on incorporating the elements of the mystical East and worshiping Jesus as an Upanishadic seer. The world, Radhakrishnan laments, is becoming rootless, drifting unguided. Writing soon after the Second World War and the sufferings caused by the Indian partition, Radhakrishnan commended the Vedanta as a possible solution to a world that had been torn apart: "The great religious tradition of India which has had a continuous life from the seers of the Upanishads and the Buddha to Ramakrishna and Gandhi, may perhaps help to re-integrate this bruised, battered, broken world and give to it the faith for which it is in search."[156] Everything will be fine, Radhakrishnan assures us, when the world comes to its senses and begins drawing its spiritual resources from the Upanishads and thinking like a Vedantin. Just as the Christian missionaries offered the Christian Gospel as a remedy for the spiritual ills of India, an enlightened "colonial" like Radhakrishnan seemed to be falling into the same old mental habit of the colonizers. Radhakrishnan, who dismissed Karl Barth as a "crusader and a fundamentalist," seems to end up himself as an advocate for Sanskritic, Brahmanical Hinduism and a champion of Upanishadic ideals.[157] His is one of the countless cases of the colonized finishing up as a spiritual colonizer, though a benign one. As the rishis of his beloved Upanishads would put it, your so-called adversary is no longer the wicked "other" but also you: "This one I am, that one I am (*tat tvam asi*)" (Chandogya Upanishad 6.10).

8

A Minjung Messiah

On a cool November day in 1970, Jeon Tae-il, a tailor and an activist, disgusted at the poor working conditions in South Korean factories, immolated himself in Pyunghwa Market in Seoul. His dramatic act was also an indirect protest against then-president Park Chung-hee's authoritarian rule. The event shocked Korea, and opened the eyes, especially, of otherwise donnish and dreamy theologians to a new perspective. Reflecting on the incident, a staid Korean New Testament scholar, well-schooled in the German historical critical tradition, wrote: "A big change occurred in my life as the Korean military dictatorship increased its oppression. It provided me a chance to see everything, including history, in a totally different way. This was when I met 'minjung.'"[1] The scholar, Korean professor Ahn Byung Mu (1922–1996), is the principal concern of this chapter, and was one of the pioneers of minjung theology, a contentious theology that emerged in the 1980s.

Prior to his conversion, the search for the historical Jesus had been Ahn's "life-long task." To this end, he had set off for Germany, where the work of Rudolf Bultmann, venerated by a generation of scholars, had a great impact on him. In an interview, Ahn confessed that he would not have pursued his theological studies if it had not been for Bultmann. By the time Ahn reached Germany Bultmann had retired, but fortunately his student Günther Bornkamm took Ahn under his wing. It was a time when a renewed search for the historical Jesus was just emerging after kerygmatic theology had reigned supreme and put an end to any serious quest, at least in Germany.[2] Even the arrival of the New Quest could not completely shake off skepticism about the historical Jesus, and the Gospels were still being treated not as depositories of biographical details of Jesus, but as bearers of the kerygma.

Unfulfilled in his personal mission to seek afresh the historical Jesus, Ahn returned home. As he later recalled, it was the Jeon Tae-il incident and the prevailing political unrest in South Korea that led to his liberation from the web of "the western thought frame that [had] coiled around" him for such a long time.[3] These events made Ahn realize that "the traditional, kerygmatic theology could give no helpful answers" to the cries of the oppressed.[4] The political upheaval and the unrest in the country led him to see everything from the minjung perspective. As he stated later: "I have tried to re-illuminate the Jesus-events in today's minjung movements."[5] He envisioned his task as to "liberate or save Jesus," who was enmeshed in the doctrinal elaborations of the institutionalized churches and thus estranged from the life of ordinary people. His language reflected a kind of altar-call experience: "I newly met Jesus whom I had never truly met until then."[6]

Before we come to the chief concern of this chapter, two inevitable but necessary digressions, one about Ahn, and the other, about minjung theology. First, Ahn was probably the first proper professional New Testament scholar to emerge in Asia, and, alongside Shūsaku Endō (profiled in Chapter 9), was a pioneer Asian who engaged seriously in the search for the historical Jesus. Asia has produced a fine crop of theologians who have used the Bible extensively in their writings—such as Kosuke Koyama, Aloysius Pieris, C. S. Song, M. M. Thomas, and Kwok Pui-lan, to name a few—but none have been professionally trained in Biblical Studies as the discipline is defined in the academy.

Second, Ahn suffered for his theological position and was imprisoned for the radical politics he advocated. This was a time when theologians were killed or locked up for their theological stance. The Catholic priests Camilo Torres from Columbia and Michael Rodrigo from Sri Lanka were both assassinated by the ruling authorities for siding with the poor. Although Ahn escaped such a fate, nonetheless he was imprisoned and psychologically tortured.

Third, Ahn's hermeneutics was undertaken at a time when theology as a mere intricate and complex set of arguments was being replaced by an exercise in involvement and a reflection on human struggle and exploitation. It was Gustavo Gutiérrez who introduced the notion that the first act in theology is commitment and praxis, with theology following as a "second step" and critically reflecting on the Word of God in the light of the involvement.[7] Although there is no direct acknowledgment, Ahn became the proponent of this radical way of doing theology, emphasizing commitment and analysis over applying predetermined theological formulations to the changing realities of Korea.

And fourth, Ahn will be remembered for his study of *ochlos* (the crowd) in the Gospel of Mark and making it the counter community. He made it difficult to think about Jesus without the ochlos who were the minjung of the time, or to imagine the minjung of the Gospels without Jesus. His two often-photocopied articles for classroom use, "Jesus and the Minjung in the Gospel of Mark," and "The Transmitters of the Jesus-Event," are fine examples of rigorous research.[8] Even if he had not written anything after these two articles, they are enough to preserve his legacy and will remain as a monument to his lasting contribution to biblical scholarship.

Now about Minjung theology. The 1970s were a time when contextual theologies were emerging as resistance against a Western theology that posed as universal, normal, and axiomatic. Two particularly vibrant Asian theologies surfaced at that time: the Filipino theology of struggle, and the Korean minjung theology.[9] Both arose as a critique of dictatorship—of Ferdinand Marcos in the Philippines, and Park Chung-he in South Korea. Filipino theology was not a theology *about* the struggle, but *of* and *in* the struggle, developed *by* the Filipinos. Minjung theology was different in that it was not only a political discourse, but also an intensely cultural one.[10]

The lazy way to describe minjung theology is to dub it the Korean version of Latin American liberation theology, which was emerging as an important force at that time. This description is unfair to minjung theology, however. The Minjung are not the proletariat as the Marxistfueled liberation theology would like to describe them—they are much more than this socioeconomic description. Who are the minjung? Korean minjung theologians are consistently adamant in refusing to define who the minjung are. They come up with vague descriptions, such as that the minjung are "politically oppressed," "economically exploited," "socially alienated," and "culturally and intellectually kept uneducated," but also agents who change society and history. The word minjung is composed of two Chinese characters—*min* (people) and *jung* (mass)—that together mean a large group or mass of people. The term was used in the fourteenth century during the Yi dynasty to describe those who were excluded from the ruling *yangban* class. Minjung is nevertheless a malleable concept. For instance, during the Japanese occupation of Korea, most Koreans other than the indigenous collaborators were reduced to minjung status. More to the point, minjung is defined in relation to those who wield power at a given time. Ahn was reluctant to define who were the minjung, except for indicating that they were a vibrant and a varying category. If one goes through his writings, it becomes clear that the sinners mentioned in the Gospels were none other than the minjung, the class of people who were structurally estranged and treated harshly. They are not the poor and weak, the object of other's help. More specifically, it was the minjung who bore "powers that made Jesus to be Jesus."[11]

The Historical Jesus in the History of Korea

On the occasion of the hundredth anniversary of the Korean church, Ahn surveyed the manner in which Jesus had been introduced to Korea. He identified two portrayals—a "doctrine-oriented" Christ and the "de-doctrinized" Jesus. The first portrayal was the preserve of and largely propagated by the mainstream churches under the influence of missionaries, and had a significant hold on the majority of Korean Christians. In this church-hierarchy-induced construal, Jesus was presented in an abstract doctrinal form as a largely isolationist and conservative figure who transcended culture and history. Such a Jesus became an object of belief and provided an escape from the harshness of life. This dogmatic Christ, Ahn noted, did not speak to key historical events in Korea, such as Japanese colonial rule, the Shinto worship enforced by the invaders, the March First Movement, and the founding of the Communist Party.

The other was a de-doctrinized human Jesus. This Jesus, Ahn observed, came in two types—"de-historicized" and "historical." The de-historicized Jesus was an "ideal man" and a "suffering man" whom one was expected to "follow," "learn" from, and "live together" with. The problem with the suffering-man image, Ahn noted, was that it had been "beautified" and so failed to take note of the historical seriousness of the pain Jesus suffered. In contrast, Jesus as a "historical person" emerged as a way of responding to the different political and social contexts of Korea. For instance, when socialism swept through Korea in the aftermath of the Russian revolution, the idea of Jesus as a "friend of the proletariat" and social reformer came into prominence among a few intellectuals, but these "sprouts of historical consciousness" were crushed with the imposition of Japanese colonialism. During the 1960s, influenced by the secular theologies of the West, echoing Dietrich Bonhoeffer, Jesus was perceived as the "man for others," living in the shanty towns of Korea. This Jesus was still regarded as the one who offered salvation to individual souls. Then, in the 1970s, the idea of salvation changed, and was replaced with liberation, which described an emancipation of both individuals and the social order. In this new scenario, Jesus was presented as freeing people from the "evils of the political and economic structures." On this foundation, another new perspective on Jesus emerged—Jesus as a "friend of Minjung." Naturally, for Ahn, this was the only valid image because it had not only "ample proofs in the Synoptics," but also spoke to the minjung of Korea.[12] He dismissed summarily the earlier constructions of Jesus by the Korean churches as "wistful understanding, stimulated by the request of those days."[13] What differentiated Jesus the liberator from Jesus a friend of the minjung was the latter Jesus's preference for a class of people who are "structurally alienated and inhumanly treated."[14] Such a perception of Jesus as the friend of minjung, however, was, and remains, a marginal view held mostly by a small number of intellectuals.

A Korean Jesus, a German Christ

Ahn's search for the historical Jesus is different from that of the Western pursuits. In many respects, it is intertwined with the period of "No Quest" but still sharply distinct from it. The first obvious difference is the personality of Jesus. While the Western search was obsessed with Jesus as a single person and portrayed him variously as a cynic, a charismatic, an eschatological prophet, or a sage, Ahn was seeking a collective persona whose identity was inseparable from and enmeshed in that of the minjung. While Bultmann considered Jesus "as one existence" and argued for an "existential solidarity with Jesus," Ahn insisted on experiencing Jesus "socially," "collectively," and "historically."[15] Ahn argued that such a collective concept, or what he called the "sociability" of Jesus, was found in Christological titles such as Son of Man and Son of God. To strengthen and legitimize his case, he enlisted an array of Western scholars, such as Walther Zimmerli, E. Schweizer, F. Hahn, and C. H. Dodd, who advocated the acknowledgment of collective connotations. This collective understanding of Jesus was clearly a radical departure from what Ahn considered the individualistic and bourgeois ideology of the historical critical method.

While Ahn agreed with the questers of the time that the Gospels were "not the personal biography of Jesus," he passionately maintained that they were the "history of Jesus' minjung movement."[16] They were stories of the growth and expansion of Jesus and the minjung. For Ahn, to understand the historical Jesus, it was important to recognize who was with him, and who his companions were. Traditionally, those who moved around Jesus had been treated as "secondary background characters" and as a foil to prop up the protagonist Jesus, a characterization that Ahn believed led to the loss of the historicity of Jesus's life.[17] The search for a historical Jesus is part of the social biography of the minjung. Ahn's repeated refrain was, "Where there is Jesus, there is the Minjung. And where there is the Minjung, there is Jesus."[18] In other words, Jesus needed the minjung as much as the minjung needed him.

Whereas the Western quest was enmeshed in the binary understanding of "historical Jesus" and "Christ of faith," Ahn yearned for the flesh-and-blood historical Jesus. This duality might sound plain and hackneyed now, but when Ahn began his theological studies in Germany, the kerygmatic Christ remained an "unchallengeable presupposition."[19] The rise of the form-critical method had turned scholars, especially German scholars, away from writing historical accounts of Jesus and toward a focus on the kerygma. Their staunch conviction was that the story about Jesus was told "from faith, for faith," and what was left in the Gospels was the kerygma of Jesus, not his personal history.

While scholars like Barth and Bultmann abandoned the search for the historical Jesus, Ahn was determined to find out who this historical person was. He even accused the Western scholars of "block[ing] the way to the historical Jesus."[20] As Ahn later bemoaned, as a result of the skepticism of these scholars, the historical Jesus had "become insignificant and the kerygma has become the sole concern of biblical scholars."[21] For the dialectical theologians like Karl Barth, the "Word" or the kerygma had become the staple of the Christian message. For them, faith meant faith in God's "Word," not in the historical reconstruction of an engaging human Jesus. What was important was not the "Christ after the flesh" but the Christ of kerygma proclaimed meaningfully for one's existence. This life-changing "Word" was heard through proclamation or preaching. As Bultmann put it, "access to Jesus Christ exists only in the preaching," and it was only in this act of proclamation that the Word "confronts the hearer here and now."[22] In other words, the "Word" becomes salvational in the present through the pulpit.

Ahn's mantra had been that "In the beginning there was the event, not the kerygma. This event was of course the Jesus-event. The kerygma concentrates on the meaning of Jesus' death and Resurrection. Yet, before the kerygma, there was the actual suffering and Resurrection of Jesus."[23] The kerygma, Ahn wrote, was "not a product of Jesus or one of his followers, but rather it evolved along with them, as the 'event.'"[24] Ahn blamed kerygmatic theologians for making historical events related to Jesus into an abstract idea. "Strictly speaking," he wrote, "kerygmatic theology did not exist first, but was preceded by the testimony of the eye-witnesses to the event of Jesus' death on the cross."[25] He also disputed the claim that one encountered Jesus through the pulpit. For him, one was confronted by Jesus not through preaching but in the liberative experience of the Crucifixion. What was encountered was not the "Word" demanding existential decision, as the German theologians had argued, but the historical and material life experiences of Jesus.

For Ahn, kerygma and the historical Jesus were ineluctably connected. Unwittingly, he initiated a search for the historical Jesus that became the main thrust of the New Quest for the historical Jesus, with scholars trying to move back through kerygma to seek the Jesus who was hidden behind it. He disagreed with this approach, however, writing: "One should methodologically move forward from the event to the kerygma, rather than to go backwards from the kerygma to the event."[26] While retaining a healthy respect for the kerygma, Ahn attempted to seek Jesus couched behind it. He wanted a more substantial role for Jesus than the dialectical theologians allowed for—the historical Jesus.

Ahn's outlook also differed from the German understanding of the Synoptic tradition. Unlike them, Ahn was not skeptical about the historical value of the Synoptics, but regarded them as providing "unique historical material about Jesus."[27] Synoptic traditions, in Ahn's view, were not a "product of the literary interest but the product of Jesus' minjung movement." Ahn's firm belief was that the "life and works of Jesus cannot be recognized fully in disconnection with the history of that movement originated by him."[28] He found fault with the redaction critics for paying "little attention to the audience of Jesus" and for "preferring to concentrate on theology" rather than on "redactional statements and redactional arrangements" of the Gospels—and more specifically, for overlooking the Gospel writers' emphasis on the people and their relationships with Jesus. This, in Ahn's view, was "crucial for understanding the identity and mission of Jesus."[29]

Another difference between the German critics and Ahn was the way they handled the oral tradition. The conventional argument of form-critics was that the sources behind the Gospel material were circulated in small units and existed separately with no connection to each other, were devoid of historical or cultural contexts, and were used for preaching, teaching, and in worship. More specifically, they did not offer anything of biographical interest, the only exception being the Passion narratives. Form-critics largely discounted the creative power of the evangelists in utilizing these sources. But Ahn saw the oral forms of the Gospels differently. He advanced the notion that the oral tradition went back to the tradition of the minjung, who had borne witness to the events of Jesus and preserved the stories surrounding him and the minjung. He also differentiated between the transmitters of the tradition of the Christ-kerygma and the Jesus-kerygma. The Christ-kerygma, he believed, had been devised by the early church for political reasons, whereas the Jesus-kerygma had been the work of the minjung. The upholders of the Christ-kerygma, wanting to please the Roman authorities and to be part of Jewish tradition (because Judaism enjoyed official status), turned the stories into abstract dogma, and couched them in metaphysical terms, whereas the Jesus-kerygma was mostly in the form of stories and rumors (his word). He assumed that it was the ordinary people who had handed on the pre-Synoptic sources and events related to Jesus in the form of rumors. It was the stories preserved by the minjung that helped to liberate Jesus, who had been "imprisoned in the cement of the dogma," and placed him "where the Minjung today are living."[30] The Jesus-kerygma was not the product of the powerful class but the labor of the minjung, who told the story of Jesus not as a biography of an individual person but as their own collective story. They saw their own life situation corresponding with the sufferings of Jesus. It was due to the prevailing political situation that the stories about Jesus had to be circulated secretly. They were preserved in the form of rumors and were circulated by the minjung.[31] They did so in order to safeguard the truth about the historical Jesus and to offer a counternarrative to the church's version. Ahn conceded that preserving these "rumors" was not an easy task. Even Mark, to his credit, who preserved some of the minjung experiences, ended up compromising with the kerygmatic Christology of the powerful.

Unlike the Germans, Ahn was not looking for the authentic words of Jesus but for the liberating potential of words that were attributed to him. There was an attempt at that time to recover the very words of Jesus before the current Jesus Seminar made it a lifelong obsession. Joachim Jeremias, who would hardly have counted himself as one of the New Questers, tried to seek the voice of Jesus in words like "Abba" and "Amen."[32] But Ahn was more keen to clarify the social and historical character of the words of Jesus, which, sadly, had been "desocialized," and to determine the "economic, political, cultural makeup of the people" to whom these words were addressed.[33] He could not separate the social character of the words of Jesus and their audience, namely, the rejected class of Galilee. These words were meant not as a call to faith in Christ but as a way to relieve them of their predicament.

Ahn accorded a different position and political role to Galilee. The form-critics assumed that Galilee was a symbolic construction of the early church, created for "literary or theological purposes." For Ahn, Galilee is important for three reasons: key events such as the Resurrection took place there; the minjung came from there; and as a rural region it stood in contrast to the urban Jerusalem. More specifically, the minjung of Galilee took a stance against the ruling class of Jerusalem.

The minjung of Galilee were important: they were the victims of Roman occupation, which had resulted in economic misery and military dictatorship; they were under the authoritarian regime of Herod Antipas; they were discriminated against by the people of Judea, who looked on them condescendingly; they were at the receiving end of the brutal and oppressive measures of the Jerusalem temple authorities; and they were exploited by absentee landlords. After the arrest of John the Baptist, Jesus did not go to the city; he headed for the countryside of Galilee. Ahn claimed that as a scholar he was concerned with such "geopolitical facts," which drew him "closer to the historical Jesus." Thus, as Ahn claimed, his quest differed "from any metaphysical search for the essence."[34]

One of the crucial differences between the Western search for the historical Jesus and this Asian version is that the Asian search does not stop with the first-century figure of Jesus but tries to understand Jesus as the "living Christ of the present."[35] According to this view, Christ was not a once-and-for-all event that happened way back in Jerusalem in the life of Jesus of Nazareth, but is instead a continuous happening, occurring and reappearing in various minjung events, like a "volcanic lava vein erupting continuously on the ceaseless flow." Minjung events in Korean history are Christ events and Christ is active in all minjung events. The uprisings of the minjung, then, are seen as a kind of Christ event.

Finally, the Western quest was trying make sense of twentieth-century industrialized and secular Europe and attempting to make Jesus meaningful to a people who had come of age, whereas Ahn was attempting to find a Jesus for the minjung, who were yet to become human. Political events like Jeon Tae-il's self-immolation, the Kwang ju revolt, and the democratic movements in Korea made Ahn and the Korean intellectuals realize that minjung liberation and national liberation were inevitably intertwined. It was in this Korean context that Ahn discovered Jesus. He wrote: "I encountered historical Jesus freshly and vividly. Minjung theology emerged in this process; in short, it was formulated through discovering minjung and Jesus in unity."[36]

As I indicated earlier, Ahn did not completely distance himself from the German pursuit. He gladly pressed into service some of their findings to buttress his case. An example of Ahn's collusion with the European search was his treatment of the Christological titles. He relegated and downgraded all of them except two—the Son of Man, and the Son of God—which strengthened his vested theological interests, as we saw earlier. Like Bultmann and his colleagues, Ahn did not find it useful to search for the historical man Jesus behind titles such as the Messiah; he found such an exercise to be "neither practical nor important."[37] He did not even try to explain these titles as post-Resurrection confessions of the early followers of Jesus, as most theologians do. Instead, he urged that "we should search for the meaning in his life-style."[38] For him, these titles neither referred to, nor were illustrative of, the personal life of Jesus. What counted most were the lifestyle choices Jesus had made, such as forgoing all material possessions and securities of life, cutting himself off from family attachments, and more crucially, overturning the value system so that those who exalted themselves were humbled, and the humble were exalted. The most outstanding example of "the core of the activity of the historical Jesus" was his unconditional acceptance of the minjung, the very people who were left abandoned by the establishment of the time, and his willingness to stand by them.[39] More than the Christological titles, what was critical to Ahn was that it was only through such activities that one could come to know Jesus. When the incarcerated John sent his disciples to ask Jesus, "Are you he that should come? or look we for another?" his reply was not an uncomplicated yes or no. He simply told him of the events effected by him: "The blind receive sight, the lame walk, the lepers are cleansed, the deaf hear, the dead are raised, and the good news is proclaimed to the poor." Ahn's message was that one should not rely on the titles to know who Jesus was, but should look for him in the events that occurred to and because of him—and a sure way to see this was to notice the effects of these events on the minjung.

Jesus, Friend to the Minjung

Ahn claimed that historical information about Jesus was "no more than fragmentary knowledge," but that did not prevent him from providing historical details of the life of Jesus.[40] It was E. P. Sanders who mooted the idea of settling the bare facts about Jesus, and Ahn followed suit. Starting with different presuppositions and using different methodologies, Sanders came up with fifteen "almost indisputable facts" about Jesus, whereas Ahn restricted his list to eleven such undeniable "facts."[41] Sanders's list included: Jesus was from Galilee; he was a carpenter by profession, without formal education, and neither married nor raised a family; he was a wandering ascetic preacher; the people whom he befriended were the villagers; he possessed the power to heal and exorcise devils; his public life was very brief; he had very little influence over the people whom he encountered; and he entered Jerusalem, purged the Temple, and was crucified as a criminal by the combined efforts of the Jewish religious authorities and the Roman government. The glaring omission in these bare facts was the Resurrection appearances. Sanders's main motive in producing his list was more historical than theological. He saw his task as freeing "history and exegesis from the control of theology" and his findings were not "pre-determined by theological commitment."[42] In contrast, Ahn's chief concern was both theological and historical. For him, the search for the historical Jesus and "our enthusiasm to follow him are inseparably linked."[43]

In Ahn's construction, Jesus comes across as a local villager without any cosmopolitan pretensions. Galilee, where Jesus was active, was depicted as a territory untainted by outside influences. The location of his ministry was largely the countryside and he hardly travelled beyond the

Palestinian territories. There was no evidence that he had any interest in Hellenism, or visited cities that were under Hellenistic culture and influence. He did not speak in metaphysical, intellectual, or philosophical language, but in the rural, folksy vernacular of the minjung, which came out of daily life. Or, as Ahn described it, it was the "minjung language from start to finish."[44]

Just like the minjung, Jesus was poor and did not have many material possessions. That he told his disciples to "have nothing but a staff" was a clear indication of his lifestyle. But Ahn's Jesus was not the conventional hermit or the mystic, remote from the hurly-burly of life. Instead he was fully involved in politics and saw his task as destroying the "structure of evil."[45]

Ahn's Jesus was cut off almost completely from his Jewish roots. The way Jesus organized his life, and his teaching method, were not "rabbi-like."[46] He never invoked the Torah or summoned the names of Jewish ancestors, as the rabbis of his time did. He acted as if he had "received full authority directly from God."[47] In other words, God's truth was discerned by Jesus not through the scriptures or human-made laws, but through the direct revelation of God. Ahn was very categorical about how this revelation was effected: "God's will is revealed in the event of Jesus."[48] The God whom Jesus proclaimed was not the Yahweh of the Hebrew scriptures who manifested a "tension between love and justice," but a God who sided with the minjung "completely and unconditionally."[49] The purpose of this revelation was not simply to curse the rich and to bless the poor, but also to point out the "paradox" that the salvation of the rich could "only be found through the poor."[50] This notion of the minjung as mediators of God's word may be inconceivable to those raised on knowing the divine through natural revelation, or through hearing it from the sacred texts.

The central contribution of Ahn's Jesus seems to be simply showing his solidarity with the minjung. He does not reform the structures that caused their misery. This Jesus does not organize the ochlos into a resistance force. He does not furnish them with any political program or want to lead them. He does rebuke those who attack them but he does not rebuke or demand anything from them. What he does mostly is to stand "passively" with them. What made Jesus different was his companionship with the minjung—the people who had been abandoned and alienated by the political and religious establishment of the time.

Ahn regarded the miracles of Jesus as the "most concrete and important" activity within his minjung movement, and considered them the events that had greatest impact on it.[51] Most of the beneficiaries of the healings were not wealthy or powerful, the exception being the synagogue official. Echoing the views of historical-criticism, Ahn conceded that the miracles were not objective accounts but went through many contextual changes to meet the theological demands of the writers. Contradicting Bultmann, Ahn asserted that all the miracle stories contained the "simplicity of the *minjung*" and lacked "elements of kerygma."[52] Ahn also dismissed the Enlightenment view of the miracles as mythical and individual acts, and interpreted them essentially as a collective phenomenon and part of the minjung story. In Ahn's reckoning, they were "social acts."[53]

Ahn challenged the conventional dual thinking that cast Jesus as the initiator and the people as complaisant objects of his healings. Ahn's contention was that the request to perform them came primarily from the minjung. The credit for healing did not go to Jesus himself either, but was often attributed to the faith of those who were healed. Most of the healings were about the ostracized being restored to their community. The healed experienced not only a new life but also a "new life within the minjung movement."[54] Back then, those suffering from diseases such as blindness, leprosy, and hemorrhage were seen as deserving excommunication on the grounds that they would pollute the environment for others, so those who were cured were able to restore their dignity and humanity by being sent back to their families and villages.

For Ahn, healing miracles were not only a social but also a political act. One example was the casting out of demons. Ahn interpreted exorcisms performed by Jesus as a struggle against the "old sovereign power" on behalf of the minjung. The conquering of Satan by Jesus, for instance, was presented as evidence for the "coming of the sovereignty of God."[55] Ahn attributed political motives to the story of the curing of the Gadarene demoniac, too. The actual focus of the event was the expulsion of Satan, and Satan was none other than the Roman empire. In other words, casting out Satan was an anti-colonial activity directed against the occupying Roman power.

In contrast to Paul, Ahn portrayed Jesus as defying the social conventions of the time and championing the cause of the women who were "the *minjung* of the *minjung*" (italics in original)—they were triply exploited, by the state, religious structures, and at home. True, Jesus had twelve male disciples, but, disregarding the social norms of the day, he surrounded himself with women "who carried out the mission of the gospels just as the apostles did."[56] When women's rights conflicted with patriarchal society, Ahn was keen to point out how often Jesus sided with the women. A conspicuous case was Jesus's attitude to divorce, which was heavily stacked against women. Jesus's speech mirrored the everyday language of women. The words he used, such as bread, breasts, bosom, salt, and banquet, were all associated with women. These words were not merely figures of speech but indicated in the mind of Jesus the pivotal role that women were going to play in the Kingdom. He imagined both male and female having equal space. For instance, if he referred to two men working in the field, he also narrated the story of two women at the mill. Similarly, if a shepherd rejoiced at the finding of a lost sheep, there was also a woman showing delight at discovering a lost coin.

In Ahn's scheme of things, it was women who played the vital role in helping Jesus to decide his mission in life. Unlike Endō's Judas (we will hear of him later), who convinced Jesus of his final destiny, it was the unnamed woman (Mary? or Martha?) who poured perfume on the head of Jesus, preparing him for the Crucifixion and so influencing his decision. "You must die" was conveyed through the act of the pouring of oil. Ahn's proposition was that it was the minjung woman who "performed a crucial act" that "strengthened Jesus' consciousness and decision." In other words, the "final decision was made" not "solely by Jesus himself, as heroism is defined" but by those women gathered around him. The woman remained silent while pouring oil, but her action indicated to Jesus that his "path [had] already been determined." Ahn could be accused of reiterating the idea of a male redeemer rescuing the women, but his redeemer was not a macho Messiah. Women's hope, Ahn wrote, lay not in "an iron-fisted, dominating Messiah but in one who would stand by them."[57]

In Ahn's reconstruction, Jesus comes out as a closet Zealot. Ahn reckoned that Zealots were part of the minjung and at the same time different from them. In his words: "The Zealots, in their social character and position, have some things in common with the *ochlos*, but the Zealots have a clear purpose which the *ochlos* do not have."[58] The clear purpose of the Zealots was to liberate Jews from foreign rule and exploitation. They were not simply mindless armed insurgents but had "ideologies." Zealots flocked to Galilee, a place where people longed for a new world, and it was in this very territory that Jesus preached the coming of the Kingdom of God. Jesus's intimate connection with Zealots was evident in his having two apostles who belonged to a Zealot group that included the flawed Judas Iscariot, and Peter, whose name was Simon Bar-Jona (which could be interpreted as "terrorist"). With such close links, Ahn concluded that it was "hard to deny that Jesus was intimately connected with the Zealot party."[59]

For Ahn, Zealots were not bandits as the Romans called them in order to discredit their cause, but the champions of the Palestinian peasants. An example of the Zealots' support for the Galilean farmers was their act of burning the ledgers that contained the names of those who owed money, thus making the collection of outstanding dues from the people impracticable. The aim was to "abolish the debts of the Galilean minjung."[60] Ahn cited Josephus to make this claim. He perceives the Zealots as the inheritors of "the spirit of Hasidem" and participants in the Maccabean War, their priority being to occupy and purge Jerusalem of its foreign hegemony. Ahn's postulation was that "Jesus stood within this struggle of the minjung and his entrance into Jerusalem and cleansing of the Temple reflected this struggle."[61] Like the Zealots, Jesus fundamentally rejected the Temple, which was responsible both for the economic exploitation of the minjung and for corrupting the Jewish people's faith in Yahweh. More significantly, the Temple was the pivotal link in the abuse of the Jewish minjung by the Roman rulers. Rejection of the Temple was the first step in realizing liberation from the Romans, the goal of the Zealots and one that was seen as having the support of Jesus. Ironically, Jesus was betrayed by Judas, a Zealot who was "ideologically disappointed with Jesus."[62]

In Ahn's construal, Jesus is portrayed as a person who was continually in conflict with two groups of people—the Jewish religious leaders and the ruling Roman authorities—who together acted as a "single enemy" in threatening the interest of the minjung. This warning of Jesus was illustrative of their threat: "Be careful. Watch out for the yeast of the Pharisees and that of Herod" (Mark 8.17). Jesus continually clashed with the Pharisees because they were the people who "interfered in the relationship between him and his minjung."[63] Jesus confronted them because the minjung were being disadvantaged by their "formalistic interpretation" of the law. He also opposed the Roman Empire and the Herodians because they caused the minjung's economic misery. It was these rulers' land-grabbing and taxation policies that went against the poor. More alarmingly, Jesus viewed the Roman rulers as usurping God and taking over God's throne.

In response, Jesus proclaimed the imminent coming of the Kingdom, which promised to overthrow all ruling powers. The sharpest criticism of the ruling power was found in Jesus's saying: "You know that those foreigners who call themselves kings like to order their people around. And their great leaders have full power over the people they rule. But don't act like them" (Mark 10.42–44). Ahn conceded that there were no records of Jesus's direct confrontation with the Romans, but the Herodians' plot to kill him at the beginning of his ministry was an indication of the danger he posed to the existing political order. His sentence to death by the power of the Roman court as a political agitator was another proof that he was a threat to the Roman Empire.

Ahn portrayed Jesus as a person who opposed both privatization of property and the accumulation of power by a privileged few. His Jesus saw his task as restoring the land, wealth, and power that had fallen into the hands of private owners to the status of *kong*—a Korean concept meaning that which cannot be privatized. Palestine was the prime example of how different invaders had privatized lands and resources. The repentance that Jesus preached was not, as Western interpreters explained, for individual moral lapses, or about a changed inner attitude, but involved a "concrete act that restores *kong* and makes possible the return of that which belongs to God." Reading from such a perspective, Ahn argued that the enigmatic saying of Jesus "Give back to God what belongs to God" meant giving back to the people the land that had been commonly owned and unprivatizable. As Ahn put it, "repentance was inconceivable if perceived independently of the issue of privatization."[64] The harsh statements Jesus aimed at the rich were designed to remind them that the guiding principle of their lives was not "to own" but to acknowledge that the land, and the wealth, belonged to God.

For Ahn, the Kingdom of God was not a static concept but an evolving one. Initially, it meant the return of the state of Israel, where the sovereignty of God ruled supreme over any human authorities. This was the model envisaged by prophets as an antidote to corrupt and evil kings. Then the idea that the Davidic dynasty would usher in the reign of God, advocated by the ruling classes, emerged as a way of giving hope to people who were under frequent harassment from foreign countries. While these two expectations of the Kingdom of God were deeply immersed in the political realities of the time, a third sense of the Kingdom of God arose, too, that was rooted in and expressed through a religious and apocalyptic vision. Ahn's Jesus, however, envisaged a Kingdom that transcended narrow Jewish territorial, national, and religious expectations, or, as he put it, was "beyond Judaism."[65]

The Kingdom that Jesus had in mind did not essentially center around Israel, but Ahn acknowledged that it would be "un-Israelite" and "irresponsible" to think about it without them. That outsiders had priority was exemplified in the words of Jesus: "The Gentiles will be the first to participate in the kingdom, before the Jews." The Kingdom that Jesus envisaged had echoes of the vision of Isaiah, which anticipated salvation for all humanity (2.2–4.1, 49.6–7). Ahn's Jesus did not perceive the Kingdom along a dynastic line but from the perspective of the minjung. The minjung movement was openly connected to the impending arrival of the Kingdom, and the expulsion of the Romans was the main focus of the movement. The Last Supper, which has been "sacramentalized and dehistoricized "in the process of transmission, was, in Ahn's view, the decisive battlefield for this coming of the kingdom. The Kingdom, in other words, was a "process of struggles" and not an "object of contemplation."[66]

The Kingdom that Jesus proclaimed was not about royal banquets, or a return to covenant loyalties, but about sharing, especially food. The disparity between the poor and the wealthy, and the widening gap between urban and rural areas, meant that people could not envision a Kingdom without a concern for food. Ahn writes that it was "natural for the poor to regard the coming of the kingdom of God as the distribution of wealth (food sharing)." For Ahn, the Kingdom meant the "reality of eating together," which was epitomized in the communal consumption of food with alien and alienated people. If happiness was regarded as the primary feature of the kingdom, then Ahn claimed that nothing was more important to the poor than the "happiness of eating." Noting that the petition for daily bread in the Lord's Prayer followed "thy kingdom come," Ahn was puzzled as to how the church could ignore "so important and so intimate a relationship" between the Kingdom and eating together.[67] For Ahn, more than the imperial connotations of "Kingdom," its experience of communal eating was important.

In spite of a communal feel about the Kingdom at times, Ahn's understanding of it sounds remarkably like the existential approach envisaged by Bultmann. Just as Bultmann's idea of the Kingdom confronted people with a radical decision, Ahn, too, wrote that its abrupt arrival called "for our decision and repentance."[68] In line with his German mentor, Ahn, too, believed that the Kingdom was not the work of human effort but demonstrative of God's grace and initiation.

Ahn's Jesus was the victim of political violence and his crucifixion was a historical event, so Ahn criticized kerygmatic theology for turning it into a dehistoricized affair, reducing it to a religious symbol and making it into an object of worship so that the cross experience had lost its relationship with the reality of suffering. Ahn wrote: "*This petrified cross does no longer associate with the suffering people, but does serve as a dogma to interrogate and judge the sinners.*" For Ahn, the Passion story was based on a "historical fact." Jesus's death had nothing to do with superhuman sacrifice on the part of Jesus. It was about the death of a weak person who was as powerless as the minjung. Jesus was killed by the "strong power of the structural evil of the world."[69]

The contents of the Passion story resonated with the life and struggles of the minjung, who were its propagators. The death of Jesus, in keeping with Ahn's thinking, was not an individual experience but a collective minjung event. The betrayal, trial, and execution that Jesus went through were not the lonely happenings of one man but embodied the life and fate of the minjung, who went through these indignities daily. Ahn was unequivocal about who died on the cross. It was not "Jesus of Nazareth who was deserted, unduly judged and executed on the cross, but minjung."[70] On the cross Jesus did not self-importantly claim, "I did it for you"; instead his desperate last cry "why have you forsaken me" was a cry of disillusion on behalf of the minjung. This distressed scream represented the minjung's accumulated anger, resentment, bitterness, and sorrow. Ahn was convinced that the minjung had told the story about the Passion of Jesus not as "his story, but as their own story."[71]

Unlike the Crucifixion, the Resurrection for Ahn was not a historical event. He indicated that there was not a "single hint about an immediate resurrection anywhere in the Passion-histories"; rather Passion announcements had presupposed it.[72] The "main concern" was not the resurrected Jesus, but how Resurrection was "realized in the community," for this varied according to historical circumstances.[73] The experience of the Resurrection was not universal but limited to the believers of Jesus. More importantly, it was realized only by those who "shared his sufferings and not by onlookers"—that is, the newly resurrected Jesus was identified and acknowledged only by his followers and not by the people who had executed him, like Pilate or Caiaphas. In other words, it was not an objective event open to all; instead it was limited to the few faithful.

Ahn distinguished between the Resurrection event and the Resurrection kerygma, which was mainly the work of Paul, expressed in his Corinthian correspondence (1 Corinthians 15.3–6). Ahn found a number of discrepancies between what Paul had to say and the Gospel narratives. The omission of women, and the mention of the risen Jesus appearing to five hundred men, for example, were "unimaginable" in the Gospel context. By simply describing the death of Jesus as being in accordance with the scriptures, Paul failed to mention where, by whom, and why Jesus was executed. In Ahn's view, the Resurrection as an event and Resurrection as kerygma were developed independently, and the latter was invented to reinforce the apostolic authority of the church. Ahn's risen Jesus was not the "church's resurrected Lord," nor seen through the eyes of the faithful, but perceived through the minjung experience of Jesus. Ahn thus criticized Paul for "suppress [ing] the *minjung* tradition."[74]

A Minjung Emancipator

Although Ahn respected Eastern sages like the Buddha and Confucius, he remained committed to Jesus as the decisive figure. The Buddha had seen human suffering from birth, through aging and sickness, to death. He overcame temptations and finally achieved spiritual enlightenment and nirvana. He was engaged during the next forty years of his life in his quest to save humanity. But this mission to save humanity, unlike the mission of Jesus, Ahn complained, was not motivated or aimed to save the oppressed. It was made possible by the demands of a great king who entreated Buddha to manifest great mercy and compassion. Although Ahn discussed at length the temptations that Jesus underwent, he was silent with regard to the similar temptations that Buddha himself experienced. Like mainstream Western scholars, Ahn failed to entertain the idea of a possible influence of Eastern thought on nascent Christianity.

As regards Confucius and Jesus, Ahn points out that both realized their potential before they reached forty. Neither was able to see their vision being fulfilled in their lifetime. Unlike Confucius, Jesus did not train himself for a government office, nor did he want to become part of the political elite. Whereas Confucius pursued a life of scholarly learning, Jesus stood on the side of the poor and as a result was put to death. Confucius, too, had a messianic vision. Saddened at the division of China, Confucius appealed to the monarchs to unite, and expected the restoration of the Chou dynasty. This was analogous to Israel's Messiah restoring the Kingdom of David. Yet whereas Confucius was keen on restoring earthly kingdoms and idealized monarchs, Jesus perceived his ideal goal as the "destruction of all human thrones for the realization of the sovereignty of God."[75]

In Ahn's estimation there was a fundamental difference between Jesus and his counterparts Buddha and Confucius: the Asian masters did not engage in what Ahn called Galilean activity—activity that involved liberating the "minjung from tyranny." Jesus did not enter the public ministry after reaching a certain point in his spiritual life, or come up with a specific political plan to change the world. Ahn's proposition was that Jesus entered his public life on the occasion of a "particular political event," namely the arrest of his comrade (Ahn's word) John the Baptist. After John had been arrested, Jesus went to Galilee. The significance of this move was to liberate "the people who sat in darkness."[76] The redactional remarks in Mark and Matthew were sure indications of the "deep relationship between Jesus and this area." His going to Galilee was a turning point in Jesus's life that neither Buddha nor Confucius had experienced. It is the emancipatory work in Galilee that made the difference between Jesus and the Eastern masters like the Buddha and Confucius.

Reflections, Observations

The grim and harsh political conditions under which the first-generation minjung theologians labored has changed remarkably, so that today there is a semblance of democracy and freedom for these scholars. (Like today's smartphones, minjung theologians are identified as first generation, second generation, and so on.) The minjung theology that Ahn and others pioneered has morphed into various Korean contextual theologies such as unification theology and environmental theology. Recently, a sexual minorities movement called Iban (otherwise known as the LGBQT community) has been in dialogue with minjung theology for mutual help in the fight for rights.[77] The identity of the minjung, which was never fully defined, has also changed. Those theologians who carry the original DNA of minjung theology see immigrant workers, war victims, displaced persons, and disabled people as the new minjung. That is, "minjung" now extends beyond the once nationally and ethnically defined concept to include people who have been made victims by global politics and economics.

In these days of free-market thinking, the type of exegesis that Ahn was engaged in, which combined the rigors of historical criticism with social appeal, might have a retro feel about it. The heightened political environment in which Ahn undertook his exegesis has long gone. The current Korean theologians do not have the experiential advantage of living through harsh political and economic realities; they have come of age during a wealthier and prosperous phase in Korea, and so they fail to grasp or relate to what it feels like to be on the underside of history. After the democratization of Korea, the new crop of theologians talks not about minjung but about "national people" and "citizens" who submissively incorporate national aspirations for the realization of their own hopes and dreams.[78]

Some of the exegetical work that sounded so exciting and made Ahn an important biblical scholar has little purchase now. His innovative work on the ochlos as poor will run into difficulty today. Recent studies have demonstrated that his beloved minjung were a complex group of people and not as innocent and downtrodden as he portrayed them. James Crossley has shown that "sinners," among whom Ahn places his ochlos, are "lawless, idolatrous, violent, oppressive, rich and hate the poor" and so could well have been seen as siding with the very people who were responsible for the economic injustice in Galilee.[79] What is evident is that the ochlos was a wide-ranging collection of people composed of both oppressed and oppressors—not a single group consisting of victims and the poor, as Ahn would like to portray them. His other pet theme—Galilee—will also likely come under severe scrutiny. Even before Western scholars like Sean Freyne, Richard Horsley, and Douglas Oakman took up the topic, Ahn drew attention to Galilee and its social and political significance for the message of Jesus. But his overtly simplistic and one-dimensional reading of Galilee as the land of poverty and protest may not have the same gripping appeal today. In fact, Galilee studies has since become a subdiscipline in biblical studies, and the search for the historical Galilee has yielded a contradictory picture. It was not a "den of minjung" as Ahn would have us believe.[80] Current scholarship presents a far more complex region. It was not only a land stricken with poverty, but also one that supported an economically prosperous society.[81]

In line with liberation theology, Ahn also had a romantic and idealized view of the poor minjung. He ignored the pliable nature of the ochlos. It was the ochlos who were stirred up by the chief priests, which led to the release of Barabbas by Pilate, and it was the same crowd that cried "Crucify him." Ahn, however, casually dismissed them as the Jerusalem minjung who had been "infected with the disease of avarice for money" and blamed the Jerusalem authorities for contaminating them with such material inducements.[82] He also ignored the examples of ordinary people who could be vicious to their own people. The Parable of the Unmerciful Servant (Matthew 18.21–35) is a notable example of a servant who was forgiven by the master for not paying his debts, yet then was cruel to a fellow servant who had failed to pay the money owed to him.

The Kingdom of God that Ahn comes up with ignores those biblical passages that support the colonializing tendencies of the Kingdom. His imagined alternative conveniently overlooked royal paraphernalia associated with the Kingdom such as sitting on the throne of glory and passing judgment. These were clear signs of power and dominance associated with and exercised by the Kingdom (Matthew 19.28, Luke 22.29–30). What Ahn fails to notice is that buried beneath the anticolonial oratory of Jesus there lurks imperial thinking that speaks the language of control, supremacy, and judgment.

The trouble with Ahn is that he is too addicted to Bultmann, Jesus, and Minjung, not necessarily in that order, and this comes across clearly in his writings. He owed a great deal to Bultmann and acknowledged his debt profusely—he practically replicated Bultmann's methodology but couched it in minjung terms. While Bultmann wrapped up Jesus in Heidegger's language of existentialism, and incorporated the word of God theology to fit with a kerygmatic Christ as a practical and theological alternative to the historical Jesus, Ahn utilized the language of the minjung and their social and political reality to fashion his Jesus. And just as Bultmann applied chronologically inappropriate twentieth-century existential categories such as "decision," "meaning," and "either-or" to show Jesus challenging his original audience, Ahn employed minjung language to understand Jesus and his first listeners. His fondness for Jesus was apparent in his use of the phrase "my attachment to Jesus," which occurs several times in *Jesus of Galilee*.

There is a tinge of Christian triumphalism in Ahn: it looks as if he is still in the business of converting the world to his beloved Jesus. Just as Jesus gave his famous sermon on a Galilean mountaintop, the risen

Jesus, this time, urges them to "advance into the whole world." Ahn, who was well-versed in the art of historical criticism, quoted the Matthean missionary command to support his evangelical zeal without questioning its authenticity or its possible later addition.

This brings me to some of the apparent contradictions in Ahn's thinking. While he approvingly cited the Matthean missionary command, he later described it as the construction of the church, which had assumed power and authority over the years. In his words, this formulation was "the self-consciousness of the Catholicized Church." Another inconsistency is Jesus's usage of the Torah and Jewish tradition. Although Ahn claimed that Jesus neither invoked the Torah nor drew on Jewish teaching, on a number of occasions his Jesus pointed to the prophets to establish his case. One such case was his quoting of Jeremiah for his actions in the Temple. These discrepancies could be attributed to the various occasions where Ahn's writings appeared. *Jesus of Galilee,* where most of these inconsistencies occur, is a collection of essays that Ahn wrote over a period of time. Ahn, too, is liable to be charged with anti-Semitism. The vehemently anti-Temple stance that his Jesus took on bordered on prejudice against Judaism and Jewish institutions. Ahn's anti-Semitism did not come out of the European agenda of a hatred toward Jews. It was based instead on the simple fact that Jewish laws and the Temple system went against the welfare of the Galilean minjung.

Ahn's exegetical findings may come under heavy scrutiny now and be surpassed by new discoveries, but his concern for the suffering of the poor is a cause worth championing and emulating. Though not his own, his methodology—community involvement followed by theological and biblical reflection in the light of that involvement—is still a valid theological project. The "agitational contemporaneity" found in the exegesis of minjung theology is worth pursuing and reviving. His willingness to suffer physically for his radical beliefs may not be possible at a time when interpreters are judged by their management-induced research and peer-reviewed work, and when confirmation is encouraged rather than confrontation of the settled wisdom. Ahn's writings showed signs of early marks of postcolonial criticism, which came into its own after his time. He would certainly have benefited from it.

Finally, contexts may change, new theological questions and concepts may arise, and a fresh set of theologians may crop up. But certain basic hermeneutical goals remain: telling the truth to power, and telling the poor the truth about the powerful. Ahn and his fellow first-generation minjung theologians were rare exemplifiers of this hermeneutical principle. Ahn was not only an outstanding scholar, but also a compassionate human being. There is something warm about him and his writings. Although culturally and intellectually he was in a class apart from the minjung whose cause he championed, he was one of those writers whom the minjung could know was on their side. Ahn would happily settle for such an acceptance and recognition rather than for what professional critics make of his work.

9

Jesus in a Kimono

"The weakling," "the washout," a "do-nothing," "the ineffectual," "ugly and emaciated," a "miserable dog"—these were just some of the descriptions of Jesus used by the Japanese novelist Shūsaku Endō (1923–1996) in his writings. These disparaging images of Jesus would have delighted Varma and Chowdhuri, whose damning perceptions of Jesus we encountered earlier. But unlike them, Endō never used these negative and dismissive phrases with malice. His adverse and antagonistic depictions of Jesus were a way of articulating a human Jesus whose abject weakness was perceived as his unassailable strength. Endō's ambition all along had been to redesign the Christian faith so that it fits more like a Japanese kimono than the Christianity that was introduced to him by his mother, which, as he put it, came in the form of ill-fitting Western garb.

Endō was an unusual Asian writer in that he continually grappled in his novels with the question of Jesus and his relevance for a country already brimming with religious ideas. What is often overlooked is that his *A Life of Jesus* was a rare attempt by a twentieth-century Asian Christian to search for the historical Jesus in the manner of the Western quest. His historical reconstruction of Jesus blends imaginatively Gospel narratives, scholarly explorations, and artistic imaginations into a persuasive and readable story. And although there are competent essays analyzing Endō's sketches of Jesus in his novels, his *A Life of Jesus* has been neglected, especially by the biblical fraternity.[1]

The principal task of this chapter, then, is to examine his *A Life of Jesus,* and to see to what extent his portrayal of Jesus reaffirms or moves beyond the images depicted in his novels. Commentators often overlook the fact that Endō's biography of Jesus appeared halfway through his writing career. His reconstruction of the historical Jesus gave him an opportunity to weigh, check, affirm, analyze, and reconsider his own earlier imaginative configurations of Jesus in his novels such as *Silence, The Girl I Left Behind,* and *Wonderful Fool,* and then to continue to extend and amplify the same images of Jesus in his later novels such as *Samurai* and *Deep River.*

Endō's quest for the historical Jesus was motivated by two factors. One was to explain Jesus to a largely non-Christian Japanese audience, to "make Jesus understandable in terms of the religious psychology of my non-Christian countrymen and thus to demonstrate that Jesus is not alien to their religious sensibilities."[2] Linked with this was an intention to satisfy the religious mindset of his people. The Japanese instinct was to seek "in their gods and buddhas a warm-hearted mother rather than a stern father," one who "suffers with us" and who "allows for our weakness."[3] The Japanese had "little tolerance for any kind of transcendent being who judges humans harshly, then punishes them."[4] Endō said in an interview that Buddhism "came in the form of the co-suffering and forgiving Buddha, not in the form of the just, angry and punishing Buddha."[5] Endō's aim was to avoid the stern father image that often characterized Christianity and instead "depict the kind-hearted maternal aspect of God revealed to us in the personality of Jesus."[6] He was convinced that the Japanese would be more open to Jesus's motherly side.

Blending Exegesis and Eisegesis: Effortless Meeting of the Twain

In his depiction of the life of Jesus, Endō, unlike Western biographers who accorded a greater weight to the Synoptic writings, drew from all the four Gospels, but remained skeptical of their historical merit. He opined that the narratives of Jesus buried in the Gospels were not "necessarily written in the modern spirit of accurate reporting." In his view, the words of the Gospels, though presented as the precise sayings of Jesus, were no "more than a reflection of the kerygma," and the events related to Jesus were "simply legends" circulated haphazardly in various communities. He was convinced that it was not possible to "retrace the life of Jesus with *absolute precision*." Endō commented that the Gospel writers did not always stick with the "'real facts' in depicting the lives of Jesus."[7]

In making this argument, Endō distinguished between "a fact and a truth in the Bible."[8] The following brings out forcefully his thinking: "Faith far and away transcends the trivialities of non-essential fact, and because in the depths of their hearts the believers of that generation wished them so, the scenes are therefore true."[9] He acknowledged that many scenes depicted in the New Testament were not historically true, yet these nonhistorical accounts represented the truth because they had been derived from the faith of the people who believed in Jesus. He illustrated this with two events that could have grown out of people's belief. One was the Bethlehem nativity, which might not be factually correct, but "is the truth" because for most people Bethlehem symbolized the innocent spiritual space that people longed for, and was a metaphor for the "purest and the most innocent place on earth." True, Endō left out the Bethlehem scene in his biography of Jesus, yet it remained an "integral part of the true world which the souls of human beings have craved."[10] The other event was Jesus entering Jerusalem on a donkey. This scene, according to Endō, was a creation of the Gospel writers that captured vividly the "spirit then prevailing in Jerusalem and the excitement of the pilgrims."[11] Endō took a similar view with regard to truth in his two celebrated novels, *Silence* and *The Samurai*—both based on Japanese history. For him, more than the historical facts that had triggered these novels, the truth that emanated from them was important. In an interview, he said he had "no intention of writing down *jijitsu* (facts); if I did, the result would no longer be a novel. Rather, to write a novel is to record *shinjitsu* (truths), not facts . . . The art of creating a novel is to use 'truths' to reconstruct 'facts'; real 'facts' themselves are totally unimportant to the novelist."[12] Endō added that "creative composing is not to be equated with telling a lie."[13] Far more important for him than the factual veracity of these events was the wider, spiritual enlightenment they projected.

Being a novelist, Endō took liberties with the Gospel narratives in fabricating plots and at times in producing uncomplimentary portrayals of the disciples. Endō suggested that the choosing of the disciples should happen not at the beginning of Jesus's ministry as the Gospels record, but at the halfway stage, specifically at Caesarea Philippi. Endō argued that initially there were more than twelve disciples who were attracted to Jesus and most of them were the "followers of John." They still hoped that he would take up John's promise and restore the "lost purity of the Jewish religion," and, more specifically, that he would act as their leader in their struggle against Roman oppression. Their persistence was an opportunity for Jesus to test their true expectations and allegiance. Endō therefore suggested that the calling of the disciples documented at the start of his Galilean preaching in the Synoptics should be relocated to after the Caesarea Philippi incident, where Jesus had the opportunity to test their hopes and loyalty. Similarly, he proposed rearranging the sequence of the Sermon on the Mount and the feeding miracle. In his view, both these events took place on the same day and were interconnected. In Endō's reconstruction, after the feeding, the crowd urged Jesus to stand up for the Kingdom of Judah, but he stunned and silenced them in his Sermon on the Mount by saying instead to love your enemies. This, as Endō noted, "shook the crowd."

Another example of Endō's speculative exegesis is the reason he comes up with for the authorities not detaining Peter and the other disciples when Jesus was arrested. Endō surmised that there might have been a prior agreement in which Peter and the disciples pledged that they would not have any dealings with Jesus. "In exchange for the promise," wrote Endō, "they escaped arrest. That's how I see it."[14] Peter's denial of Jesus was some kind of an arrangement between the Sanhedrin and all the disciples, and it illustrated the duplicity of the disciples. Like the leading characters in his novels, all the disciples in Endō's version apostatized and all were in need of forgiveness.

Endō's imaginative eisegesis was his remarkable take on Jesus's return to Galilee after his sojourn in the Qumran territory and his ordeal with Satan. Taking advantage of the discrepancies in the biblical chronology, Endō reckoned that Jesus went straight to his mother. This return, in Endō's view, was similar to the scene in the Parable of the Prodigal Son, but with one difference. Instead of the father, it was Mary who ran and "threw her arms around his neck and kissed him affectionately." Just like the father in the parable who rejoiced at his son giving up his evil habits, it was the mother of Jesus who was relieved to see her son turning his back on the "ill-humoured image of God" that he had encountered in John's community. His speculation on the mother-and-son union, Endō claimed, was reinforced by other events: when Jesus accompanied his mother to the wedding at Cana, and when he stayed at home with her in Capernaum.

As an exegete, Endō at times defies the accepted wisdom and contributes his own exceptional expositions. The Temptation of Jesus ordeal has been interpreted variously as Jesus overcoming pride, avarice, and power; testing his role as the chosen Messiah; or as a sign of his becoming stronger than Satan. Endō perceived Jesus's wilderness experience differently. For him, it was not a kerygmatic event or a psychological drama but an actual incident that happened in the wilderness. What is more, he identified the tormentor. Unlike the biblical commentators who simply used a generic term like Satan, Endō provided an identity and a name for the tempter—the Qumran community. What happened in the wilderness was an "ideological showdown" between Jesus and the Qumran community that boiled down to this: "Pursue earthly salvation for the people and in return I promise to give you the fullness of power on earth."[15] The possibility of the encounter was further strengthened by Endō's claim that Jesus meditated not far from the Qumran monastery. Both Satan and the Qumran community had the same objective of recruiting Jesus for their cause, but Jesus resisted both.

The other example was his reading of Jesus's words on the cross, "My God, my God why hast thou forsaken me?" He discounted all the conventional understandings of the desolate cry of as a sign of despondency, sadness, complaint, and protest aimed at God for the failure to rescue him. He observed that these utterances came from Psalm 22 and that a close reading of it revealed that the agonizing words of Jesus were not about despair, as traditionally perceived, but were essentially a song of praise. In making his case, Endō draws attention to the rest of the psalm, which his audience would have been familiar with. The Gospel accounts quote simply the opening verse, which describes the hopelessness of Jesus, but the same psalm goes on to pay respect and reverence to God: "I will tell of your name to my brothers and sisters; in the midst of the congregation I will praise you." This cry, as far as Endō was concerned, was not about despair but "actually a song of praise to the Lord."[16] Analyzing other sayings of Jesus on the cross, Endō concluded that these words were a "declaration of absolute trust" rather than voiced in anger, hatred, or hostility.[17] They were not "words of pleading" but words of homage to God.

A Novelist's Vision: A Maternal Messiah

Endō's engaging biography, *A Life of Jesus,* is an attempt to "de-Westernize" Christianity so that Jesus could be made meaningful to Japanese people. Unlike other quests for the historical Jesus, which start with the analysis of the teachings of Jesus, or investigate his historical and geographical background, Endō began with an unusual pursuit: a search for a physical Jesus. What did he look like? How did he sound? The arresting opening lines of *A Life of Jesus* expressed this intention: "We have never seen his face. We have never heard his voice." Endō admitted that the Gospels were not helpful for answering such questions, that we are left to "rummage our own imaginations." Since no one had criticized Jesus for his physical looks, Endō inferred that Jesus must have had the normal physique of a preacher. Benefiting from the work of Ethelbert Stauffer, Endō imagined that Jesus might have been a "person tall in stature and well put together." In his depiction, his face looked "old beyond his years," and his eyes at times betrayed a "tinge of anguish." After the torment by the Roman soldiers, he seemed "thin." Endō let loose his novelist's imagination and described Jesus as having dark hair that parted in the middle and flowed onto his shoulders, and as sporting a customary beard and a moustache. This Jesus looked remote from the Western blue-eyed and blonde Jesus. Endō's Jesus, in his outward style, "cut no special figure," he had a boringly common name, and his life followed an "uneventful routine" that was similar to that of others. Endō reckoned, too, that Jesus was a man with a limited wardrobe. His clothes must have been shabby and worn because anyone who would discourage his disciples from having a "second coat" was unlikely to have had much to choose from himself.

Endō saw Galilee, where Jesus grew up, as a backward, "weak nation" and a "land trampled underfoot by the Gentiles." Galileans were a disparate population held together by their Jewish faith. When Endō's Jesus emerged in first-century Palestine, there was popular resentment toward two classes of people—the ruling Romans and the "priestly caste in Jerusalem." This was a time when the Galileans viewed with disapproval and hostility the enthusiastic "Romanizing of King Herod Antipas." They felt that the "purity of Judaism" and the monotheistic faith were under constant threat from their conquerors, who encouraged the worship of many gods and goddesses. The oppressive policies of Sejanus, the political mover in the court of the emperor, made the situation worse. His issuing of an order that all coinage should have the emblem of the Roman emperor, and his repealing of the powers of the Jewish leadership, especially that of the Sanhedrin and the priests, hardened the Jews. Although the Gospels did not expressly indicate how Jesus responded to this anti-Roman feeling, Endō sensed that there was a "scent of antagonism" noticeable between him and Herod, and the fact that Jesus scrupulously avoided the cities built by Herod demonstrated his resentment toward the man who was to interrogate him later in Jerusalem. The disgruntlement of the Galileans was not aimed exclusively toward the Roman imperialists and the affluent elite but also toward their own priestly class, whose priests acquired privileges simply by collaborating with the Roman empire. It had been almost five hundred years since the prophets had spoken of restoring national honor and glory in the form of the Kingdom of God. The prevailing economic privation and political oppression were dashing the hopes of the Jews for a political Messiah. It was in such an unsettled, discontented atmosphere that the people of Galilee welcomed Jesus as the "one who was to come."[18]

Like Parekh's portrait of Jesus that we looked at earlier, Endō's Jesus resembled a villager who stayed close to home, unaffected by the dominant Hellenistic culture. The opulent lifestyle of the rulers seemed to be alien to him. Just like his people, Jesus at Nazareth experienced "the stinking sweat, the misery and the penury of the working class." His literary and cultural influences were restricted to reading together with the poor villagers the books of the Old Testament. He had hardly any contact with the Roman "fashions and ways of thought." Endō utilized the work of Bornkamm to strengthen his case for a rural, regional Jesus: "We can find in the thinking of Jesus no trace of any influence from the alien Hellenistic way of life."[19] Jesus was part of the class of people facing political harassment, economic hardship, and physical infirmity, and expecting both the judgment of God on alien rulers and redemption from their oppressive rule. It was in this context that Jesus arose, announcing a God who was more willing to suffer with the people in their weakness and poverty than to lift them out of misery, or offer them national redemption.

A Life of Jesus was written with a novelist's verve and imagination. In it, Jesus comes over as a "Japanese" person whose humanity, compassion, and spirit of self-sacrifice were more pronounced than his Davidic descent, or his relationship with a mysterious "Father in heaven." Endō's Jesus did not fit in with the prophetic prescription of a Messiah. Endō was not enamored of prophetic predictions. We encounter, then, a Jesus who was eviscerated from his Jewish history and ancestry. Endō spoke expressively of the need to reconcile his "Catholicism with my Japanese blood." This meant dislodging Jesus from any Jewish connections and doctrinal entanglements and placing him within a climate of Japanese sentiment. Such a reshaping, Endō admitted, had taught him "one thing . . . , that the Japanese must absorb Christianity without the support of a Christian tradition or history or legacy or sensibility." He perceived this task as a divine burden placed on himself on behalf of his people: "This is the peculiar cross that God has given to the Japanese."[20] The question of the incompatibility of Christian faith and Japanese culture recurs in Endō's novels. In *White Man, Yellowman*, the Japanese student, Chiba, tells the disgraced French priest of the irrelevance of imported Christian doctrines such as sin, while all he knew as a yellow man was "deep fatigue."[21] In the same novel, Kimiko, the Japanese wife of the disgraced French priest, Durrand, taunted him, saying that the ideas of sin and of the atoning death introduced by the missionaries were pointless, because the Japanese had their Buddha who easily exonerated their misdeeds: "You don't know how much better the Buddha is, who forgives us the minute we say Namu Amida Buddha."[22]

The Jesus envisioned by Endō was not the patriarchal figure who came with the padres, but one who catered to Japanese sentiment, which understood the motherly, not the fatherly, love of God. He recalled an old Japanese saying that referred to the four most awful things on earth as "fires, earthquakes, thunderbolts, and fathers."[23] Endō made it clear that the Japanese much preferred a "kind-hearted maternal aspect of God," over the Jesus who was enthroned on the right hand of God, waiting to judge his enemies and reward the elect. In his recounting of the trial of Jesus, Endō's option for Luke's version is instructive. He omitted the second part of the reply, where Jesus says, "But from now on, the Son of Man will be seated at the right hand of the mighty God"—which any student of the Bible knows is a combination of Psalms (1.10.1) and Daniel (7.141), where the Son of Man was given everlasting dominance and the power to subjugate his enemies. Endō's exclusion of these words made clear his intention. This was not a Messiah who aspired to be crowned or to dispense judgment. He was not a political Messiah—a national leader who would expel foreign conquerors from the land of Judah—but one who offered a kingdom or "universe of love based on the presence of a companion."[24]

The vision that emerges of Jesus is that of a caring, divine mother—ineffectual, powerless, and an eternal companion. This is the Jesus who is often moved by compassion, and whose vulnerability comes through more decisively than his valorous kingship. When people around him were looking for power and miraculous deeds, he appeared as a man who "could accomplish nothing, the man who possessed no power in the visible world." His greatest achievement was never to have abandoned people if they were in trouble: "When women were in tears, he stayed by their side. When old folks were lonely, he sat with them quietly. It was nothing miraculous, but the sunken eyes overflowed with love more profound than a miracle."[25] Unlike the stern father, he is the eternal companion, like the mothers who "share wretched suffering" and "weep together" when people are in trouble.

In his motherly form, Jesus upholds undervalued and unwanted people, like prostitutes, and forgives them: "God is not a punishing God, but a God who asks that children be forgiven." Jesus brought this message of motherly love to balance the fatherly love of the Hebrew scriptures. Endō acknowledges that the Hebrews spoke of the maternal instincts of God, but he argues that this got lost in the idea of punishment and retribution, so that what came to prevail in the hearts of Jewish people was "fear."[26] A mother's love will not desert even those who commit crimes; it forgives any weakness, even apostasy. When he was tormented about choosing between his old beliefs and the new faith, Hasekura, the samurai in *Samurai,* felt that it was the motherly presence of Jesus that sustained him: "He is always besides us. He listens to our agony and our grief. "[27] Endō was firmly convinced that if Christianity were to have any appeal to the Japanese, it must stress the motherly love of God, the love that forgives wrongs, heals wounds, and draws others to itself.

Endō's Jesus was a reluctant performer of miracles. The Gospels were full of stories about Jesus healing the sick, and Endō felt that Jesus dealt with the afflicted in two ways. First, he healed their diseases through miraculous acts that Endō characterized in conventional terms, as "miracle stories." Second, Jesus shared with people their "pitiable sufferings" in communal experiences that Endō, in his inimitable style, called "consolation stories." Endō held the "miracle stories" in low esteem because they had been documented in writing long after the event, whereas the "consolation stories" had more merit, in his view, because they were based on eyewitness accounts. They were still fresh in the memory of the disciples, and, more significantly, recorded without any "embroidering."[28] The "consolation stories" seemed inclined to emphasize the compassionate side of Jesus. They were not about Jesus performing extraordinary feats, but about his way of embracing the unloved and the unworthy. The woman who washed Jesus's feet and the woman with the issue of blood are clear examples of consolation stories. In one case, her tears alone were sufficient to indicate to Jesus her sorrows and suffering, and in the other, the touch of her finger was enough for Jesus to know her burden of suffering and desperation. These stories are far more effective ways of demonstrating the love and care of Jesus for people who were otherwise forsaken, despised, or held in contempt. By contrast, the miracles of Jesus, which alleviated illnesses of the body, had always ended tragically. The sole concern of the blind, lame, and deaf was to be healed of their physical infirmities and not simply to be loved. The sick wanted to be cured, the lame begged to walk again, and the blind beseeched him to restore their vision—and they were furious if their hopes were left unfulfilled. The cures and healing enabled Jesus to appraise what the people thought about him and expected from him. What they wanted, it seemed, were "prodigies" and "corporeal wonders"—all of which made Jesus realize "love's futility in the world of material values" and benefits.[29] There was an acute ache hidden behind every miracle story. Endō comments that this pain Jesus felt had more theological importance than did the Enlightenment question of whether Jesus performed any of those miracles or not. Traditionally, a miracle is considered a measure and proof of Jesus's divinity. In Endō's case, it was used to authenticate Jesus's humane and compassionate side.

Endō's Jesus had only a simple message—love and sacrifice—expressed in these words: "Love your enemies, do good to those who hate you. Bless those who curse you. Pray for those who abuse you. To him who strikes you on the cheek, offer the other also. From him who takes away your coat do not withhold your cloak as well." On the face of it, his message looked hackneyed and simplistic. Read in the context envisaged by Endō, however, it looks different and energizing. These words were uttered by Jesus at a time when the crowd, in a nationalistic spirit after the feeding miracle, wanted him to lead them against the imperial rulers. To the horror of the crowd, his answer was a "flat refusal." Instead, he talked about love and self-sacrifice.

This was a kind of love they had not heard about from their lawgivers or the priests. The rabbinical Judaism on which they had been schooled did not entirely ignore love, but the rabbis had not "inculcated this ideal of love." The prophets, including John the Baptist, did not match the ideal set out by Jesus. Endō observed that "his principle of love was directly opposed to all casuist commentaries regarding the letter of the Law." What the teaching of Jesus demanded was an "impossible standard of sincerity in heart and soul, of purity, honesty, and self-denial."

His idea of self-sacrifice is expressed in these words: "Give to everyone who begs from you, and of him who takes away your goods do not ask them again. And as you wish that men would do to you, do so to them. If you love those who love you, what credit is that to you?" The spirit of sacrifice envisaged in the teaching was altogether different from what the crowd had known from the wisdom writings of the Jewish sages, or from the teachings of the Pharisees: "It was a summons to love which lies perhaps beyond the power of mere human earthlings to attempt." Endō sums up the preaching and work of Jesus: "The God of Love, the love of God—the words come easy. The most difficult thing is to bear witness in some tangible way to the truth of the words."[30] What Endō's Jesus was offering was this new way of being.

For Endō, Jesus was the most misunderstood figure both in the Bible and in history. His life and work were carried on in a "whirlpool of misconception," with his family, the crowds, his own disciples, and authorities both religious and political continually misreading him. His family and neighbors questioned his sanity. His own disciples informed on him and left him in the lurch. Endō paints a picture of the crowds as continually changing their views of him, leading to both his fame and his fall. Initially, they idolized him for his healing abilities, and later, after hearing his Sermon on the Mount, they avoided him. They again began to feel affection for him as they tried to pin their messianic hopes on him, yet they eventually rejected and betrayed him when he spoke about his death at the Last Supper. Finally, they swapped him for an agitator.

Jesus became the object of the dreams of different people. The vast majority of those who knew him saw him as John the Baptist, or Elijah, or any of the prophets of the old dispensation who could become their leader and help to realize their "limited and partisan dreams." While the crowds were ambivalent about Jesus, however, the Pharisees, the Sadducees, and the council of the Sanhedrin saw him as an "insidious self-appointed reformer of Jewish religion and as an agitator" who could incite the crowd. The ultra-nationalists expected him to overthrow the Romans and restore the pride of the Jews. The Zealots eyed him as a possible leader who would resort to armed struggle. Finally, there were women, old people, and the sick who looked upon him as a "holy man displaying deeds of power" in healing their illnesses. Apparently, when alive, no one understood or appreciated Jesus. His earthly life was marked by rejection, ridicule, betrayal, and abandonment. Only after his death were they "able to grasp what kind of person he really was." In his earthly life, Jesus "embraced the simplicity of living," and he lived a life of being a companion to the unwanted, which the disciples found "ineffectual." It was his death that enabled the disciples to discern what "lay hidden behind the weakness."[31]

Although Jesus was seen as a loyal, close companion for those who needed care, Endō's Jesus did not have any friends of his own; he was instead a solitary figure who was "completely alone" when he was with his own disciples, or even when he was among the crowd. One sentence strikingly captures the isolation of Jesus: "We can see the figure of Jesus standing near the shore of the Lake of Galilee, completely alone, even when surrounded by his disciples and by the crowds."[32] In Endō's re-telling, Jesus revealed his true vocation not to his closest disciples but to the Samaritan woman, a stranger, indicating that he had no one close to him with whom to share his inner thoughts. He looked isolated and mystified, a "figure standing quietly in the crowd."[33]

Endō's Jesus is not always a solemn and sober figure who spends most of his time with "filthy and ugly" people. Endō presents a picture of Jesus enjoying himself at the wedding at Cana, where, to use a modern phrase, he seemed to enjoy clubbing. It was an unusual moment for Jesus to make merry after the hard winter he had endured with John and his followers in the inhospitable wilderness of Judea. Along with the villagers he enjoyed the wine and "broke out in audible laughter with one cup on another." The mixing with the revellers is an indication that Jesus by no means wore only a "grumpy face."[34]

Endō regarded the Passion and death of Christ as "the climax to the entire Bible." He commented that "for a scribbler of novels" like him, "this particular drama" would never go "stale." The descriptions of Jesus's death in the Gospels were far more "effective than most of the classic tragedies in literature." In the scene of his death, Jesus was "more than merely a human hero" because no "other tragic drama introduces to the stage a sacred aureole to match the halo which radiates from the Holy one."[35]

Endō's Jesus dies on the cross weak, alone, and in agony. This spectacle of the anguished Jesus, smeared with his "own sweat and blood," Endō reckoned, allowed the crowd and the disciples to witness a Jesus whom they had not seen before. The crowd had known Jesus as a miracle worker who cured everyone's pain. Now they saw him as a person who could not even ease his own pain. He did not resist, nor did God come to his rescue. In the eyes of the crowd, he had changed from being a "wonder worker to feckless has-been." The cross was also a revelation to Jesus. It is there that he learns about God's silence. When Jesus cried out in agony, the answer was a dead silence from God. Endō observes that "God only left him alone to suffer." Endō, in a confessional tone, notes: "The quintessence of what Jesus taught us comes home to me not so much from that dynamic Jesus in Galilee as from this helpless Jesus from the cross."[36]

God's abandonment of Jesus and this change of perception point to a recurring theme in Endō's novels. In *Silence*, Rodrigues, the Portuguese priest, came to Japan with an image of Jesus that radiated "vigor and strength," "majesty and glory."[37] When Rodrigues was tortured, however, the Jesus he gazed upon looked weary, haunted, and in despair. As Endō put it, "To me the most meaningful thing in the novel is the change in the hero's image of Christ."

The achievement of this weak, ineffectual, and helpless Jesus was that he became more compelling to the disciples in death than in his lifetime. For Endō, it is here that the essential clue to the mystery of the Resurrection is to be found. For him, "the meaning of the resurrection is unthinkable if separated from the fact of his being ineffectual and weak."[38] Jesus dying on the cross, weak and alone, made the disciples ashamed and uncomfortable and spurred them on to post-Easter heroism. It is the sheer humanity of this dying man that allows people to identify with him.

As to who was responsible for the death of Jesus, Endō is ambiguous and does not single out anyone in particular. In his view, Jesus suffered for and poured out his love for everyone, even those who put him to death. As an outsider, he felt that he was not in a position to blame either the Romans or the Jews other than by writing that "Jesus was put to death by people whom he never ceased to love." This includes not only the Roman rulers and the high priests, but also his own disciples, who misunderstood him and for their own safety were willing to betray him. Endō maintained that Pilate had been pressured by members of the Sanhedrin and the high priests and had made his execution order reluctantly. He would have let Jesus off with a lesser punishment like flogging, but the priests had threatened, "If you let this man go, you are no friend of Caesar."[39]

Endō saw an inescapable connection between the Passion and the Resurrection of Jesus. He acknowledged that the Resurrection of Jesus was the "pivotal point of the passion narrative and indeed a key to the entire New Testament." He regarded it not as a historically objective event, however, but as a subjective, private experience that changed into valiant heroes the bunch of feckless disciples who had deserted and betrayed Jesus. Endō cited Bultmann to validate his case: "Jesus rose from the dead in virtue of disciples' faith."[40]

Jesus's Resurrection had a "firm grip on the imagination of the Jews" of the time, but it was not like the reappearance of Elijah in the form of John the Baptist.[41] The disciples experienced something else: an event that turned their spineless, fickle, treacherous group into courageous and inspirational men. The act that prompted the transformation of these "weaklings, cowards and no-goods" might have been the words of Jesus from the cross: "Father, forgive them; for they know not what they do." Instead of being angry at them and invoking the wrath of God on them for their betrayal, Jesus, to the disciples' astonishment, prayed for their salvation. In the words of Endō:

> And regarding those who deserted him, those who betrayed
> him, not a word of resentment came to his lips. No matter what
> happened, he was the man of sorrows, and he prayed for nothing
> but their salvation. That's the whole life of Jesus. It stands out
> clean and simple, like a single Chinese ideograph brushed on a
> blank sheet of paper.[42]

Such a charitable attitude was "inconceivable" to the disciples, yet Jesus spoke the inconceivable. While at the height of his torment on the cross,

Jesus "amiably continued his desperate effort on behalf of those who had deserted and betrayed him." As Endō put it, "no hero can be expected to forgive anyone who betrays him."[43]

Endō described this transformative moment in the lives of the disciples as "electrifying." It was for them not "an abstract mediation" but a "non-metaphorical, tangible realization." Endō argued that this moment was enough to produce a "radical switch in their scales of values" and to turn upside down what they had previously held to be true. It was the very moment that a "powerless Jesus" became an "all powerful one," for they finally began to see his true worth. The cry of love on the cross was an event that led them to call Jesus "Christ, the Son of God," and persuaded the disciples that the "resurrection of Jesus was a *fact*."[44] This veneration of Jesus by his disciples, Endō claimed, was unique. Other charismatic leaders such as the teachers of righteousness of Qumran were not adored by their adherents after their death in the manner of Jesus. Their message mostly stayed within their local communities, whereas the disciples of Jesus took the faith from the Jewish environment to the Gentile world. The disciples would have remained cowards if something more hadn't happened. Endō admitted that the New Testament did not explicitly state the psychological mood of the disciples, but "between the lines" one could read it. Endō remarked that as a "solitary novelist in the orient" he could "sense that much." On speaking about the experience of the disciples, Otsu, himself a reject from the Roman Catholic Church, put it succinctly and compellingly in *Deep River*: "He died, but he was restored to life in their hearts." It is this resurrected Jesus who wanders "through India and Vietnam, through China, Korea, Taiwan."[45]

Unlike other Asian Christians whom we have studied here, Endō did not show any personal interest in the risen Christ except for his effect on the cowardly and traitorous band of men who were transformed into a group of courageous and inspirational figures in history. For Endō, the preaching of Jesus and his parabolic stories, the utterances from the cross, his acceptance of his enemies, and his prayers for their salvation were more than enough to show what kind of a person Jesus was. Essentially, the way he lived, and his concern for the very people who had betrayed and deserted him, outweighed any miraculous rising from the dead.

Jesus, John, and the Essenes: Unlikely Associates

In Endō's reckoning, the relationship between John the Baptist and Jesus was a very complicated one. Jesus felt a great deal of affection and admiration for John, even as he wanted to remain aloof and detached from him. Jesus worked independently of John and did not carry out any of his baptismal practices. His view of John was summed up neatly in the answer he gave to his disciples' query. He told them that John was far greater than a prophet, and among those born of women there had risen no one greater than him. But Jesus added a caveat: the least in the Kingdom was greater than John.

Jesus was in total sympathy with John when he castigated the Sadducees and Pharisees, and his stay with the Baptist and his community was a real changing point in Jesus's life. It was here that Jesus came to understand the daily grind that his people had to endure to earn their daily bread. He also found that John's "ascetical image" was "forbidding." It was in the wilderness of Judea that he could feel the need for a different perception of God from that offered by John. The "stern-father image" of a God who raged and punished people against the background of a doomsday scenario alienated John's followers. From that moment onward, Jesus realized that his people needed a more calming and reassuring God, rather than the "grim, censorious deity" of John, which, according to Endō, Jesus could not identify with. From then on, Jesus distanced himself from John. Endō cites a Johannine verse to sum up Jesus's attitude to John and his community: "Jesus for his part would not trust himself to them—not even to the Baptist's followers."[46]

Endō speculated that it was through John that Jesus might have some tenuous connection with the Jewish ascetic sect, the Essenes. Endō was aware that there was no mention of this group in the Gospels, and he was keen to point out that on a number of issues, Jesus differed from the Essenes. Their belief in an earthly messianic figure; the exclusive nature of the salvation they preached; and their practice of offering no hope to the unwanted in society deterred Jesus from associating with them.

Jesus and Judas: A Troubled Relationship

The relationship that Endō paints between Jesus and Judas Iscariot who betrayed Jesus is an intriguing one. In Endō's portrayal, Judas, one of the most hated figures in the Gospels, and humanity's worst sinner, emerges as an enlightened figure who actually knew the role that Jesus had to play, and surreptitiously abetted him in achieving it. Endō used his novelist's imagination and arrived at this rehabilitated image of Judas well before the discovery of the Gospel of Judas, which provided a new perspective on the personality and understanding of Judas.[47] Interestingly, it took four decades for another novelist, the Israeli writer Amos Oz, to attempt to redeem Judas's treacherous image.[48]

Endō offers a picture of a mutual admiration and distrust between these two men. Judas's understanding of himself and his feelings toward Jesus are summed up this way: "He loved Jesus as he loved himself and he hated Jesus as he hated himself."[49] Endō reckoned that Judas was closer to Jesus than the Gospels led us to believe. The fact that Jesus trusted the money box with Judas was an indication of his confidence in him.

In Endō's imagination, Judas was the only one who really understood the "true intent" of Jesus's mission, and his eventual fate, namely his arrest, torture, and death. It was at Bethany that Judas first realized, even before the other disciples, that Jesus was not the Messiah that people were hoping for. The crowd gathered in Jerusalem and rallied behind Jesus, shouting "Jesus for Messiah, Jesus for Messiah." Jesus was lodging in Bethany, and Mary, hearing the words, suddenly produced a jar of costly perfume and poured it on the feet of Jesus. Her gesture was not an act of hospitality but an act that befitted a Messiah. If he was the Messiah, as the crowd presumed, then he should be anointed with the oil. While those present were visibly touched, it was Judas who recognized the significance but also the futility of Mary's anointing. He knew that Jesus had no intention of becoming the Messiah whom the people hoped for. In a "chilling" tone, he told those present "clearly that Jesus will never become the Messiah that everybody seeks."[50] When Jesus said to Judas, "Do quickly what you have to do," this urging, in Endō's estimation, was not in a tone of condemnation for his devious act, but a tone of recognition for Judas's understanding of Jesus's role. Much of this was already captured in Endō's most celebrated novel, *Silence.* The *fumie* (Japanese image of Jesus or Mary) of Jesus tells Rodriquez, the apostate priest: "Just as I told you to step on the plaque, so I told Judas to do what he was going to do. For Judas was in anguish as you are now."[51]

Unlike in the Gospels, the betrayal of Jesus was not a single person's act. Endō's Judas was the only one to grasp the idea that Jesus would be betrayed not just by himself but by all the disciples. Endō writes: "To put it bluntly, like Judas they turned traitor on him." While all the Gospels were clear that it was Judas who betrayed Jesus, they did not provide the reason for this act. Endō challenges the traditional version in the Gospels, in which Judas had simplistic motives, as recounted in John's Gospel: "Were he the owner of a simple mentality, he would have quit the master long before." It was not extreme dislike of Jesus, as often presumed, that led to his betrayal, since in Endō's portrayal, whatever the Gospels say of him, Judas "did believe in Jesus." In Endō's view, Judas had a naivety about him. He thought Jesus might change his mind. That he persisted with Jesus, and was the only one to follow the master after the other disciples had abandoned him, indicated his belief that Jesus might reverse his intention and restore the ancient glory and hope of Israel. It was disappointment about this that led Judas to guide the temple police to Gethsemane. Foolishly, Judas believed that Jesus would somehow escape and would not be sentenced to death.

Judas was not a cold-hearted snitch, as the popular imagination has it. He despised himself even before he betrayed Jesus. After realizing his mistake, Endō portrayed him as going through a whole gamut of emotions—"loathing himself, then excusing himself, hating the master, then loving him." Money was not crucial to him, and he felt that the amount offered was a complete insult to the life and work of Jesus. Endō tells his readers that Judas was not proud of what he did. There was a "twist in his face" and this was a moment of torment, isolation, "self-savagery," "self-hatred." In Endō's retelling, Judas was not the betrayer, but was the one who was betrayed by Caiaphas, who "double-crossed" him. In other words, the archetypical betrayer was also betrayed.

In Endō's presentation, Judas was not merely a compliant disciple. He not only questioned the motive underlying Jesus's planned death, but also told Jesus what people truly wanted from him. The following encapsulates the true expectations of the people:

> Master, you have resolved to meet death in order to become the eternal companion of all mankind. The people's demand, however, is different . . . Obviously they wanted only to be cured, the cripples wanted only to be able to walk, the blind wanted only to see. That's human nature.[52]

The more Jesus looked worn out on the cross, the more Judas was fascinated by him. Jesus with sunken eyes, looking older than his years, appearing more wretched, "exerted some indescribable fascination for Judas." Jesus, in his turn, understood Judas's suffering. Endō notes that when Jesus was being rejected, jeered at, and spat upon, Judas felt a certain resemblance between himself and Jesus—a recognition that he also would die, and he, too, would be cursed by people. Endō found that there was a "strange analogy between the betrayer and the betrayed," united as they were in their own failure, rejection, and agony. In Endō's portrayal, Judas is not a wicked person, as most perceived him, but a flawed human who suffers as well. More importantly, Jesus appreciates this man so much that he not only loved him but also died for him: "Jesus poured out his love even on the man who betrayed him." Tellingly, Judas was saved through the very suffering of his master, suffering in which he had had a hand.

The depiction of Judas in *A Life of Jesus* is in a sense like that of the fallen priest Durant in the *Yellow Man*. He, too, betrayed Jesus, and sold his soul. It would have been better had he never been born, but unlike Judas he was too weak to hang himself. In Endō's imagination, Judas appears as a complicated figure who had mixed feelings toward Jesus, both love and loathing. Yet his betrayal was the thankless job he undertook so that Jesus could fulfill his mission. He was an indispensable but doomed character in the story of Jesus.

A Passive and Nonconfrontational Jesus

Endō's biography of Jesus is part historical, part personal, and part hermeneutical. He resourcefully musters the works of leading biblical scholars of the time to make his points. Endō's *A Life of Jesus* should be seen as a novelist's way of weaving facts about the historical Jesus into a speculative, imaginative, and credible narrative. Endō's Jesus is free from reference to his Jewish background and from apocalyptic urgency, and those who use the Jewish or Greco-Roman background to explain Jesus will be disappointed. Endō's method is like that of the nineteenth-century Western orientalists—to simplify, isolate, and exaggerate. His employment of the Japanese maternalistic instinct is an obvious case in point. His passive, nonconfrontational Jesus feeds into the oriental image of the East as effeminate.

In a sense, Endō was an old-fashioned evangelical. He saw himself as a mediator of the evangelizing spirit of Christianity to his people, and in his narratives, Jesus alone has the power to save humanity. Endō wrote that the image that he presented in his biography of Jesus would not go to waste if it could "strike a spark of vital appreciation of Jesus even in readers" who had no knowledge or previous contact with Christianity.[53] His writings are about God's all-embracing love to the world, exemplified in the universal spirit of the resurrected Jesus. Jesus is projected as the "eternal companion of mankind everywhere" and his kingdom of love is available to "all mankind." Endō made a bold claim that "Jesus represents all humanity." Endō's strong claim for Christianity comes out in two of his novels. In *White Man, Yellowman*, Father Brou's conviction was that, as in the miracle of Cana, Catholicism would transform the heretical pantheistic gods of Japan. He tells the disgraced priest Durand that the Japanese "gods will be conquered" and "Catholicism will swallow up the pantheism in another miracle of Cana."[54] And in *Deep River*, Otsu, the excommunicated Catholic priest, speaks of Jesus as the all-embracing love of God.

Although he acknowledged that God had many faces, Otsu tells his former lover that Jesus "is everywhere" and "can be found in Hinduism and in Buddhism as well."[55] Endō's unacknowledged Jesus in other religions resonates with Vatican II's condescending inclusivist theology of an anonymous Jesus present in other faiths.

Conservative Christians raised on high-octane exclusivist Christological doctrines will find Endō's portrayal of Jesus theologically deficient and unappealing, and will likely view the weak, ineffectual nature of Endō's Jesus not as his strength, but as his failure. All central Christian doctrines—the Fall, the Virgin Birth, the Incarnation, the Trinity—are missing. He hardly mentions Jesus's divinity. Endō says nothing of Jesus's birth even when there is a fleeting reference to it; instead he spiritualizes it. In short, he leaves out incidents that show the authority and power of Jesus. Like most of the interpreters studied here, Endō pays little attention to the doctrine of atonement or to Hebraic prophecy. Endō's Jesus does not fulfill Jewish Old Testament expectations. Nor is Endō interested in the theological interpretations contained in the prophetic message. Endō admits that in his portrayal of Jesus he does not touch on "every aspect of his life," and acknowledges that these omissions will disappoint many.[56] To such critics he writes:

> My way of depicting Jesus is rooted in my being a Japanese
> novelist. I wrote this book for the benefit of Japanese readers
> who have no Christian tradition of their own and who know
> almost nothing about Jesus.[57]

Endō was not the first Japanese to suggest a Christianity without Western doctrinal and institutional trappings. Uchimura Kanzō (1861–1930) advanced this notion in the 1920s and initiated what came to be known as the Non-Church Movement—a movement thoroughly self-governing and independent of Western theological control and denominational influence.[58] Where Endō and Uchimura differed was in the type of indigenous cultural resources they used to make Christianity relevant to Japan. While Endō drew heavily on the maternal impulses in Japanese culture and limited its value to his own people, Uchimura, who envisaged world domination for Japan, was trying to graft Christianity onto Bushido, the Japanese "high" culture. He believed that a Christianity enhanced by Bushido values would save the world. In his weekly magazine, Uchimura wrote: "Christianity engrafted upon Bushido will be the finest product of the world. *It* will save, not only Japan, but the whole world."[59]

Endō's *A Life of Jesus* came out in the 1970s. In that era, Jesus was presented as a "countercultural guru" persuading his followers to try out new ways of living, to challenge traditional power structures, to free themselves from conventional social restraints, and to think of themselves as belonging to part of a wider human community. Endō's Jesus, by contrast, was involved with individuals who were struggling to cope with their newly found faith. This Jesus does not save nations or communities, but individuals who have been marginalized by society, or individual Christians tortured for their faith. The salvation, he offers, too, is different. It is not from sin and guilt that Jesus redeems people, but from the "loneliness and hopelessness that come with being sick or being poor." He draws people from "forlorn hopelessness," but does not himself establish enduring friendships or stable relationships.

This was also the time that Latin American and African American liberation theologies were bursting upon the scene with a Jesus who blatantly sided with the poor and challenged the social structures that had produced such people. Endō's Jesus does not show any emancipatory interest. In liberation theology's mission, following Jesus meant replicating his radical stance. The power that Endō's Jesus provides is instead paradoxical, speaking of weakness as strength. This is a Jesus who does not encourage political agitation but asks people to become weak to gain power. Endō wrote: "A person begins to be a follower of Jesus only by accepting the risk of becoming himself one of the powerless people in this visible world."[60]

Endō's Jesus does not get angry at the powerful or the oppressive structures. The only incident where Jesus shows some anger is at the Temple when he drives out the merchants. Endō does not interpret this event as a political protest intended to challenge the Romans or to question the meaningless spirituality of the priests. Since neither the Sanhedrin nor the Temple guards make any move to arrest Jesus, Endō speculates that Jesus's rage in this incident might have been his way of inviting his own arrest.

In Endō's construal, Jesus is not a subversive sage or a radical social prophet. He is deeply rooted in a Japanese middle-class milieu and shows particular sympathy to those who suffer for their faith and not for their political beliefs. This Jesus caters to the spiritual needs of the upper crust of Japanese society such as the samurai who were faced with religious questions, but he does not address the burakumins, the outcasts of Japanese society who frequently encounter discrimination and ostracism. He is not the one to be found in the bars and slums of Tokyo. To seek such a Jesus, one has to look at the novels of Rinzō Shiina, where Jesus is found among the despised, the "scum" of Japan. Or one can go back to an earlier work like Toyohiko Kagawa's *Before the Dawn* (1925), which describes the inequalities and sufferings of the people even more vividly. As one reviewer put it, in Kagawa's writing, "The life of the slum emerges with amazing clarity."[61]

The companionship offered by Endō's Jesus could be mistaken for a mere sentimental gesture. Even those who were with him found that simply standing by was unhelpful. Judas, for instance, told Jesus that companionship was not enough and that people expected something more than merely a perpetual presence:

> Master, you have preached a love that has no real meaning in the real world. Your kind of love does not pay off. You aspire to becoming the eternal companion of all the misfortunate people. Yet these misfortunates, would they not themselves prefer to receive the three hundred denarii I speak of?[62]

Again, just before he betrays Jesus, Judas tells him:

> Rabbi, you say that God is love. But where is God's love in the harsh realities of life? Does God keep silence in the face of hardships? . . . Rabbi, you say there is nothing more valuable than love. But men crave something more. Men want action, they want it now. It's only human nature to want something practical.[63]

Endō introduced the idea of a compassionate God before Marcus Borg discovered it for Western audiences. Both perceived compassion as a critique of the dominant ideology of Jesus's day. One saw it as a potent antidote to the severe image of the father God, and the other as a sharp contrast to the holiness and purity of the day. Whereas Endō injected a maternal aspect into it, and made it a virtue for individuals, Borg's compassion was gender-neutral but had a social and political vision.[64] Endō was not, of course, the first one to envision Jesus as a mother. Before him there was Narayan Vaman Tilak (1861–1919), the Brahmin convert who in his poetry brought out the maternal image of Jesus: "Tenderest Mother-Guru mine, Saviour, where is love like thine?"[65] More recently, Asian Christian feminist theologians have reconfigured Jesus as a mother out of their own experience of exploitation and degradation. They might find Endō's mother-image patronizing and unduly romantic.[66]

Endō, who seriously opposed Western imports of Jesus, ended up mirroring them. Like the missionaries, he presented a Jesus who comforted and cared for individuals' personal needs rather than showing solidarity with the subjugated masses, or any interest in social restructuring. It is almost a cliché to say that everyone fashions a Jesus to meet their own needs, and unconsciously imitates the very Jesus they conjure. Endō created a powerless Jesus and wanted his followers to become the "powerless people in this visible world." That is a big ask and a challenge for a country like Japan, which had tainted colonial adventures in the past but is now a superpower envied and resented by its Asian neighbors.

CONCLUSION

Our Jesus, Their Jesus

Just as the Bible in Asia is not a stand-alone text but has to be read in conjunction with religious texts of the East, so, too, Jesus has to be understood in relation to the region's spiritual sages. Without this context, Jesus simply does not make sense. A. J. Appasamy articulates the challenge: "How does he compare with the great religious leaders of the world such as the Buddha, Muhammad, Krishna, Zoroaster, Confucius and others? Does he really differ from them or is he in the same class with them?"[1] In a continent already crowded with religious texts and sacred figures, the influence of Jesus is unclear.

These Asian portrayals that we have looked at have all the marks of colonizer-colonized confrontations, complicities, imitations, and transgressions, and they were a curious mix of colonial and anti-colonial. They were colonial in the sense that they assumed that Asian spirituality was superior to the West's, and anti-colonial in that they weakened and de-centered the triumphalistic picture of Jesus forged by the missionaries. Some Indians even harbored a hope that such a savior would be reborn in India and save the world. Rabindranath Tagore spoke for many when he wrote about yet another male savior: "Today I live in the hope that the Saviour is coming—that he will be born in our midst in this poverty-shamed hovel which is India. I shall wait to hear the divine message of civilization which he will bring with him, the supreme

249

word of promise that he will speak unto man from this very Eastern horizon to give faith and strength to all who hear."[2] These Asian configurations of Jesus might appear, frustratingly, to be replicating the familiar orientalist binarism that assigned science, rationality, and objectivity to the West, and spirituality, intuition, and subjectivity to the East, but these thinkers were in fact much more sophisticated than this allegation. In their anxiety to challenge the West, coupled with their unwillingness to admit the colonialists' assertion about their inferiority, they unearthed cultural elements from their indigenous sources. One of these elements was an interior spirituality. The underlying perception was that the West, in achieving material prosperity through its scientific and industrial achievements, had lost the higher notion of spirituality, whereas Asia, in spite of its technical backwardness, still had the potential to offer spiritual leadership to the West. What the West needed, in order to have any lasting stake in the world, were the fundamental essences of Asia such as moderation, austerity, stability, and self-control.

These Asian portraits were prime examples of the colonized returning the very prescription that the colonizer had handed to them. Western orientalists like Max Müller and others had routinely reminded Hindus that their religious tradition has been preserved in its purity in the original textual sources and that they should seek to discover them in the ancient manuscripts. In a stunning reversal, these Hindu reformers took it on themselves to upend the claim by reminding Christians that the original message of Jesus was preserved in the Gospels. They refused to accept the Jesus proclaimed by the missionaries, retorting: "I have gone direct to the Bible to ascertain the genuine doctrines of morality inculcated by Christ."[3] These presentations exhibit early signs of the postcolonial trait of "talking back" (or "writing back") to the empire, without much of the angst so evident in modern-day postimperial Indian novels.

Most of these Asian articulations of Christ were done in the context of the "cultural fusion" generated by colonial rule. Acutely conscious of being Asian writers, these thinkers were trying to attract both an indigenous and a wider audience. Writing in the language of the colonialist power, they brought Asia into dialogue with the West. They enriched their own indigenous tradition by introducing Western techniques and thought into it. Unfortunately, the reciprocal process never happened. While Hindu reformers like Ramanathan, Radhakrishnan, and Parekh showed a great interest in Jesus and made room for him in the Vedantic, Saiva Siddhanta, or Bhakti traditions as a seer, or a guru, or a God-conscious person, Christian missionaries either derided these theological constructions, or secretly believed that some of these authors might eventually turn to Christianity, which never happened. Sadly, their contributions went unnoticed in the West. Present-day minority hermeneuts experience the same neglect.

These Asian portrayals straddle the era of the first search for the historical Jesus and the No Quest period. In a sense, they were the forebears of the kerygmatic Christ, which became the signature contribution of the next phase, known as the New Quest. One can imagine these Asian scholars sporting a mysterious oriental smile in their *samadhis* (final resting places) when the New Quest invested deeply in the kerygma of Jesus. The Jesus these Asians were searching for was not found behind the Gospel traditions but enshrined in the Gospel kerygma. Their work anticipated, and so is the unacknowledged precursor of, the kerygmatic Christ advanced by Ernst Käsemann, who was trying to unearth a Jesus in the Gospels after the impasse created by the German no-biography Jesus. These Eastern interpreters also broke the artificial, and sharp, division between the Jesus of history and the Christ of faith, which had created an interpretative pecking order that equated the Jesus of history with truth and described the Christ of faith as mystical and mawkish. In addition, they transformed the quest for the historical Jesus into a yearning for the *anubhava*—the embodiment—of Brahman, or, as the Mundaka Upanishad put it: "Verily he becomes Brahman, who knows Brahman" (Chapter 3, 2.9).

While most of the Western representations of Jesus envisaged him as a person with universal outlook and appeal, Asians saw him as a villager with a narrow ethnic perspective who needed Asian influences to make him universally acceptable. They all felt that he was inhibited by the worldviews and ethos of his time. His earlier nationalistic outlook, especially evidenced in his notorious dealing with the Syrophoenician woman, offered them an easy target to expose his xenophobic tendencies. He came across as a simple Galilean who lacked Hellenistic and Greek civilizational sophistication, and who had little interest in theoretical concepts like atonement and justification. More to their liking, he never set foot inside a church. He neither called himself a God nor claimed to have risen on the third day. Some of them found his moral teachings, which came out of his peasant context, unsuitable for the modern world. And some even rebuked him for not practicing what he preached—showing love to enemies.

Of the Asian thinkers, only three had any interest in telling everything about Jesus: Kingsbury, Parekh, and Endō, who wrote full-length Jesus books. Even they were not searching for the historical facts about Jesus, but only for particular aspects of his life or personality that might eventually contribute to a bigger picture. They were looking for an inward, invisible, dwelling of the eternal in Christ, or, as Sen put it, an "Invisible Supreme Essence."[4] They were not excited by the historical details, but by the inner spiritual power he possessed. They all included spirituality, God-consciousness, and a renunciant lifestyle in their pictures of Jesus.

Their real hermeneutical coup was to usurp and offer an alternative to the Kingdom of God propagated as an ideal state. These Hindus did not simply spiritualize the Kingdom: they were much more original. Living under oppressive colonial rule, they found the idea of the Kingdom of God suspiciously defective. While the missionaries, in concert with the British raj, offered Christ's kingdom as a model for good governance and a paradise on earth, these Indians promoted an individually focused oneness with Brahman as superior to any human order. They viewed any relationship between the state and the individual with wariness. Instead, they proposed as the ideal model a metaphysical relationship between the individual and God as delineated in the Vedantic doctrine of Advaita, in the process redefining this Upanishadic concept as a unifying political force for a free India no longer shackled under British rule. The recuperation of the Vedic concept was more than an exercise in nostalgia. These authors repurposed an ancient idea to disturb a cherished Christian notion.

East and West: Different Trajectories

There are certain common interests as well as drastic divergences in the Asian and Western searches for the historical Jesus. I readily concede that the amalgamated view that I present here might undervalue the much more refined and subtle shades of meaning found in the work of individual theologians. The Western search is about a Jesus who proclaims the Good News, and the other is about a Jesus who preaches Vedantic ideals of individual holiness. One is about a Jesus preoccupied with recruitment, and the other is about enlightenment, inner growth, and fulfillment. One is about the divine self-emptying to take human form, and the other is about the deification of the human. One was impelled by modern rationalistic values, and the other was spurred on by the orientalist and missionary defamation of Asian cultures and religions.

For both, the search for a historical Jesus was also a search for selfhood, national identity, and character. In one case, it was about Christian distinctiveness, and in the other, Asian sensibilities and spirit. Both were pursuits for an uninterpreted Jesus and relied largely on the Synoptic Gospels. While the Western enterprise was eager to free Jesus from the tangled textual layers, Asians had an additional task of extricating Jesus from colonial associations. Both followed the nineteenth-century liberal program of appealing to Jesus himself, against the subsequent dogmatic accretions. Or, as Schweitzer observes, the biographers of Jesus "turned to the Jesus of history as an ally in the struggle against the tyranny of dogma."[5] In the Asian case, the Jesus of the Gospels served another purpose. The ethical significance of Jesus became a template for contrasting the behavior of the British and the missionaries. They used it as a way of exposing the dichotomy between British behavior and the teachings of Jesus. Swami Vivekananda found the divergence between their preaching and practice "startling." The Western search was driven and directed by the idea of an apocalyptic Jesus who anticipated God's intervention in human history and the beginning of the new age. Although there were precedents in Hindu thought for God taking human form to rescue the world whenever the unrighteous reigned, Indian searchers did not see Jesus as an avenging avatar but upheld him as a moral harbinger who would revolutionize the world through his spirituality and the example of his renunciant life.

The Western search was obsessed with finding parallels for Jesus amid the ancient Hellenic heroes and sages, charismatic holy men, or millennial prophetic preachers and Cynic philosophers. The crucial question for them was whether Jesus fitted in with these known types, or was different from them, that is, whether he subverted existing practices and offered an alternative. The Asian search, by contrast, was about how to respect, acknowledge, and accord Jesus a place among the numerous illustrious religious figures such as the Buddha, Zoroaster, and Confucius. These Asian thinkers, especially the Hindus, were relentless in their affirmation that "God lives and reigns far beyond . . . [Jesus's] own little neighbourhood."[6] All of them believed, to use the words of Pandipeddi Chenchiah, that Jesus could not be "understood in a single context."[7] Some ideas, such as the Incarnation of Jesus, God dwelling in a human being, may be repugnant and unintelligible to Jews, but the Asians claimed that it made sense to Hindus.

Most of the Western searchers wrapped themselves in Christian sentiment and announced that Jesus was distinct from other ancient figures. The idea of Jesus as an exemplary hero continues in the New Quest; Marcus Borg, for example, portrayed him as an "alternative teacher of wisdom." The Asian quest for Jesus did not see him as a unique person, but perceived him as one who was engaged in work similar to that of the Asian seers, and welcomed him and such teachers "as God's revelation in history." Each one of them was a messenger of God, "bearing a distinct message of glad tidings which he contributed to the cause of religious enlightenment, and progress." For Radhakrishnan, the Buddha and Jesus are "expressions of one great religious movement."[8] What these thinkers were against was binding themselves as "slaves to any particular person as the only chosen prophet of God." Their persistent appeal had been that humanity should "freely honour all of them, and gratefully accept from each what he has to deliver."[9]

Asian and Western interpreters accord varying authority to the Gospel narratives. Both concede that the Gospels have only a limited historical purchase for recovering the actual Jesus because of the already interpreted nature of these documents. But while Western interpreters recognize the historical uncertainties surrounding Jesus yet continue to seek him in his sayings and the titles attributed to him in the Gospels, Asian searchers confine themselves to the narrative values and moral precepts left in the Gospels. For them, the narrative importance of the Gospels lies in their rich and diverse portrayals of Jesus.

There is also a difference in these groups' methodological approach. Westerners go to the Gospels with historical questions. For them, everything related to Jesus—or, for that matter, Christianity—is tied to historical facts. Consequently, Western research is marked by a series of historical questions: When did the Incarnation take place? Where are the historical locations of ministry? What happened in the last week of Jesus's life in Jerusalem? If Jesus died on the cross, when and where was he crucified, and who was responsible for his death? If he did rise on the third day, where was the empty tomb, and who witnessed the post-Easter appearances? Asian interpreters paid scant respect to these historical details. They had a different set of priorities, and asked large questions: Where do we locate Jesus within the pantheon of the religious masters of Asia? What sort of spirituality did he advocate? What kind of austere and renunciant living did he promote? Was he part of the imperial project? Which of his characteristics resonate with Asian sentiments? Was he the conduit through whom godliness was manifested? Did he help to awaken God-consciousness in human beings? Was he a person who had divine consciousness, showed moral sensitivity, and was willing to subordinate himself to the will of God? For these scholars, whether historical events surrounding Jesus occurred two thousand years ago did not matter; what was crucial was the ongoing, interior recurrence of these events in one's life. They allegorized, or metaphorized, historical events such as the cross and the Resurrection so that they became not events that happened in the past, but mediations of continuous spiritual experience. Their message was that dispassionate scientific research would not lead to the historical Jesus; instead, reenacting his words and his asceticism in one's own life would show the way to him.

For most Asian interpreters, principles mattered more than historical personalities. For them, historical figures were only conduits and personifications of religious truths; crucial for them were the values these personalities signaled and propagated. They had much less regard for religions that derived strength from individual saints. For them, it was not lone individuals that mattered but the ideas these seers disseminated. What counted most was these leaders' potency to challenge and transform lives, and their gift to awaken the divine hidden in individuals. The Indian reformers are not alone in this. There were Western thinkers, too, who made personality secondary to ideas. When Meister Eckhart spoke about Christ, he was not in any way imagining the historical Jesus, but an idea of Christ whose words and actions are interpreted symbolically. Similarly, for Kant, Christ is the idea of human perfection.[10]

Asian interpreters were not interested in finding a single Jesus, the Son of God who existed long ago, but the divinely embodied jnani who could make every human being divine. Their firm belief was that "what is possible for a Gautama or a Jesus is possible for every human being."[11] What they were looking for were the sanctifying and illuminating qualities in Jesus that would carry humankind heavenward. He is portrayed as representing perfect humanity and showing what a human being should be in this life. Their vision was that Jesus was aligning with God to enable humankind to realize our divine potential—God in every human being.

The Asian construals of Jesus were unapologetically popular and aimed at a mass audience; they never had any pretensions of being academic. Schweitzer was critical of such portrayals of the life of Christ aimed at the "needs of the man in the street." He was wary of spreading the "assured results broadcast among the people."[12] Besides aiming for a mass market, these Asian interpreters unashamedly sought a figure relevant to oriental sensibility, thus willfully violating the frequent warning of Western scholars about the perils of contemporizing Jesus. Their work was exactly what Schweitzer in schoolmasterly fashion had excoriated as an attempt to "reconcile the Germanic religious spirit with the spirit of Jesus of Nazareth."[13] For him, such depictions are an act of "historic violence" that "injures" both history and theology.[14] Whereas Schweitzer solemnly pronounced that Jesus refused to be "detached from his own time," these Asian interpreters were trying to drag him into their time and context. Their aim was to extricate Jesus from his historical moorings so that he could live at any time, including in the present. What they were looking for was not the Jesus of "then" but a Jesus of "now." Gandhi's words encapsulated their mood: "It would be poor comfort to the world if it had to depend upon a historical God who died 2000 years ago. Do not then preach the God of history, but show him as he lives today through you."[15]

Pots and Kettles, Beam and Speck

Several criticisms leveled against Asian approaches to Jesus could just as easily be directed toward Western approaches. One is that Asian depictions of Jesus, or, for that matter, any contextual construal of his life, are situation-bound, subjective portraits. In contrast, Western academic renditions are hailed as transcending regional and ideological biases, as maintaining impeccable scientific objectivity, and as exemplars of solid scholarship. As Halvor Moxnes has shown, however, contextual appropriations are not the sole preserve of minority hermeneutics; they are strongly prevalent among the Western scholars who claim that they painstakingly follow the historical-critical method. Scrupulously analyzing the portraits of Jesus by German, French, and British scholars, Moxnes has demonstrated that their portrayals reflect the social, political, and cultural contexts of their Western interpreters. What is worse, they are exposed as being confessional and nationalistic.[16] Many years ago, Adolf Deissmann wrote that "all great movements in the history of our race have been determined by conditions of the heart of the people, not by intellect," and that "the triumph of the cult of Christ over all other cults" was due to the fact that it "took deep root in the heart of the many."[17] The difference is that Asian interpreters openly and unabashedly admit their partialities and preconceptions, whereas Western scholars hubristically claim their work as a precise, logical, and a scientific project, which it is evidently not. The historical Jesus, whether constructed by the West or by Asian interpreters, will always remain an emotional reconstruction.

Asian renditions of Jesus are often dismissed as reductive simplifications, but the same criticism could be made of Western representations.

Whether the quest for Jesus is driven by historical, social-science, rhetorical, or literary methods, and by theoretical, theological, philosophical, or ideological presuppositions, it ends up projecting a Jesus of the interpreter's own imagination and ideals. Under the pretense of objectivity, Western scholars have produced a variety of Jesuses to suit their vested interests—such as Jesus the social prophet (Richard Horsley), Jesus the charismatic Jew (Géza Vermes), Jesus the magician (Morton Smith), Jesus the Jewish sage (Ben Witherington), Jesus the Cynic philosopher (F. Gerald Downing), Jesus the itinerant radical (Gerd Theissen), Jesus the millenarian prophet (Dale Allison), and Jesus the *mamzer* rabbi (Bruce Chilton). To these one could add Jesus as the Eastern seer, the Saiva jani, the minjung, or the Jain Tirthankara. Passionate advocates of one cause or another will always see what they want to see, finding meaning where it may not exist. The so-called historical Jesus is invariably an idealized picture drawn from the interpreter's fancy and from fads.

Asian interpreters are criticized for paying too much attention to a spiritual Christ and too little to his historicity. What Western scholars do not realize is that for much of the time, for the Christian church, the only Jesus that mattered was not the rationally unearthed historical Jesus but an intuitively experienced Christ of faith. Many scholars considered constructing the life of Jesus to be a methodologically impracticable and theologically pointless endeavor. Schweitzer, in his monumental work, wrote that "to know Jesus and to understand him requires no scholarly initiation. Nor does one need to grasp the details of his public ministry or to be able to arrange them into a 'Life of Jesus.'"[18] He was convinced that in the end people's relationship with Jesus was "ultimately of a mystical kind."[19] He expanded this point in the closing pages of his book:

> But the truth is, it is not Jesus as historically known, but Jesus as
> spiritually arisen within men, who is significant for our time and
> can help it. Not the historical Jesus, but the spirit which goes
> forth from him and in the spirits of men strives for new influ-
> ence and rule, is that which overcomes the world.[20]

He also offered a hermeneutical health warning: "And further we must be prepared to find that the historical knowledge of the personality and life of Jesus will not be a help, but perhaps even an offence to religion."[21] Schweitzer was not alone in advocating this mystical relationship. Rudolf Bultmann, too, proposed that what mattered for theology was only the Christ of faith. He openly acknowledged the futility of searching for the historical Jesus: "We must frankly confess that the character of Jesus as a human personality cannot be recovered by us. We can neither write a 'life of Jesus' nor present an accurate picture of his personality."[22] What is critical is not the knowable historical Jesus, but the Christ known by faith. For Bultmann, "it is *faith in the kerygma*, which tells of God's dealing in the man Jesus of Nazareth."[23] It is in this proclamation that one hears the Word and is personally challenged. This was what Asian thinkers were saying all along. What is clear is that, not only for the Asian interpreters, but also for Western scholars, the mystically encountered, risen Christ overrides the historical Jesus. Historical understanding has given way to intuition and inward realization, a development that Asian scholars have been anticipating for years.

Asian thinkers have been reprimanded for traces of anti-Semitism in their work, and admittedly, the Jesus that emerges in Asian writings is almost disconnected from Judaism, its scriptures, history, hopes, leaders, and teachings. Jesus has been decontextualized, or, to be specific, de-Judaized to fit into the narrative of these Hindu reformers, as a universal apolitical and spiritual figure. These Asians' attempts to portray Jesus as non-Jewish, however, were not like the ideologically motivated and massive de-Judaizing process that went on in the days of National Socialist Germany.[24] They were not doctrinally anti-Semites of the Nazi variety, nor was their anti-Jewish feeling based on a notion of Aryan superiority. Some of their work appeared before the modern European oppression and before genocidal loathing became a sinister way of targeting Jews, though some of them parroted the prevailing notions. None of them envisaged an Aryan Christ or an ethnically non-Jewish Jesus. Although they often blatantly and unashamedly invoked their Aryan identity and heritage in glorious terms and employed phrases like "the Aryans, our forefathers," or "we Hindu Aryans," they never proposed an Aryan Jesus. He was simply described as "an Asiatic in race, as a Hindu in faith."[25] Even Vivekananda, the Hindu reformer, never claimed Jesus as an Aryan, though he argued that one of the fundamental sayings of Jesus—"I and my Father are one"—was an "Aryan idea" and outrageously declared, without providing any evidence, that "almost all Christianity is Aryan." For him, Jesus remained "the true son of the Orient." He constantly reminded the missionaries that they often forgot that "the Nazarene himself was an Oriental of Orientals. With all your attempts to paint him with blue eyes and yellow hair, the Nazarene was still an Oriental."[26]

Asian portrayals of Jesus as an Asiatic or an oriental was a deliberate hermeneutical move on the part of the Hindu reformers. One reason was political. At a time when missionaries were describing Indians as being "degraded by Asiatic effeminacy," these Asians reminded them that "almost all the ancient prophets and patriarchs venerated by Christians, nay even Jesus Christ himself, a Divine Incarnation and the founder of Christian faith, were ASIATICS." If missionaries thought it was "degrading to be born or to live in Asia," this would "directly reflect upon" those venerable biblical figures.[27] All they did was to replace his Jewishness with Asiatic traits that fitted with their specific hermeneutical needs. What they were after was a Jesus who was essentially that essential mix of being an Asiatic in race, and a Hindu in faith.[28]

Another reason for the insistence on a non-Jewish Jesus had to do with cultural and continental pride. These reformers projected the Orient as the cradle of civilizations and a birthplace of religions and religious figures, or, as one of them claimed, as a "Golgotha of power and learning." Their persistent plea was that "without one exception, all the Messengers were Orientals." For them, Zoroaster, Buddha, and Jesus were respectively Persian, Hindu, and Jewish representatives of the one yearning of human souls, whose archetypal expression was found in the Upanishads and the Bhagavad Gita. Added to this was another cultural claim, that Christianity was an Eastern religion: "Christianity was founded and developed by Asiatics, and in Asia."[29] These interpreters believed that Christianity was essentially an Eastern religion that had been gradually taken over and infused with the Western muscular spirit. They emphasized Christianity's Eastern orientation in order to show that Dharmic religions like Hinduism or Buddhism were not in any way inferior to the biblical religion.

For Asian thinkers, the Jewish element of Jesus's life story was theologically, culturally, and religiously irrelevant. Their aim was not to dominate or erase the Jewish part of this history, but to match the prevailing racial and theologically triumphant narrative by asserting that they, the Asians, should be considered equal to the Christian Anglo-Saxon invaders. Their purpose was to reconcile an Asiatic spirit with the spirit of Jesus. Their projection of oriental, Eastern spirituality became a countercultural lifeboat riding a tsunami of unhelpful Asian stereotypes propagated by the missionaries. Asian interpreters' construction of Jesus as an oriental man, and Christianity as an Asiatic faith, was their way of seizing the other from a position of strength rather than from one of self-doubt. What their seemingly anti-Semitic manifestation demonstrates is that a colonized people, when faced with defamation and humiliation, can summon and enlist indigenous resources to resist the colonizer from an alternate center, a center that has a different set of rules and is not itself easily neutered or co-opted.

Writing about Jesus has never been a straightforward business. The whole enterprise is immersed in an author's strong personal faith, complicated ideological interests, and internecine institutional interventions and control. Although it is seen as an intellectual exercise, it is basically an emotional activity. As a topic of research it is enticing, and has deep roots in Christian commitment, but the quest for the historical Jesus is eminently a personal affair. Even the diehard proponents of the historical-critical method eventually betray their confessional intentions. The following words of Marcus Borg illustrate this apologetic mood: "Believing in Jesus does not mean believing doctrines about him. Rather, it means to give one's heart, one's self at its deepest level, to the post-Easter Jesus who is the living Lord, the side of God turned towards us, the face of God, the Lord who is also the Spirit."[30]

The questions that used to govern the quest for the historical Jesus have become ridiculously anachronistic, for three main reasons. First, the historical context has changed. The Western quest for Jesus was undertaken at a time when rationalism, scientific methods, nationalism, and democratic processes were threatening the stronghold of the church. It was against this forceful and intrusive secular mood and culture that a Jesus was sought who could offer a radical alternative to the emerging civil society. The Western quest was pervaded by a plea to protect and promote Jesus as a secure shield against the threat of modernity.

Second, most of the churches of the West today do not exercise as much religious authority as they once did, and their congregations no longer suffocate under their doctrinal pronouncements. The task of freeing Christian believers from ecclesiastical and dogmatic control—a task that initially prompted the Jesus search—is therefore a much less relevant pursuit today. With dwindling church membership in the West, and most people drawing their spiritual sustenance from outside church circles, appealing directly to a historical Jesus who could act as an arbiter of later doctrinal accruals seems almost superfluous. And third, historical criticism, which had a firm grip, has given way to new critical approaches that have exposed the limitations of historical investigation. The liberal theology from which Western searchers tried to rescue Jesus has given rise to numerous theologies focused on causes such as ecological, gender, and transgender concerns, to which the Gospel Jesus makes hardly any reference.

What the Western quest did was to impose on Jesus the modern cult of personality and turn him into a highly individualized citizen of the Western world during the Enlightenment. This was in sharp contrast to the Mediterranean understanding of self, which is regarded as non-individualistic and tied up with household, family, clan, and tribal kinships. How a peasant from the dusty desert became the hero of green and pleasant Europe will remain a mystery. For Asians, especially for the Korean minjung, what was important was Jesus not as a singular person but as a collective event in which the followers of Jesus are embodied.

The quest for the historical Jesus perpetuates the notion that one needs religious heroes to grasp the divine. The heroic biographies simultaneously celebrate the idea of spiritual heroes as conduits for God's self-disclosure and limit other avenues for experiencing the divine. The biblical narratives themselves offer different ways of encountering God, such as through historical events, liturgical experience, cultic remembrances, nature, and ordinary everyday occurrences. The heroic biographies obscure other ways, such as art and music, in which people can feel the divine and encounter God.

What the Western searchers self-importantly call the historical Jesus, then, is not historical but a series of imaginative constructs. Vengal Chakkarai might have gone too far when he bluntly called Western biographies of Jesus "well-spun speculations," but indeed the quest for such a narrative is essentially a search for the already interpreted, reconstructed, and memorialized Jesus of the Gospels.[31] And what we find in the Gospels and the New Testament, as historical-criticism has relentlessly reminded us, are not factual details of Jesus's life but a series of confessional statements and judgments generated by the early supporters of Jesus. The Western search for Jesus was not strictly about the historical Jesus but about a Jesus portrayed in the biblical narratives as a teacher, redeemer, an apocalyptic hero, or all of these. What the Western biographers were dealing with and unearthing was not the historical Jesus, but, to use the phrase of Keshub Chunder Sen, the "Christ of the Gospel."[32]

The quest for the historical Jesus seems in a way to be a futile enterprise, so it is well worth asking whether there is any purchase in undertaking it. There are several compelling reasons for its discontinuance. For most of its history, Christianity grew through telling or retelling stories about Jesus. In the nascent church, the story of Jesus was told though Passion narratives, and later his early life was captured in the Gnostic Gospels, which were a mixture of legends and imagination. The devotional, pietistic, and symbolic Jesus disseminated through these discourses proved to be attractive and drew people's attention. The search for the historical Jesus, by contrast, has been a fairly recent and exclusive enterprise, undertaken over the last two hundred years or so, and restricted to a few academics.

In addition, even if we succeed in finding the "original," "real" Jesus, in the end, he is just a man, and complex at that. If we simply go by the records, during his earthly life he was an insignificant figure. What he was supposed to have said was not particularly original or earth-shattering. His sayings about loving one's enemies were already familiar in Jewish and Mediterranean circles before the Gospel writers implied that they were his own invention. The redeeming activity that he was engaged in has countless counterparts in the ancient world. The renunciant life he led has several parallels in Asia. More importantly, if one is looking for an anchor and direction, one is left with a complex and disturbingly contradictory figure in Jesus. For every progressive pronouncement he made, there is equally an oppressive statement attributed to him. What Swami Vivekananda said long ago about the difficulty of a vast portion of humanity rallying under a single person remains valid: "It is in vain we try to gather all the peoples of the world around a single personality."[33] In an increasingly diverse multicultural world, the possibility of a single person, or for that matter one religion, holding together the varying requirements and aspirations of humankind is difficult to entertain.

Other problems confound the effort to find and retell the story of the historical Jesus. First, no quest for Jesus is final. Each search for the historical Jesus is marked by subsequent correction and castigation. No doubt, the current biases of the New Quest, including those of contemporary biographers—whose feelings and perceptions will unavoidably be included in their writings—will one day be questioned and amended as well. Second, despite the many biographies of Jesus, we hardly ever hear his own voice. Like other ancient figures, Jesus can only be reconstructed through legends and perceptions that accrued around him. What is said about Cleopatra is equally true of Jesus: "We cannot hope to hear Cleopatra's true voice, and are forced to see her through secondary eyes; eyes already coloured by other people's propaganda, prejudices and assumptions."[34]

Finally, there is no obviously smooth and straight way of constructing a historical Jesus—indeed, our worst hermeneutical folly is to entertain the notion that ending up with a tidy image of Jesus is even possible. This predicament is poignantly captured by Margarlitha, a character in Sarah Joseph's novel *Othappu*.[35] Margarlitha wants to tell the story of Jesus to her children, but she hesitates to depend on, or draw from, the canonical sources. Her experience in a convent and later in the secular world has shown her that the ethics and ethos of first-century Palestine will not translate to the new, globalized India in which her children are growing up. We learn that she would like to begin anew the story of Jesus, but the novel ends with a blank page, presumably hinting at what some scholars are coming to realize as well: the impossibility of reconstructing a meaningful, straightforward history of Jesus in the modern era.

NOTES

INTRODUCTION

1. For a concise and clear periodization of the quest for the historical Jesus, see Helen K. Bond, *The Historical Jesus: A Guide for the Perplexed* (London: T&T Clark, 2012).

2. Daniel L. Pals, *The Victorian "Lives" of Jesus* (San Antonio: Trinity University Press, 1982).

3. R. S. Sugirtharajah, "An Interpretative Forward," in R. S. Sugirtharajah, ed., *Asian Faces of Jesus* (Maryknoll, NY: Orbis Books, 1993), 3.

4. C. J. den Heyer, *Jesus Matters: 150 Years of Research* (Valley Forge, PA: Trinity Press International, 1997), 114.

1. JESUS IN THE SUTRAS, STELE, AND SURAS

1. Albert Schweitzer, *The Quest of the Historical Jesus: A Critical Study of Its Progress from Reimarus to Wrede* (London: A. C. Black, 1910), 14.

2. James Legge, *The Nestorian Monument of Hsî-an Fû in Shen-hsî, China* (London: Trubner and Co., 1888); P. Y. Saeki, *The Nestorian Monument in China* (London: Society for Promoting Christian Knowledge, 1916), 1–97; P. Y. Saeki, *The Nestorian Documents and Relics in China* (Tokyo: Academy of Oriental Culture, 1937), 18–41; A. C. Moule, *Christians in China before the Year 1550* (London: Society for Promoting Christian Knowledge, 1930), 27–77; Martin Palmer, *The Jesus Sutras: Rediscovering the Lost Religion of Taoist Christianity* (London: Piatkus, 2001); Ray Riegert and Thomas Moore, *The Lost Sutras of Jesus: Unlocking the Ancient Wisdom of the Xian Monks* (London: Souvenir Press, 2003), 3–42; and Li Tang, *A Study of the History of Nestorian Christianity in China and Its Literature in Chinese: Together with a New*

English Translation of the Dunhuang Nestorian Documents, 2nd rev. ed. (Frankfurt am Main: Peter Lang, 2004).

3. Palmer, *Jesus Sutras,* 174.

4. *Mir'āt al-Quds (Mirror of Holiness): A Life of Christ for Emperor Akbar,* translated and annotated by W. M. Thackston (Leiden: Brill, 2012).

5. Moule, *Christians in China before the Year 1550,* 65; Saeki, *Nestorian Monument in China,* 166.

6. On the Chinese emperor sending his minister, see Saeki, *Nestorian Monument in China,* 208.

7. Edward Maclagan, *The Jesuits and the Great Mogul* (London: Burns, Oates, and Washbourne, 1932), 24.

8. Tang, *Study of the History of Nestorian Christianity,* 149.

9. Kalikinkar Datta, "Akbar the Great," in R. C. Majumdar, H. C. Raychaudhuri, and Kalikinkar Datta, *An Advanced History of India: Fourth Edition with an Appendix on Bangladesh* (Madras: Macmillan India Limited, 1978), 451.

10. *Mir'āt al-quds,* 205.

11. Ibid., 140.

12. Ibid., 151.

13. Palmer, *Jesus Sutras,* 166.

14. Ibid., 166.

15. Saeki, *Nestorian Monument in China,* 132.

16. Saeki, *Nestorian Documents and Relics in China,* 55.

17. Palmer, *Jesus Sutras,* 63.

18. Saeki, *Nestorian Documents and Relics in China,* 165.

19. Palmer, *Jesus Sutras,* 203.

20. Saeki, *Nestorian Documents and Relics in China,* 165.

21. Palmer, *Jesus Sutras,* 160.

22. Riegert and Moore, *Lost Sutras of Jesus,* 82.

23. Saeki, *Nestorian Documents and Relics in China,* 182.

24. Riegert and Moore, *Lost Sutras of Jesus,* 124.

25. Saeki, *Nestorian Monument in China,* 194.

26. Ibid., 164, 195.

27. Riegert and Moore, *Lost Sutras of Jesus,* 125.

28. Ibid., 83.

29. Ibid., 125.

30. Tang, *Study of the History of Nestorian Christianity in China,* 139.

31. Jay G. Williams, *The Secret Sayings of Ye Su: A Silk Road Gospel* (New York: Universe, 2004), 5.

32. Saeki, *Nestorian Documents and Relics in China,* 55.

33. Palmer, *Jesus Sutras,* 204.

34. Saeki, *Nestorian Documents and Relics in China,* 214.

35. A. Rogers, "The Holy Mirror; or, The Gospel According to Father Jerome Xavier from the Original Persian," *Asiatic Quarterly Review* 10 (July– October 1890): 200.

36. Saeki, *Nestorian Monument in China,* 191.

37. John Foster, *The Church of the T'ang Dynasty* (London: SPCK, 1939), 112.

38. Samuel H. Moffett, *A History of Christianity in Asia,* vol. 1: *Beginnings to 1500,* revised and corrected edition (Maryknoll, NY: Orbis Books, 1998), 306.

39. Legge, *The Nestorian Monument of Hsî-an Fû in Shen-hsî, China,* 55.

40. Ramsay MacMullen, "Christianity Shaped through Its Mission," in A. Kreider, ed., *The Origins of Christendom in the West* (Edinburgh: T & T Clark, 2001), 97.

41. Legge, *The Nestorian Monument of Hsî-an Fû in Shen-hsî, China,* 52.

42. John M. Hobson, *The Eastern Origins of Western Civilization* (Cambridge, UK: Cambridge University Press, 2004), 140.

43. Ibid., 139.

44. K. N. Chaudhuri, *Asia before Europe: Economy and Civilization of the Indian Ocean from the Rise of Islam to 1750* (Cambridge, UK: Cambridge University Press, 1990), 54.

45. Riegert and Moore, *Lost Sutras of Jesus,* 63.

46. Tang, *Study of the History of Nestorian Christianity in China,* 142.

47. Saeki, *Nestorian Documents and Relics in China,* 226.

48. Palmer, *Jesus Sutras,* 60.

49. Saeki, *Nestorian Documents and Relics in China,* 214.

50. On the Mughals' appreciation for gardens, see C. Villiers-Stuart, *Gardens of the Great Mughals* (London: Adam and Charles Black, 1913).

51. Moffett, *A History of Christianity in Asia,* vol. 1, 311.

52. Percival Spear, *The Nobobs: A Study of the Social Life of the English in Eighteenth-Century India* (London: Oxford University Press, 1963), xi.

53. Ian Gillman and Hans-Joachim Klimkeit, *Christians in Asia before 1500* (Richmond, VA: Curzon Press, 1999), 278.

54. Zhao Fusan, *Christianity in China* (Manila: De La Salle University Press, 1986), 15.

55. Ibid., 15.

56. Spear, *The Nobobs*, xiv.

57. J. S. M. Hooper, *The Bible in India with a Chapter on Ceylon* (London: Oxford University Press, 1938), 37.

58. Edward D. Maclagan, "The Jesuit Missions to the Emperor Akbar by E. D. Maclagan C.S. from Notes Recorded by the Late General R. Maclagan, R.E," *Journal of the Asiatic Society of Bengal* 65, pt. 1, nos. 1–4 (1896): 108.

2. THE HEAVENLY ELDER BROTHER

1. John E. Johnson, "Tai-Ping-Wang, and the Chinese Rebellion of 1853–1862," *New Englander* 30, no. 116 (1871): 389.

2. Franz Michael, ed., *The Taiping Rebellion: History and Documents. In Collaboration with Chung-Li Chang*, vol. 2: *Documents and Comments* (Seattle: University of Washington Press, 1971), 20; and Theodore Hamberg, *The Visions of Hung-Siu-tshuen, and Origin of the Kwang-si Insurrection* (Hong Kong: China Mail Office, 1854), 24. Hong Xiuquan is also known as Hung-Siu-Tshuen.

3. Sinim, mentioned in Isaiah 49.12, is supposed to be China.

4. For earlier accounts, see Thomas T. Meadows, *The Chinese and Their Rebellions Viewed in Connection with Their National Philosophy, Ethics, Legislation, and Administration: To Which Is Added, an Essay on Civilization and Its Present State in the East and West* (London: Smith, Elder and Co., 1856); and William J. Hail, *Tsêng Kuo-Fan and the Taiping Rebellion: With a Short Sketch of His Later Career* (New Haven, CT: Yale University Press, 1927). For more current scholars' accounts, see Eugene Powers Boardman, *Christian Influence upon the Ideology of the Taiping Rebellion, 1851–1864* (Madison: University of Wisconsin Press, 1952); Yuan Chung Teng, "Reverend Issachar Jacox Roberts and the Taiping Rebellion," *Journal of Asian Studies* 23, no. 1 (1963): 55–67; Jonathan Spence, *God's Chinese Son: The Taiping Heavenly Kingdom of Hong Xiuquan* (London: Flamingo, 1996); and Thomas H. Reilly, *The Taiping Heavenly Kingdom: Rebellion and the Blasphemy of Empire* (Seattle: University of Washington Press, 2004). For documents of the Taipings, see Michael, *Taiping Rebellion*.

5. Reilly, *Taiping Heavenly Kingdom*, 4–5.

6. Compilation Group for the History of Modern China Series, *The Taiping Revolution* (Peking: Foreign Language Press, 1976), 31.

7. W. A. P. Martin, *A Cycle of Cathay; or, China, South and North with Personal Reminiscences: With Illustrations and Map.* 3rd ed. (New York: Fleming H. Revell, 1900), 137.

8. The Four Books are *The Great Learning, Doctrine of the Mean, The Analects,* and *The Works of Menicus.* The Five Classics are *The Book of the Odes, The Book of Documents, The Book of Change, The Book of Rites,* and *The Spring and Autumn Annals.*

9. Hamberg, *Visions of Hung-Siu-tshuen*, 10.

10. Michael, *Taiping Rebellion*, vol. 2, 62.

11. For the letter, see S. Y. Teng, *The Taiping Rebellion and the Western Powers: A Comprehensive Survey* (Oxford, UK: Clarendon Press, 1971), 185.

12. Philip A. Kuhn, "Origins of the Taiping Vision: Cross-Cultural Dimension of a Chinese Rebellion," *Comparative Studies in Society and History* 19, no. 3 (1977): 352.

13. Hamberg, *Visions of Hung-Siu-tshuen*, 22.

14. Ibid., 21.

15. Michael, *Taiping Rebellion*, vol. 2, 240.

16. Teng, *Taiping Rebellion and the Western Powers*, 337.

17. Ibid., 328.

18. Compilation Group for the History of Modern China Series, *Taiping Revolution*, 171–172.

19. Lytton Stratchey, *Eminent Victorians* (Luton: Andrews UK, 2012), 242.

20. All these documents are in Michael, *Taiping Rebellion*, vols. 1–3.

21. Ibid., vol. 2, 408–415.

22. Joseph Edkins, "Narrative of a Visit to Nanking," in J. R. Edkins, ed., *Chinese Scenes and People* (London: James Nisbet and Co., 1863), 295.

23. Meadows, *Chinese and Their Rebellions*, 422. Emphasis in the original.

24. Edkins, "Narrative of a Visit to Nanking," 298.

25. Michael, *Taiping Rebellion*, vol. 2, 108.

26. Edkins, "Narrative of a Visit to Nanking," 294.

27. Ibid., 297.

28. Teng, "Reverend Issachar Jacox Roberts and the Taiping Rebellion," 64.

29. Edkins, "Narrative of a Visit to Nanking," 297.

30. J. C. Cheng, *Chinese Sources for the Taiping Rebellion, 1850–1864* (Hong Kong: Hong Kong University Press, 1963), 86; Michael, *Taiping Rebellion,* vol. 2, 231.

31. Cheng, *Chinese Sources for the Taiping Rebellion,* 86.

32. Ibid., 86.

33. Michael, *Taiping Rebellion,* vol. 2, 231.

34. Edkins, "Narrative of a Visit to Nanking," 272.

35. Cheng, *Chinese Sources for the Taiping Rebellion,* 83; and Michael, *Taiping Rebellion,* vol. 2, 227.

36. Michael, *Taiping Rebellion,* vol. 2, 229; and Spence, *God's Chinese Son,* 83.

37. Cheng, *Chinese Sources for the Taiping Rebellion,* 86; and Michael, *Taiping Rebellion,* vol. 2, 231.

38. Hail, *Tsêng Kuo-fan and the Taiping Rebellion,* 94.

39. Cheng, *Chinese Sources for the Taiping Rebellion,* 88.

40. Ibid., 90; and Michael, *Taiping Rebellion,* vol. 2, 236.

41. Cheng, *Chinese Sources for the Taiping Rebellion,* 91; and Michael, *Taiping Rebellion,* vol. 2, 237.

42. Ibid.

43. Michael, *Taiping Rebellion,* vol. 2, 159.

44. Ibid.

45. Cheng, *Chinese Sources for the Taiping Rebellion,* 91, and Michael, *Taiping Rebellion,* vol. 2, 237.

46. Michael, *Taiping Rebellion,* vol. 2, 245.

47. Ibid., 57.

48. Ibid., 100.

49. Ibid., 589.

50. Ibid., 102.

51. Spence, *God's Chinese Son,* 264.

52. Ibid., 135.

53. Kuhn, "Origins of the Taiping Vision," 359.

54. Archie Lee to author, private email, n.d., in author's possession.

55. Cheng, *Chinese Sources for the Taiping Rebellion*, 84; and Michael, *Taiping Rebellion*, vol. 2, 228.

56. Michael, *Taiping Rebellion*, vol. 2, 373.

57. Ibid., 114.

58. Ibid., 156.

59. Ibid., 156–157.

60. Ibid., 234–235.

61. Ibid., 225.

62. Ibid., 31.

63. Teng, *Taiping Rebellion and the Western Powers*, 121.

64. Jack Gray, *Rebellions and Revolutions: China from the 1800s to 1900s* (Oxford, UK: Oxford University Press, 1990), 62.

65. For Hong's annotations to the Bible, see Cheng, *Chinese Sources for the Taiping Rebellion*, 81–91, and Michael, *Taiping Rebellion*, vol. 2, 220–237.

66. Edkins, "Narrative of a Visit to Nanking," 274.

67. For the various perspectives of the Western missionaries toward the Taipings, see Teng, *Taiping Rebellion and the Western Powers*, 173–205; and R. Covell, *Confucius, the Buddha and Christ: A History of the Gospel in Chinese* (Maryknoll, NY: Orbis, 1986), 174–181.

68. Teng, *Taiping Rebellion and the Western Powers*, 202.

69. Meadows, *Chinese and Their Rebellions*, 418.

70. For Martin's letter to his mission board, see Ralph R. Covell, *W. A. P. Martin: Pioneer of Progress in China* (Washington, DC: Christian University Press, 1978), 85.

71. Joseph Edkins, *Religion in China Containing a Brief Account of the Three Religions of the Chinese with Observations on the Prospects of Christian Conversion amongst That People* (London: Trübner and Co., 1878), 199.

72. Hail, *Tsêng Kuo-fan and the Taiping Rebellion*, 100.

73. Gray, *Rebellions and Revolutions*, 63.

74. Joseph Edkins, *The Religious Condition of the Chinese* (London: Routledge, Warnes, and Routledge, 1859), 282. The Fifth Monarchy refers to the militant puritans who believed that they were successors to earlier Assyrian, Perian, Greek, and Roman monarchies. They believed that force should be used to inaugurate the reign of God.

75. For Martin's second letter to U.S. Attorney General Caleb Cushing, see Covell, *W. A. P. Martin*, 85.

76. Michael, *Taiping Rebellion*, vol. 2, 114.

77. Ibid., 225.

78. Ibid., 33.

79. Edkins, "Narrative of a Visit to Nanking," 274.

80. J. W. Colenso, *The Pentateuch and Book of Joshua Critically Examined* (London: Longman, Green, Longman, Roberts, & Green, 1862), 13.

81. Edkins, "Narrative of a Visit to Nanking," 292.

82. Michael, *Taiping Rebellion*, vol. 2, 234; ibid., 268.

83. Johnson, "Tai-Ping-Wang, and the Chinese Rebellion of 1853–1862," 399–400.

84. *The Challenge of Basic Christian Communities: Papers from the International Ecumenical Congress of Theology, February 20–March 2, 1980, São Paulo, Brazil*, ed. S. Torres and John Eagleson, trans. J. Drury (Maryknoll, NY: Orbis Books, 1981).

85. Martin, *Cycle of Cathay*, 142.

86. For newspaper articles by Karl Marx on the Taipings, see Marx, "Articles on China, 1853–1860," https://www.marxists.org/archive/marx/works/1853/china /index.htm (accessed July 16, 2017).

87. Michael, *Taiping Rebellion*, vol. 2, 314.

88. Teng, *Taiping Rebellion and the Western Powers*, 106.

89. Brian F. Le Beau, "Christopher Columbus and the Matter of Religion," *Kripke Center for the Study of Religion and Society*, online newsletter (October 1992). See http://moses.creighton.edu/csrs/news/F92-1.html (accessed July 16, 2017).

3. A JUDEAN JNANA GURU

1. M. Vythilingam, *The Life of Sir Ponnambalam Ramanathan in Two Volumes*, vol. 1 (Colombo: Ramanathan Commemoration Society, 1971), 329.

2. Ponnambalam Ramanathan, *The Gospel of Jesus According to St. Matthew Interpreted to R. L. Harrison by the Light of the Godly Experience of Sri Parananda* (London: Kegan Paul, Trench, Trubner & Co., 1898), 96.

3. Ibid., 53.

4. Ponnambalam Ramanathan, *An Eastern Exposition of the Gospel of Jesus According to St. John Being an Interpretation Thereof by Sri Parananda* (London: William Hutchinson, 1902), 222.

5. Ponnambalam Ramanathan, *The Culture of the Soul among Western Nations* (New York: G. P. Putnam's Sons, 1906), 105.

6. R. Lilavati, *Western Pictures for Eastern Students: Being a Description of the Chief Incidents of a Journey Made by That Distinguished Scholar, Statesman and Sage, Sri P. Ramanathan, K.C., C.M.G., from Ceylon to the United States of America in 1095–1906* (London: W. Thacker & Co, 1907), 75.

7. Ramanathan, *Gospel of Jesus According to St. Matthew*, 125.

8. Ramanathan, *Eastern Exposition of the Gospel of Jesus*, 175.

9. Ibid., 153. Emphasis in the original.

10. Ponnambalam Ramanathan, *The Spirit of the East Contrasted with the Spirit of the West, Being a Lecture Delivered by Ponnambalam Ramanathan, K.C., C.M.G. before the Brooklyn Institute of Arts and Sciences at Its Opening Meeting of the Season of 1905–1906* (New York: G. P. Putnam's Sons, 1905), 10, 15.

11. Ramanathan, *Gospel of Jesus According to St. Matthew*, 256.

12. Ramanathan, *Eastern Exposition of the Gospel of Jesus*, 152.

13. Ibid., 42, 59. Emphasis in the original.

14. Ramanathan, *Gospel of Jesus According to St. Matthew*, 194.

15. Ramanathan, *Culture of the Soul among Western Nations*, 118.

16. Ibid., 119.

17. Ramanathan, *Gospel of Jesus According to St. Matthew*, 6.

18. Ibid., 7. Emphasis in the original.

19. Ibid., 251. Emphasis in the original.

20. Thomas Thangaraj, *The Crucified Guru: An Experiment in Cross-Cultural Christology* (Nashville: Abingdon Press, 1994), 89–105.

21. Ramanathan, *Culture of the Soul among Western Nations*, 154.

22. Ramanathan, *Eastern Exposition of the Gospel of Jesus*, 115. Emphasis in the original.

23. Ibid., 146.

24. Ibid., 122.

25. Ramanathan, *Gospel of Jesus According to St. Matthew*, 255.

26. Ramanathan, *Eastern Exposition of the Gospel of Jesus*, 210. Emphasis in the original.

27. Ibid., 207.

28. Ramanathan, *Spirit of the East Contrasted with the Spirit of the West*, 20.

29. Ramanathan, *Culture of the Soul among Western Nations,* 18.

30. Ponnambalam Ramanathan, "The Miscarriage of Life in the West," *Hibbert Journal* 7 (1909): 7.

31. Lilavati, *Western Pictures for Eastern Students,* 105.

32. Ramanathan, *Gospel of Jesus According to St. Matthew,* 46. Emphasis in the original.

33. Ibid., 46.

34. Ibid., 10.

35. Ramanathan, *Eastern Exposition of the Gospel of Jesus,* 197.

36. Ramanathan, *Gospel of Jesus According to St. Matthew,* 34. Emphasis in the original.

37. Ibid., 64.

38. Ramanathan, *Eastern Exposition of the Gospel of Jesus,* 69.

39. Ramanathan, *Gospel of Jesus According to St. Matthew,* 8. Emphasis in the original.

40. Ibid., 233.

41. Ibid.,166.

42. Ramanathan, *Eastern Exposition of the Gospel of Jesus,* 55. Emphasis in the original.

43. Ramanathan, *Culture of the Soul among Western Nations,* 119.

44. Ramanathan, *Eastern Exposition of the Gospel of Jesus,* 156.

45. Ramanathan, *Gospel of Jesus According to St. Matthew,* 191. Emphasis in the original.

46. Ramanathan, *Culture of the Soul among Western Nations,* 156.

47. Ramanathan, *Eastern Exposition of the Gospel of Jesus,* 74.

48. Ibid., 74.

49. Ramanathan, *Culture of the Soul among Western Nations,* 98.

50. Ramanathan, *Gospel of Jesus According to St. Matthew,* 206.

51. Ramanathan, *Eastern Exposition of the Gospel of Jesus,* 120.

52. Ramanathan, *Gospel of Jesus According to St. Matthew,* 206.

53. Ibid., 209.

54. Ramanathan, *Eastern Exposition of the Gospel of Jesus,* 7.

55. Ibid., 30.

56. Ibid., 7. Emphasis in the original.

57. Ibid.

58. Ramanathan, *Gospel of Jesus According to St. Matthew*, 195.

59. Ramanathan, *Culture of the Soul among Western Nations*, 81.

60. Ramanathan, *Eastern Exposition of the Gospel of Jesus*, 34.

61. Ramanathan, *Culture of the Soul among Western Nations*, 210.

62. Ibid., 97.

63. Ramanathan, *Eastern Exposition of the Gospel of Jesus*, 34.

64. Ramanathan, *Gospel of Jesus According to St. Matthew*, 139.

65. Ibid., 35.

66. Ibid., 82.

67. Ibid., 96.

68. Ramanathan, *Culture of the Soul among Western Nations*, 230. Emphasis in the original.

69. Ibid.

70. Ibid., 2.

71. Ibid., 34. Emphasis in the original.

72. Ramanathan, *Gospel of Jesus According to St. Matthew*, 70.

73. Ibid., 86.

74. Ramanathan, *Eastern Exposition of the Gospel of Jesus*, 150.

75. X. Irudayaraj, "The Guru in Hinduism and Christianity," *Vidyajyoti* 39, no. 8 (1975): 338–351; X. Irudayaraj, "Christ—the Guru," *Jeevadhara: A Journal of Christian Interpretation* 2, no. 9 (1972): 241–249; V. Paranjoti, *Saiva Siddhānta* (London: Luzac and Co., 1954), 92–97; and Thangaraj, *Crucified Guru*, 35–58.

76. T. Ganapathy, *The Philosophy of the Tamil Siddhas* (New Delhi: Indian Council of Philosophical Research, 1993), 13.

77. Ibid., 20.

78. Ramanathan, *Culture of the Soul among Western Nations*, 116.

79. Ramanathan, *Gospel of Jesus According to St. Matthew*, 215. Emphasis in the original.

80. Ramanathan, *Eastern Exposition of the Gospel of Jesus*, 200.

81. Ganapathy, *Philosophy of the Tamil Siddhas*, 13.

82. For the characteristics of siddhas, see ibid., 5.

83. Ibid., 15.

84. Ramanathan, *Eastern Exposition of the Gospel of Jesus*, 291.

85. Ramanathan, *Gospel of Jesus According to St. Matthew*, 128.

86. Ramanathan, *Culture of the Soul among Western Nations*, 98.

87. Ibid., 244.

88. Ramanathan, *Gospel of Jesus According to St. Matthew*, 207.

89. Ramanathan, *Culture of the Soul among Western Nations*, 98.

90. Ramanathan, *Eastern Exposition of the Gospel of Jesus*, 106.

91. Ibid., 2.

92. Ibid., 116.

93. Ramanathan, *Culture of the Soul among Western Nations*, 184.

94. Paranjoti, *Saiva Siddhānta*, 92.

95. Ramanathan, *Eastern Exposition of the Gospel of Jesus*, 30.

96. Ganapathy, *Philosophy of the Tamil Siddhas*, 197.

97. Ramanathan, *Eastern Exposition of the Gospel of Jesus*, 30.

98. Ibid., 225.

99. Ramanathan, *Gospel of Jesus According to St. Matthew*, 10, 23. Emphasis in the original.

100. Ramanathan, *Eastern Exposition of the Gospel of Jesus*, 242.

101. Lilavati, *Western Pictures for Eastern Students*, 105.

102. Ramanathan, *Culture of the Soul among Western Nations*, 53.

103. Ramanathan, *Eastern Exposition of the Gospel of Jesus*, 6.

104. Ramanathan, *Spirit of the East Contrasted with the Spirit of the West*, 21.

105. Ramanathan, *Gospel of Jesus According to St. Matthew*, 24.

106. Ramanathan, *Culture of the Soul among Western Nations*, 238.

107. Ibid., 81. Emphasis in the original.

108. Ibid.

109. Lilavati, *Western Pictures for Eastern Students*, 105.

110. Ramanathan, *Spirit of the East Contrasted with the Spirit of the West*, 30.

111. Ibid., 27. Emphasis in the original.

112. Lilavati, *Western Pictures for Eastern Students*, 46. Emphasis in the original.

113. For the differences between the Advaita and Saiva Siddhanta, see Paranjoti, *Saiva Siddhānta*, esp. 44.

114. Ramanathan, *Eastern Exposition of the Gospel of Jesus,* 31.

115. Ibid., 268.

116. Lilavati, *Western Pictures for Eastern Students,* 106.

117. Ramanathan, *Culture of the Soul among Western Nations,* 126.

118. Ibid., 161.

119. Paranjoti, *Saiva Siddhānta,* 144.

120. Ramanathan, *Culture of the Soul among Western Nations,* 126.

121. Ramanathan, *Spirit of the East Contrasted with the Spirit of the West,* 29.

122. Lilavati, *Western Pictures for Eastern Students,* 11.

123. Ramanathan, "Miscarriage of Life in the West," 7.

124. Surendra Kumar Datta, *The Desire of India* (London: Young Peoples' Missionary Movement, 1908), 255.

4. THE NONEXISTENT JESUS

1. Arthur Drews, *The Christ Myth: Revised and Enlarged Third Edition,* trans. C. Delisle Burns (London: Fisher Unwin, 1910), 7–9.

2. Thakur Kahan Chandra Varma, *Christ a Myth: The Historicity of Christ Proving the Christ of the New Testament a Myth and the Gospels Spurious,* 12th ed. (Lahore: K. C. Varma, 1928).

3. A. Lebeau, *The Historicity of Christ* (Trichinopoly: Indian Catholic Truth Society, 1925).

4. Varma, *Christ a Myth,* 6.

5. Chowdhuri, *In Search of Jesus Christ* (Calcutta: Brahma Mission, 1927), 410.

6. Ibid., 410.

7. Ibid., 312.

8. Ibid., 30.

9. Varma, *Christ a Myth,* 162.

10. Chowdhuri, *In Search of Jesus Christ,* vi.

11. Albert Schweitzer, *The Quest of the Historical Jesus: The First Complete Edition,* ed. John Bowden (London: SCM Press, 2000), 257.

12. Chowdhuri, *In Search of Jesus Christ,* 145.

13. Ibid., 8.

14. Varma, *Christ a Myth,* 74.

15. Chowdhuri, *In Search of Jesus Christ*, 261.

16. Ibid., xxiii.

17. Varma, *Christ a Myth*, 155.

18. Ibid., 82.

19. Ibid., 9.

20. Chowdhuri, *In Search of Jesus Christ*, 217.

21. Ibid., 22.

22. Ibid., 360.

23. Ibid., 179.

24. Varma, *Christ a Myth*, 10.

25. Chowdhuri, *In Search of Jesus Christ*, 242.

26. Ibid., 371.

27. Ibid., 137.

28. Ibid., 2.

29. Ibid., 250.

30. Ibid., 258.

31. Ibid., 2.

32. Ibid., 423.

33. Ibid., 30.

34. Varma, *Christ a Myth*, 32.

35. Chowdhuri, *In Search of Jesus Christ*, 66.

36. Ibid., 184.

37. Ibid., 414.

38. Ibid., 244.

39. Ibid., 217.

40. Varma, *Christ a Myth*, 64.

41. Ibid., 41.

42. Ibid., 56.

43. Louis Jacolliot, *The Bible in India: Hindoo Origin of Hebrew Revelation of Science* (London: John Camden Hotten, 1870).

44. Chowdhuri, *In Search of Jesus Christ*, 418.

45. Ibid., 124.

46. Ibid., 19.

47. Ibid., 204.

48. Ibid., 221.

49. Ibid., 222.

50. Ibid., 116.

51. Ibid., 188.

52. Ibid., 157.

53. Varma, *Christ a Myth,* 29, 26.

54. Chowdhuri, *In Search of Jesus Christ,* 313.

55. Ibid., 356.

56. Ibid., 420.

57. Ibid., 381.

58. Varma, *Christ a Myth,* 65.

59. Chowdhuri, *In Search of Jesus Christ,* 407.

60. Ibid., 209.

61. Ibid., 423.

62. Schweitzer, *Quest of the Historical Jesus,* 4.

63. Arthur Drews, *The Witnesses to the Historicity of Jesus,* trans. Joseph McCabe (Chicago: Open Court Publishing, 1912), 299.

64. Varma, *Christ a Myth,* 71.

65. Chowdhuri, *In Search of Jesus Christ,* 266.

66. Ibid., 380.

67. Varma, *Christ a Myth,* 150.

68. Chowdhuri, *In Search of Jesus Christ,* 116.

69. Ibid., 30.

70. Ibid., 22.

71. Varma, *Christ a Myth,* 15.

72. Chowdhuri, *In Search of Jesus Christ,* 220.

73. Ibid., 221.

74. Ibid., 41, 266; Schweitzer, *Quest of the Historical Jesus,* 399.

75. Varma, *Christ a Myth*, 142.

76. Ibid., 143.

77. Ibid., n.p.

78. John C. B. Webster, *The Christian Community and Change in Nineteenth-Century North India* (Delhi: Macmillan Company of India, 1976), 112.

79. Chowdhuri, *In Search of Jesus Christ*, 41.

80. Ibid., 188.

81. Varma, *Christ a Myth*, 163.

82. Chowdhuri, *In Search of Jesus Christ*, 3.

83. T. B. Macaulay, "Minute of the 2nd of February 1835," in G. Young, ed., *Speeches by Lord Macaulay with His Minute on Indian Education* (London: Oxford University Press, 1935), 345–361.

5. A JAFFNA MAN'S JESUS

1. Francis Kingsbury and G. E. Phillips, *Hymns of the Tamil Saivite Saints* (London: Oxford University Press, 1921), 8.

2. Francis Kingsbury, *How I Became a Christian* (London: Christian Literature Society, 1907), 9.

3. Ibid.

4. There is little on the life of Kingsbury. For a brief introduction, see R. F. Young and S. Jebanesan, *The Bible Trembled: The Hindu-Christian Controversies of Nineteenth-Century Ceylon* (Vienna: Institut zur Indologie der Universitat Wien, 1995), 156–157; S. R. H. Hoole, "C. W. Thamothrampillai, Tamil Revivalist: The Man behind the Legend of Tamil Revivalism," *Nethra* 2, no. 1 (1997): 15–20.

5. Kingsbury, *How I Became a Christian*, 24.

6. Kingsbury and Phillips, *Hymns of the Tamil Saivite Saints*.

7. Francis Kingsbury, *Jesus of Nazareth: His Life and Teaching* (Madras: Authors' Press and Publishing House, 1924).

8. Francis Kingsbury, *The Life of Jesus* (Colombo: H. W. Cave & Co, 1932).

9. Ibid., xi.

10. Francis Kingsbury, *The Life of Jesus in Tamil* (Colombo: Ilangabhimani Press, 1939).

11. Kingsbury, *Life of Jesus*, v–vi.

12. Ibid., xxx.

13. Kingsbury, *How I Became a Christian*, 27.

14. Kingsbury, *Jesus of Nazareth*, vii.

15. Kingsbury, *Life of Jesus*, vi.

16. Ibid., xxviii.

17. Kingsbury, *Jesus of Nazareth*, vii.

18. Kingsbury, *Life of Jesus*, 96.

19. Ibid., 114.

20. Ibid., 16.

21. Kingsbury, *How I Became a Christian*, 10.

22. Kingsbury, *Life of Jesus*, 21.

23. Ibid., 44.

24. Ibid., 113. Emphasis in the original.

25. Ibid., 67.

26. Ibid., 115.

27. Ibid., vii.

28. Ibid., viii.

29. Ibid., 83.

30. Ibid., 72.

31. Kingsbury, *How I Became a Christian*, 29.

32. Kingsbury, *Life of Jesus*, 115.

33. Ibid., 31.

34. Ibid., 28.

35. Ibid., 20. Emphasis in the original.

36. Ibid., 68.

37. Ibid., 5.

38. Ibid., 39.

39. Ibid., 68.

40. Ibid., 68.

41. Ibid., 109.

42. Ibid., viii.

43. Kingsbury, *How I Became a Christian,* 27.

44. Kingsbury, *Life of Jesus,* 109.

45. Ibid., 109.

46. Ibid., 84. Emphasis in the original.

47. R. S. Sugirtharajah, *Asian Biblical Hermeneutics and Postcolonialism: Contesting the Interpretations* (Sheffield, UK: Sheffield Academic Press, 1999), 29–53; and R. S. Sugirtharajah, *The Bible and Asia: From the Pre-Colonial Era to the Postcolonial Age* (Cambridge, MA: Harvard University Press, 2013), 84–92.

48. On "dogmatic Christianity and the traditions of Hinduism," see P. Chenchiah, "Jesus and Non-Christian Faiths," in G. Job, ed., *Rethinking Christianity in India* (Madras: A. N. Sudarisanam, 1938), 49.

49. Kingsbury, *How I Became a Christian,* 11.

50. For a survey of lives of Jesus during this period, see W. P. Weaver, *The Historical Jesus in the Twentieth Century, 1900–1950* (Harrisburg, PA: Trinity Press International, 1999).

51. K. Zvelebil, *Lexicon of Tamil Literature* (Leiden: E. J. Brill, 1995), 669.

52. Kingsbury, *Life of Jesus,* 112.

53. Kingsbury, *How I Became a Christian,* 25.

54. E. J. Sharpe, *Not to Destroy but to Fulfill: The Contribution of J. N. Farquahar to Protestant Missionary Thought in India before 1914* (Uppsala: Swedish Institute of Missionary Research, 1965), 87.

55. Kingsbury, *How I Became a Christian,* 26.

6. JESUS AS A JAIN TIRTHANKARA

1. For a convenient introduction to Sen's life, thought, and contribution, see *Keshub Chunder Sen: A Selection,* ed. D. C. Scott (Madras: Christian Literature Society, 1979).

2. M. C. Parekh, "Selections from the Gujarati Autobiography," in R. Boyd, ed., *Manilal C Parekh, 1885–1967; Dhanjibhai Fakirbhai, 1895–1967: A Selection* (Madras: Christian Literature Society, 1974), 32.

3. Manilal C. Parekh, "The Spiritual Significance and Value of Baptism," in R. Boyd, ed., *Manilal C Parekh, 1885–1976; Dhanjibhai Fakirbhai, 1895–1967: A Selection* (Madras: Christian Literature Society, 1974), 61.

4. Ibid., 56.

5. Manilal C. Parekh, *A Hindu's Portrait of Jesus Christ: A Gospel of God's Free Gift of His Sonship* (Rajkot: Sri Bhagavata Dharma Mission, 1953), 331.

6. Manilal C. Parekh, *Brahmarshi Keshub Chunder Sen* (Rajkot: Oriental Christ House, 1926); Parekh, *Sri Swami Narayana: A Gospel of Bhagwat-Dharma or God in Redemptive Action* (Rajkot: Sri Bhagwat-Dharma Mission House, 1936); and Parekh, *Sri Vallabhacharya: Life, Teachings and Movement. A Religion of Grace* (Rajkot: Sri Bhagavata Dharma Mission, 1943).

7. Manilal C. Parekh, *The Gospel of Zoroaster: The Iranian Veda* (Rajkot: Sri Bhagwat-Dharma Mission House, 1939).

8. Parekh, *Hindu's Portrait of Jesus Christ*.

9. Parekh, "Selections from the Gujarati Autobiography," 54.

10. Ibid., 46.

11. Ibid., 34.

12. M. C. Parekh, "An Autobiographical Sketch," in R. Boyd, ed., *Manilal C Parekh, 1885–1967; Dhanjibhai Fakirbhai, 1895–1967: A Selection* (Madras: Christian Literature Society, 1974), 28.

13. Parekh, *Hindu's Portrait of Jesus Christ*, 247.

14. Parekh, "Spiritual Significance and Value of Baptism," 56–57.

15. Parekh, "Autobiographical Sketch," 29.

16. R. S. Sugirtharajah, *The Bible and Asia: From the Pre-Colonial Era to the Postcolonial Age* (Cambridge, MA: Harvard University Press, 2013), 103–117.

17. Parekh, *Brahmarshi Keshub Chunder Sen*, 106.

18. Parekh, *A Hindu's Portrait of Jesus Christ*, 247.

19. On Sen's approach, see K. Chunder Sen, *Keshub Chunder Sen's Lectures in India* (London: Cassell & Company, 1901), 424.

20. Parekh, *A Hindu's Portrait of Jesus Christ*, 348.

21. Parekh, *Sri Swami Narayana*, 224.

22. Ibid., 282.

23. Parekh, *A Hindu's Portrait of Jesus Christ*, 564.

24. Ibid., 118.

25. Ibid., 117.

26. Parekh, "Autobiographical Sketch," 24.

27. Parekh, *A Hindu's Portrait of Jesus Christ*, 145.

28. Ibid., 349.

29. Ibid., 349.

30. Ibid., 213.

31. Parekh, "Autobiographical Sketch," 27.

32. Brahmabandhab Upadhyay, "Are We Hindus," in J. Lipner and G. Gispert-Sauch, eds., *The Writings of Brahmabandhab Upadhyay: Including a Resume of His Life and Thought*, vol. 1 (Bangalore: United Theological College, 1991), 24.

33. P. Chenchiah, "Jesus and Non-Christian Faiths," in G. Job, ed., *Rethinking Christianity in India* (Madras: A. N. Sudarisanam, 1938), 49.

34. M. C. Parekh, "The Christian Religion and the Jains," *National Christian Council Review* 46, no. 3 (1926): 142.

35. Parekh, *Hindu's Portrait of Jesus Christ*, 373.

36. Ibid., 373.

37. Ibid., 374.

38. Ibid.

39. Ibid., 375.

40. Keshub Chunder Sen, *Keshub Chunder Sen's Lectures in India* (London: Cassell & Company, 1904), 21.

41. Keshub Chunder Sen, *The Brahmo Samaj: The New Dispensation or the Religion of Harmony, Compiled from Keshub Chunder Sen's Writings* (Calcutta: Bidhan Press, 1903), 32.

42. Parekh, *Hindu's Portrait of Jesus Christ*, 447.

43. A. J. Appasamy, *The Gospel and India's Heritage* (Madras: Society for the Promoting Christian Knowledge, 1942), 35–39.

44. Parekh, *A Hindu's Portrait of Jesus Christ*, 440.

45. Ibid., 463.

46. Parekh, *Sri Vallabhacharya*, 135.

47. Ibid., 136.

48. Parekh, *A Hindu's Portrait of Jesus Christ*, 317–318, 383–384.

49. Ibid., 325.

50. Ibid., 328.

51. Ibid., 460.

52. Parekh, *Sri Vallabhacharya*, 31.

53. Parekh, *A Hindu's Portrait of Jesus Christ*, 215.

54. Parekh, *Brahmarshi Keshub Chunder Sen*, 245.

55. Parekh, *A Hindu's Portrait of Jesus Christ*, 329.

56. Ibid., 329.

57. Ibid., 515.

58. Ibid., 516.

59. Ibid., 550.

60. Parekh, "Christian Religion and the Jains," 138–145.

61. Chunder Sen, *Keshub Chunder Sen's Lectures in India* (1901), 47.

62. Parekh, "Christian Religion and the Jains," 144.

63. Ibid., 145.

64. Ibid.

65. Parekh, *A Hindu's Portrait of Jesus Christ*, 409.

66. Ibid.

67. Parekh, "Christian Religion and the Jains," 144.

68. Parekh, *A Hindu's Portrait of Jesus Christ*, 575.

69. Ibid., 574.

70. Ibid., 576.

71. Ibid., 588.

72. Ibid., 576.

73. Sen, *Keshub Chunder Sen's Lectures in India* (1904), 1–48.

74. Parekh, *Hindu's Portrait of Jesus Christ*, 170.

75. Ibid., 171.

76. Ibid., 177.

77. Parekh, "Christian Religion and the Jains," 143–44.

78. Parekh, *Hindu's Portrait of Jesus Christ*, 342.

79. Ibid., 243.

80. Ibid., 473.

81. Parekh, "Christian Religion and the Jains," 142.

82. Parekh, *Hindu's Portrait of Jesus Christ*, 394.

83. Ibid., 234.

84. Ibid., 233.

85. Ibid, 474.

86. Parekh, *Sri Swami Narayana*, 225.

87. Parekh, *Hindu's Portrait of Jesus Christ*, 291.

88. Ibid., 386.

89. Ibid., 158.

90. Ibid., 263.

91. Ibid., 541.

92. M. Gandhi, *The Message of Jesus Christ* (Bombay: Bharatiya Vidya Bhavan, 1964), 7.

93. Parekh, *Hindu's Portrait of Jesus Christ*, 247.

94. Parekh, "Selections from the Gujarati Autobiography," 42.

95. Parekh, *Hindu's Portrait of Jesus Christ*, 335.

96. Albert Schweitzer, *The Quest of the Historical Jesus: A Critical Study of Its Progress from Reimarus to Wrede* (London: A. C. Black, 1910), 399.

97. M. M. Thomas, *The Acknowledged Christ of the Indian Renaissance* (London: SCM Press, 1969); Michael Amaladoss, *The Asian Jesus* (Maryknoll, NY: Orbis, 2006).

98. Shūsaku Endō, *A Life of Jesus* (Tokyo: Charles E. Tuttle, 1979).

99. Parekh, *Hindu's Portrait of Jesus Christ*, 248.

100. Ibid., 297.

101. Ibid.

102. Ibid., 296.

103. Parekh, "Selections from the Gujarati Autobiography," 53.

104. Parekh, *Sri Vallabhacharya*, 195.

105. Ibid., 196.

106. Parekh, *Gospel of Zoroaster*, 60.

107. Parekh, *Brahmarshi Keshub Chunder Sen*, 173.

108. Ibid., 109.

109. Ibid., 171.

110. Sen, *Keshub Chunder Sen's Lectures in India* (1901), 391; Parekh, *Hindu's Portrait of Jesus Christ*, 385.

111. Sen, *Keshub Chunder Sen's Lectures in India* (1904), 26.

7. AN UPANISHADIC MYSTIC

1. S. Radhakrishnan, *The Hindu View of Life* (London: George Allen & Unwin, 1927), 21.

2. S. Radhakrishnan, *Eastern Religions and Western Thought* (Oxford, UK: Clarendon Press, 1939), 338.

3. Radhakrishnan, *Hindu View of Life*, 37.

4. S. Radhakrishnan, "My Search for Truth," in R. A. McDermott, ed., *Basic Writings of S. Radhakrishnan* (Bombay: Jaico, 1972), 37.

5. Robert N. Minor, *Radhakrishnan: A Religious Biography* (Albany: State University of New York Press, 1987); S. Gopal, *Radhakrishnan: A Biography* (London: Unwin Hyman, 1989); and K. Satchidananda Murty and Ashok Vohra, *Radhakrishnan: His Life and Ideas* (Albany: State University of New York Press, 1990).

6. Radhakrishnan, "My Search for Truth," 40.

7. Ibid., 37.

8. S. Radhakrishnan, "The Religion of the Spirit and the World's Need: Fragments of a Confession," in Paul A. Schilpp, ed., *The Philosophy of Sarvepalli Radhakrishnan* (New York: Tudor, 1952), 9.

9. Radhakrishnan, "My Search for Truth," 39.

10. Ibid.

11. S. Radhakrishnan, *East and West in Religion* (London: George Allen & Unwin, 1933), 47.

12. Ibid., 58.

13. Radhakrishnan, *Eastern Religions and Western Thought*, 272.

14. S. Radhakrishnan, *The Present Crisis of Faith* (New Delhi: Orient Paperbacks, 1970), 63.

15. Radhakrishnan, *Eastern Religions and Western Thought*, 272.

16. Radhakrishnan, *East and West in Religion*, 66.

17. Radhakrishnan, *Eastern Religions and Western Thought*, 197. For the Indian mystical influence, Radhakrishnan quoted Dean Milman's *History of Christianity*, which advanced the theory of permanent Indian settlement in the deserts of Egypt (197).

18. S. Radhakrishnan, "Reply to Critics," in P. A. Schilpp, ed., *The Philosophy of Sarvepalli Radhakrishnan* (New York: Tudor, 1952), 807.

19. S. Radhakrishnan, *Indian Religious Thought* (Delhi: Orient Paperbacks, 2006), 110.

20. Radhakrishnan, "Reply to Critics," 812.

21. S. Radhakrishnan, *Recovery of Faith* (Delhi: Hind Pocket Books, 1956), 147.

22. S. Radhakrishnan, *The Bhagavadgita: With an Introductory Essay Sanskrit Text, English Translation and Notes* (Bombay: George Allen & Unwin India Private, 1948), 28.

23. S. Radhakrishnan, *East and West: Some Reflections. Beatty Memorial Lectures* (London: George Allen & Unwin, 1955), 73.

24. S. Radhakrishnan, *The Heart of Hindusthan* (New Delhi: Rupa & Co., 2002), 72; Radhakrishnan, *East and West*, 71.

25. Ibid., 73.

26. Ibid., 73.

27. Ibid.

28. Ibid., 72.

29. R. Otto, *The Kingdom of God and the Son of Man: A Study in the History of Religion* (London: Lutterworth Press, 1938), 16; Radhakrishnan, *Eastern Religions and Western Thought*, 171.

30. Radhakrishnan, *Eastern Religions and Western Thought*, 176.

31. Ibid.

32. Ibid., 174–175.

33. Ibid., 171.

34. Radhakrishnan, *East and West*, 44.

35. Ibid., 79.

36. Radhakrishnan, *Eastern Religions and Western Thought*, 160; see also Otto, *The Kingdom of God and the Son of Man*, 187.

37. Radhakrishnan, *East and West*, 70.

38. Radhakrishnan, *Eastern Religions and Western Thought*, 173; see also Rhys T. W. Davids, "What Has Buddhism Derived from Christianity?" *Journal of the Pali Text Society* 7 (1923): 43.

39. Ibid.

40. Radhakrishnan, *Eastern Religions and Western Thought*, 172.

41. Ibid., 173.

42. Radhakrishnan, *The Bhagavadgita*, 48; Radhakrishnan, "Religion of the Spirit and the World's Need," 42.

43. Radhakrishnan, *Heart of Hindusthan*, 87.

44. Radhakrishnan, "Religion of the Spirit and the World's Need," 42.

45. Radhakrishnan, *Heart of Hindusthan,* 75.

46. Ibid.

47. Radhakrishnan, *Eastern Religions and Western Thought,* 176.

48. Ibid., 324.

49. Radhakrishnan, *East and West in Religion,* 58.

50. Radhakrishnan, *Heart of Hindusthan,* 77.

51. Radhakrishnan, *Eastern Religions and Western Thought,* 165.

52. Ibid., 168.

53. S. Radhakrishnan, *Occasional Speeches and Writings, October 1952– February 1959. Combined Edition* (Delhi: Publications Division, Ministry of Information and Broadcasting, Government of India, 1960), 318.

54. Radhakrishnan, *Heart of Hindusthan,* 88.

55. Radhakrishnan, *Eastern Religions and Western Thought,* 168.

56. Ibid., 174.

57. Radhakrishnan, *Occasional Speeches and Writings,* 306.

58. Ibid., 307.

59. S. Radhakrishnan, *An Idealist View of Life* (New Delhi: HarperCollins, 1994),108.

60. Radhakrishnan, *Eastern Religions and Western Thought,* 176.

61. Radhakrishnan, *Present Crisis of Faith,* 62.

62. Radhakrishnan, "Reply to Critics," 808.

63. Radhakrishnan, "Religion of the Spirit and the World's Need," 808.

64. Radhakrishnan, "Reply to Critics," 811.

65. Ibid., 808.

66. Radhakrishnan, "My Search for Truth," 39.

67. Radhakrishnan, "Religion of the Spirit and the World's Need," 68.

68. Radhakrishnan, "Reply to Critics," 810.

69. Ibid., 807.

70. Radhakrishnan, *Heart of Hindusthan,* 5.

71. R. Lilavati, *Western Pictures for Eastern Students: Being a Description of the Chief Incidents of a Journey Made by That Distinguished Scholar, Statesman and*

Sage, Sri P. Ramanathan, K. C., C. M. G., from Ceylon to the United States of America in 1095–1906 (London: W. Thacker & Co., 1907), 11.

72. Radhakrishnan, *Eastern Religions and Western Thought*, 381.

73. Radhakrishnan, *Occasional Speeches and Writings*, 305.

74. Radhakrishnan, *Eastern Religions and Western Thought*, 381–382.

75. Radhakrishnan, *The Bhagavadgita*, 254.

76. Radhakrishnan, *East and West in Religion*, 58.

77. S. Radhakrishnan, *Religion and Society: Kamala Lectures* (London: George Allen & Unwin, 1947), 208.

78. Radhakrishnan, *Eastern Religions and Western Thought*, 171.

79. Radhakrishnan, *Heart of Hindusthan*, 4.

80. Radhakrishnan, *Religion and Society*, 76.

81. Ibid., 207.

82. Radhakrishnan, "Religion of the Spirit and the World's Need," 79, 80; Radhakrishnan, *Recovery of Faith*, 116.

83. Radhakrishnan, *Indian Religious Thought*, 26.

84. Radhakrishnan, *Heart of Hindusthan*, 88.

85. Radhakrishnan, "Religion of the Spirit and the World's Need," 79.

86. Radhakrishnan, *The Bhagavadgita*, 36.

87. Radhakrishnan, *Eastern Religions and Western Thought*, 176.

88. Ibid.

89. Ibid., 170.

90. Ibid.

91. Radhakrishnan, "Religion of the Spirit and the World's Need," 45.

92. Radhakrishnan, *Recovery of Faith*, 116.

93. S. Radhakrishnan, *The Religion We Need* (London: Ernest Benn, 1928), 30.

94. Radhakrishnan, *Eastern Religions and Western Thought*, 171.

95. Radhakrishnan, "Religion of the Spirit and the World's Need," 79.

96. Radhakrishnan, *Indian Religious Thought*, 106.

97. Radhakrishnan, *Present Crisis of Faith*, 68.

98. Radhakrishnan, *The Bhagavadgita*, 155.

99. Ibid., 36.

100. Radhakrishnan, *Heart of Hindusthan,* 73.

101. Radhakrishnan, *The Bhagavadgita,* 35.

102. Ibid., 31.

103. Radhakrishnan, *Heart of Hindusthan,* 74.

104. Radhakrishnan, "Religion of the Spirit and the World's Need," 68.

105. Ibid.

106. Radhakrishnan, *East and West,* 75.

107. Ibid., 78.

108. Radhakrishnan, *Recovery of Faith,* 117.

109. Radhakrishnan, *East and West,* 78.

110. Radhakrishnan, *Eastern Religions and Western Thought,* 186.

111. Ibid., 183.

112. Ibid., 186.

113. Ibid., 184.

114. Ibid., 186.

115. Ibid., 185.

116. Ibid., 186.

117. Ibid., 186.

118. Gopal, *Radhakrishnan,* 147.

119. Radhakrishnan, *Occasional Speeches and Writings,* 546.

120. Radhakrishnan, *East and West,* 130.

121. Radhakrishnan, "The Religion of the Spirit and the World's Need," 60.

122. Radhakrishnan, "Religion of the Spirit and the World's Need," 68.

123. Radhakrishnan, *East and West,* 79.

124. S. Radhakrishnan, *The Ethics of the Vedanta and Its Metaphysical Presuppositions* (Madras: Guardian Press, 1908), 1.

125. Radhakrishnan, "My Search for Truth," 40.

126. *Eastern Religions and Western Thought,* 272.

127. Ibid., 271.

128. Radhakrishnan, *Indian Philosophy,* vol. 1, 283.

129. Radhakrishnan, *Heart of Hindusthan,* 69.

130. Ibid., 79.

131. Ibid., 80.

132. S. Radhakrishnan, *Religion in a Changing World* (London: George Allen & Unwin, 1967), 154.

133. Radhakrishnan, *Heart of Hindusthan*, 76.

134. Radhakrishnan, *Indian Religious Thought*, 40.

135. Radhakrishnan, *East and West*, 120.

136. Radhakrishnan, *Recovery of Faith*, 164.

137. Radhakrishnan, *Occasional Speeches and Writings*, 299.

138. Radhakrishnan, *Recovery of Faith*, 115.

139. Otto, *The Kingdom of God and the Son of Man*, 15.

140. S. Heschel, *The Aryan Jesus: Christian Theologians and the Bible in Nazi Germany* (Princeton, NJ: Princeton University Press, 2008), 60–61.

141. R. Otto, *Mysticism East and West: A Comparative Analysis of the Nature of Mysticism* (New York: Macmillan, 1932), 196.

142. Radhakrishnan, *Eastern Religions and Western Thought*, 305.

143. Radhakrishnan, *Indian Religious Thought*, 39.

144. Stanley J. Samartha, "S. Radhakrishnan: Jesus Christ—the One among the Many," *Religion and Society* 11, no. 3 (1964): 52.

145. Radhakrishnan, *Hindu View of Life*, 23.

146. Radhakrishnan, *An Idealist View of Life*, 81

147. Ponnambalam Ramanathan, "The Miscarriage of Life in the West," *The Hibbert Journal* 7 (1909): 7.

148. K. M. Banerjea, *The Arian Witness: Or the Testimony of Arian Scriptures in Corroboration of Biblical History and the Rudiments of Christian Doctrine, Including Dissertations on the Original and Early Adventures of Indo-Arians* (Calcutta: Thacker, Spink & Co, 1875); J. N. Farquhar, *The Crown of Hinduism* (London: Oxford University Press, 1913); R. Panikkar, *The Unknown Christ of Hinduism* (London: Darton Longman and Todd, 1964).

149. Radhakrishnan, *East and West in Religion*, 24.

150. Radhakrishnan, *Eastern Religions and Western Thought*, 304.

151. Radhakrishnan, *Hindu View of Life*, 46.

152. Radhakrishnan, *Heart of Hindusthan*, 15.

153. Radhakrishnan, *Indian Religious Thought*, 75.

154. S. Radhakrishnan, "Indian Philosophy: Past and Present," in R. A. McDermott, ed., *Basic Writings of S. Radhakrishnan* (Bombay: Jaico, 1972), 107.

155. S. Radhakrishnan, *Indian Philosophy*, vol. 2 (London: George Allen & Unwin, 1923), 777.

156. S. Radhakrishnan, "The Voice of India in the Spiritual Crisis of Our Time," *Hibbert Journal* 44, no. 4 (1946): 304.

157. Radhakrishnan, *Eastern Religions and Western Thought*, 283.

8. A MINJUNG MESSIAH

1. Byung-Mu Ahn, *Jesus of Galilee* (Hong Kong: Christian Conference of Asia, 2004), xi.

2. For an easy-to-read introduction into different phases of the quest for the historical Jesus, see Helen K. Bond, *The Historical Jesus: A Guide for the Perplexed* (London: T & T Clark, 2012), 7–36.

3. Ahn, *Jesus of Galilee*, xii.

4. Ibid., 3.

5. Ibid., 4.

6. Ibid., xii. For Ahn's theological and political journey, see Volker Küster, *A Protestant Theology of Passion: Korean Minjung Theology Revisited* (Leiden: Brill, 2010), 59–78; Volker Küster, "Jesus and the Minjung Revisited: The Legacy of Ahn Byung-Mu (1922–1996)," *Biblical Interpretation* 19, no. 1 (2011): 1–18; and Jin-ho Kim, "The Hermeneutics of Ahn Byung-Mu: Focussing on the the Concepts of 'Discovery of Internality' and 'Otherness of Minjung,'" in Yung Suk Kim and Jin-ho Kim, eds., *Reading Minjung Theology in the Twenty-First Century: Selected Writings by Ahn Byung-Mu and Modern Critical Responses* (Eugene, OR: Pickwick, 2013), 13–23.

7. Gustavo Gutiérrez, *A Theology of Liberation: History, Politics, and Salvation*, trans. C. Inda and J. Eagleson (Maryknoll, NY: Orbis, 1973), 11–13.

8. Byung-Mu Ahn, "Jesus and the Minjung in the Gospel of Mark," in Commission on Theological Concerns of the Christian Conference of Asia, ed., *Minjung Theology: People as the Subjects of History* (London: Zed Press, 1983), 138–152; Byung-Mu Ahn, "Jesus and the Minjung in the Gospel of Mark," in R. S. Sugirtharajah, ed., *Voices from the Margin: Interpreting the Bible in the Third World*, rev. and exp. 3rd ed. (Maryknoll, NY: Orbis, 2006), 87–102; Byung-Mu Ahn, "The Transmitters of the Jesus-Event," *CTC Bulletin* 5, no. 3, and 6, no. 1 (1984–1985): 26–39. For an earlier version of the same article, see Byung-Mu Ahn, "The Body of Jesus-Event Tradition," *East Asia Journal of Theology* 3, no. 2 (1985): 293–309.

9. On Filipino theology, see Eleazar S. Fernandez, *Toward a Theology of Struggle* (Maryknoll, NY: Orbis, 1994).

10. For the emergence of minjung theology, its cultural and historical roots, its sources of authority, and its methodological preferences, see Commission on Theological Concerns of the Christian Conference of Asia, *Minjung Theology*; and Jung Young Lee, "Minjung Theology: A Critical Introduction," in Jung Young Lee, ed., *An Emerging Theology in World Perspective: Commentary on Korean Minjung Theology* (Mystic, CT: Twenty-Third Publications, 1988), 3–29.

11. Ahn, *Jesus of Galilee*, xiii.

12. Byung-Mu Ahn, "The Korean Church's Understanding of Jesus," *CTC Bulletin* 6, nos. 2 and 3 (1986): 29. See also Byung-Mu Ahn, "The Korean Church's Understanding of Jesus: A Historical Review," *International Review of Mission* 74, no. 293 (1985): 81–91.

13. Ahn, "Korean Church's Understanding of Jesus," 29.

14. Ibid., 28.

15. Byung-Mu Ahn, "Minjung Theology from the Perspective of the Gospel of Mark," in Yung Suk Kim and Jin-ho Kim, eds., *Reading Minjung Theology in the Twenty-First Century: Selected Writings by Ahn Byung-Mu and Modern Critical Responses* (Eugene, OR: Pickwick, 2013), 85.

16. Ahn, "Jesus and the Minjung," unpublished paper in author's possession, 16.

17. Ahn, *Jesus of Galilee*, 114.

18. Byung-Mu Ahn, "Jesus and People (Minjung)," *CTC Bulletin* 7, no. 3 (1987): 10.

19. Ahn, *Jesus of Galilee*, 2.

20. Ahn, "Jesus and People (Minjung)," 8.

21. Ahn, "Jesus and the Minjung" (unpub. paper), 2.

22. Rudolf Bultmann, *Faith and Understanding*, trans. L. P. Smith (London: SCM Press, 1969), 212, 205.

23. Ahn, "Transmitters of the Jesus-Event," 27.

24. Ahn, *Jesus of Galilee*, 7.

25. Ahn, "Jesus and People (Minjung)," 13.

26. Ahn, "Transmitters of the Jesus-Event," 27–28.

27. Ahn, "Korean Church's Understanding of Jesus," 22.

28. Ahn, *Jesus of Galilee*, 4.

29. Ahn, "Jesus and the Minjung in the Gospel of Mark" (1983), 139.

30. Ahn, "Jesus and People (Minjung)," 13.

31. Ahn, "Body of Jesus-Event Tradition," 309.

32. Joachim Jeremias, *The Prayers of Jesus* (London: SCM Press, 1967).

33. Ahn, "Jesus and the Minjung in the Gospel of Mark" (1983), 138, also (2006), 87.

34. Ahn, "Jesus and the Minjung" (unpub. paper), 1.

35. Ahn, "The Korean Church's Understanding of Jesus," 29.

36. Ahn, *Jesus of Galilee*, 4.

37. Ibid., 19.

38. Ibid., 20.

39. Ahn, "The Korean Church's Understanding of Jesus," 29.

40. Ibid.

41. For Sanders's "almost indisputable facts," see E. P. Sanders, *The Historical Figure of Jesus* (London: Penguin, 1993), 10–12.

42. E. P. Sanders, *Jesus and Judaism* (London: SCM Press, 1985), 333–334.

43. Ahn, "The Korean Church's Understanding of Jesus," 30.

44. Ahn, "Minjung Theology from the Perspective of the Gospel of Mark," 88.

45. Ahn, *Jesus of Galilee*, 105.

46. Ibid., 9.

47. Ibid., 22.

48. Ahn, "Jesus and the Minjung in the Gospel of Mark" (1983), 151.

49. Ibid.

50. Ahn, "Jesus and People (Minjung)," 11.

51. Ahn, *Jesus of Galilee*, 132.

52. Ibid., 145.

53. Ahn, "Minjung Theology from the Perspective of the Gospel of Mark," 88.

54. Ahn, *Jesus of Galilee*, 146.

55. Ibid., 148.

56. Ibid., 165.

57. Ibid., 178.

58. Ahn, "Jesus and the Minjung in the Gospel of Mark" (1983), 151.

59. Ahn, *Jesus of Galilee*, 119.

60. Ibid., 82.

61. Ibid., 238.

62. Ahn, "Minjung Theology from the Perspective of the Gospel of Mark," 89.

63. Ahn, *Jesus of Galilee*, 212.

64. Ibid., 197.

65. Ibid., 100.

66. Ibid., 107.

67. Ibid., 102.

68. Ibid., 100.

69. Ahn, "Jesus and People (Minjung)," 12, 13. Emphasis in the original.

70. Ahn, "Minjung Theology from the Perspective of the Gospel of Mark," 89.

71. Ahn, "Jesus and People (Minjung)," 13.

72. Ibid.

73. Ahn, *Jesus of Galilee*, 253.

74. Ibid.

75. Ibid., 77.

76. Ibid., 83.

77. Min-Ah Cho, "'If They Send Me to Hell, Jesus Will Rescue Me': Minjung Theology and the Iban Movement," in Yung Suk Kim and Jin-ho Kim, ed., *Reading Minjung Theology in the Twenty-First Century: Selected Writings by Ahn Byung-Mu and Modern Critical Responses* (Eugene, OR: Pickwick Publications, 2013), 184–199.

78. Yong-Yeon Hwang, "'The Person Attacked by the Robbers Is Christ': An Exploration of Subjectivity from the Perspective of Minjung Theology," in Yung Suk Kim and Jin-ho Kim, ed., *Reading Minjung Theology in the Twenty-First Century: Selected Writings by Ahn Byung-Mu and Modern Critical Responses* (Eugene, OR: Pickwick Publications, 2013), 224.

79. James G. Crossley, *Jesus and the Chaos of History: Redirecting the Life of the Historical Jesus* (Oxford, Eng.: Oxford University Press, 2015), 102.

80. Ahn, *Jesus of Galilee*, 82.

81. David A. Fiensy and Ralph K. Hawkins, eds., *The Galilean Economy in the Time of Jesus* (Atlanta: Society of Biblical Literature, 2013).

82. Ahn, "Jesus and the Minjung" (unpub. paper), 18.

9. JESUS IN A KIMONO

1. Mark B. Williams, *Endō Shūsaku: A Literature of Reconciliation* (London: Routledge, 1999); Emi Mase-Hasegawa, *Spirit of Christ Inculturated: A Theological Theme Implicit in Shusaku Endo's Literary Works* (Lund, Swed.: Lund University Centre for Theology and Religious Studies, 2004); Leith Morton, *The Image of Christ in the Fiction of Endo Shusaku* (Melbourne: Japanese Study Centre, 1994); Elizabeth Wills, "Christ as Eternal Companion: A Study in the Christology of Shusaku Endo," *Scottish Journal of Theology* 45, no. 1 (1992): 85–100; Steve Scott, "A Christ for Japan," *Third Way* 14, no. 7 (1991): 18–21.

2. Shūsaku Endō, *A Life of Jesus* (Tokyo: Charles E. Tuttle, 1979), 1.

3. Ibid.

4. Ibid.

5. Kazumi Yamagata, "Mr. Shusaku Endo Talks about His Life and Work as a Catholic Writer," *Chesterton Review* 12 (1986): 496.

6. Endō, *Life of Jesus*, 1.

7. Ibid., 41.

8. Ibid., 178.

9. Ibid., 105.

10. Ibid., 179.

11. Ibid., 107.

12. Mark B. Williams, "Inner Horizons: Towards Reconciliation in Endo Shusaku's *The Samurai*," *Japan Christian Review* 62 (1996): 79.

13. Endō, *Life of Jesus*, 106.

14. Ibid., 127.

15. Ibid., 27.

16. Ibid., 149.

17. Ibid., 150.

18. Ibid., 52.

19. Ibid., 13.

20. Shūsaku Endō, *Silence*, trans. William Johnston (London: Penguin, 1988), 14.

21. Shūsaku Endō, *White Man, Yellowman*, trans. T. Shimizu (Norwalk, CT: Eastbridge, 2006), 66.

22. Ibid., 97.

23. Endō, *Life of Jesus,* 4.

24. Ibid., 87.

25. Ibid., 173.

26. Ibid., 44.

27. Shūsaku Endō, *The Samurai* (London: Penguin, 1983), 245.

28. Endō, *Life of Jesus,* 51.

29. Ibid., 52.

30. Ibid., 71.

31. Ibid., 178.

32. Ibid., 58.

33. Ibid., 72.

34. Ibid., 33.

35. Ibid., 102.

36. Ibid., 151.

37. Endō, *Silence,* 47, 276.

38. Endō, *Life of Jesus,*145.

39. Ibid., 141.

40. Ibid., 174.

41. Ibid., 162.

42. Ibid., 173.

43. Ibid., 169.

44. Ibid., 177. Emphasis in the original.

45. Shūsaku Endō, *Deep River,* trans. Van C. Gessel (London: Sceptre, 1995), 191.

46. Endō, *Life of Jesus,* 28.

47. Elaine Pagels and Karen L. King, *Reading Judas: The Controversial Message of the Ancient Gospel of Judas* (London: Penguin, 2008).

48. See Amos Oz, *Judas* (London: Chatto & Windus, 2016).

49. Endō, *Life of Jesus,*112.

50. Ibid.,100.

51. Endō, *Silence,* 297.

52. Endō, *Life of Jesus,* 100.

53. Ibid., 2.

54. Endō, *White Man, Yellowman,* 110.

55. Endō, *Deep River,* 184.

56. Endō, *Life of Jesus,* 2.

57. Ibid., 1.

58. James T. Kodera, "Uchimura Kanzo and His 'No Church Christianity': Its Origin and Significance in Early Modern Japan," *Religious Studies* 23, no. 33 (1987): 377–390.

59. *The Complete Works of Kanzo Uchimura with Notes and Comments by Taijiro Yamamoto and Yoichi Muto* (Tokyo: Kyobunkwan, 1972), 56. Emphasis in the original.

60. Endō, *Life of Jesus,*145.

61. Louis Kronenberger, "A Japanese Novel," *Saturday Review of the Literature,* October 24, 1925, 239.

62. Endō, *Life of Jesus,* 100.

63. Ibid., 119.

64. Marcus J. Borg, *Jesus, A New Vision: Spirit, Culture, and the Life of Discipleship* (San Francisco: Harper & Row, 1987); and Marcus J. Borg, *Conflict, Holiness, and Politics in the Teachings of Jesus* (Harrisburg, PA: Trinity Press International, 1998).

65. P. S. Jacob, ed., *Experimental Response of N. V. Tilak,* Confessing Faith in India Series, no. 17 (Madras: Christian Literature Society, 1979), 102.

66. For recent images of Jesus as mother in Asian theology, see Curt Cadorette, Marie Giblin, Marylyn J. Legge, and Mary H. Snyder, *Liberation Theology: An Introductory Reader* (Maryknoll, NY: Orbis, 1992), 134–136; and Muriel Orevillo-Montenegro, *The Jesus of Asian Women* (Maryknoll, NY: Orbis, 2006), 104–111, 150–156.

CONCLUSION

1. A. J. Appasamy, *The Gospel and India's Heritage* (Madras: Society for Promoting Christian Knowledge, 1942), 26.

2. Rabindranath Tagore, *Crisis in Civilization,* rev. ed. (Calcutta: Vishva-Bharati, 1950), 22.

3. Keshub Chunder Sen, *Keshub Chunder Sen's Lectures in India* (London: Cassell & Company, 1901), 37.

4. Keshub Chunder Sen, *Keshub Chunder Sen's Lectures in India* (London: Cassell & Company, 1904), 35.

5. Albert Schweitzer, *The Quest of the Historical Jesus: A Critical Study of Its Progress from Reimarus to Wrede* (London: A. C. Black, 1910), 4.

6. Ponnambalam Ramanathan, "The Miscarriage of Life in the West," *Hibbert Journal* 7 (1909): 8.

7. *The Theology of Chenchiah with Selections from His Writings*, ed. D. Thangasamy, Confessing the Faith in India Series, no. 1 (Bangalore: Christian Institute for the Study of Religion and Society, 1966), 159.

8. S. Radhakrishnan, *Eastern Religions and Western Thought* (Oxford, UK: Clarendon Press, 1939), 186.

9. Sen, *Keshub Chunder Sen's Lectures in India* (1901), 87.

10. A. Drews, *The Witnesses to the Historicity of Jesus*, trans. Joseph McCabe (Chicago: Open Court Publishing, 1912), 299.

11. S. Radhakrishnan, *Recovery of Faith* (Delhi: Hind Pocket Books, 1956), 164.

12. Schweitzer, *Quest of the Historical Jesus*, 310.

13. Ibid., 310.

14. Ibid., 311.

15. M. G. Gandhi, *Christian Missions: Their Place in India* (Ahmedabad: Navajivan Press, 1941), 160.

16. Halvor Moxnes, *Jesus and the Rise of Nationalism: A New Quest for the Nineteenth Century Historical Jesus* (London: I. B. Tauris, 2012).

17. Adolf Deissmann, *Light from the Ancient East: The New Testament Illustrated by Recently Discovered Texts of the Graeco-Roman World* (London: Hodder and Stoughton, 1910), 396.

18. Albert Schweitzer, *The Quest of the Historical Jesus: The First Complete Edition*, ed. John Bowden (London: SCM Press, 2000), 480.

19. Ibid., 486.

20. Ibid., 399.

21. Ibid., 399.

22. Rudolf Bultmann, *Existence and Faith: Shorter Writings of Rudolf Bultmann*, trans. and ed. Schubert M. Ogden (London: Collins, 1964), 59.

23. Rudolf Bultmann, *Theology of the New Testament*, vol. 2, trans. Kendrick Grobel (London: SCM Press, 1955), 239. Emphasis in the original.

24. Peter M. Head, "The Nazi Quest for an Aryan Jesus," *Journal for the Study of the Historical Jesus* 2, no. 1 (2004): 55–89.

25. Sen, *Keshub Chunder Sen's Lectures in India* (1901), 388.

26. Swami Vivekananda, *The Complete Works of Swami Vivekananda: Mayavati Memorial Edition*, vol. 4 (Almora: Advaita Ashrama, 1923), 138.

27. *The English Works of Raja Rammohun Roy*, ed. J. C. Ghose (New Delhi: Cosmo Print, 1906), 906. Emphasis in the original.

28. Sen, *Keshub Chunder Sen's Lectures in India* (1901), 388.

29. Ibid., 33.

30. Marcus Borg, *Meeting Jesus Again for the First Time: The Historical Jesus and the Heart of Contemporary Faith* (San Francisco: Harper San Francisco, 1994), 137.

31. V. Chakkarai, *Jesus the Avatar* (Madras: Christian Literature Society of India, 1926), 124.

32. Sen, *Keshub Chunder Sen's Lectures in India* (1904), 24.

33. Swami Vivekananda, *The Complete Works of Swami Vivekananda: Mayavati Memorial Edition*, vol. 7 (Almora: Advaita Ashrama, 1923), 184.

34. I owe this quote to Nayanjot Lahiri. See Lahiri, *Ashoka: In Ancient India* (Cambridge, MA: Harvard University Press, 2016), 11.

35. Sarah Joseph, *Othappu: The Scent of the Other Side* (New Delhi: Oxford University Press, 2009).

ACKNOWLEDGMENTS

The volume you hold in your hands was made possible by an enormous amount of help from many people.

There is not an idea expressed here that has not benefited from the keen mind of Dan O'Connor. It was he who gracefully and humorously helped me to refine good ideas and reject swiftly the dreadful ones. Although he was going through a difficult time after the death of his beloved Juliet, he continued, astonishingly, to show the same enthusiasm that he extended to me nearly twenty-five years ago when I started to discuss my research with him. He is the godfather of my research.

I am fortunate to have had the care and understanding of many people at Harvard University Press, especially Sharmila Sen and Heather Hughes, who showed extraordinary patience at a time when I was going through a difficult period of poor health, and kept assuring me that an author's welfare was more important than the production of a text. I am grateful to Sharmila for pushing me to write in a style that enlivens scholarship. This is my second book with Harvard. What more can I say about the press than to recall a comment I came across in the *Guardian* that conveys my thoughts with much wit and verve: "Being published with Harvard is like being married to a duchess. The honour is almost greater than the pleasure!"

I owe a particular debt of gratitude to the supremely knowledgeable and ever-cordial staff at the Orchard Learning Resource Centre—Pat Budgen, Janet Bushnell, Lorraine Fletcher, Nigel Hardware, Helen Moreton, Rob Prince, Stephanie Rose, Marta Slaska, Dorothy Vuong,

Susan Wiyzell, and Sian Wyre, and especially those at the interlibrary loan department for tracking down materials as far away as a remote community library in New York.

My thanks go as well to Julie Carlson for the careful and sensitive way she copyedited the manuscript, and to Ralph Broadbent for his attentive and astute proofreading.

I am grateful to a number of people who helped me to obtain materials without which this volume would have been the poorer: Shashikala Alva, William Emilsen, Chanhee Heo, S. Jebanesan, David Joy, Israel Selvanagyam, and Arulanantham Thevagunananthan.

Finally, a thank you to my wife, Sharada, who continues to be a never-ending source of inspiration and encouragement, and without whose scholarly support I could not have ventured out on any of my research projects.

INDEX